The Chivalric Epic in Medieval Italy

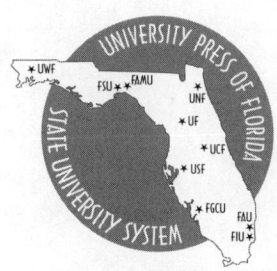

Florida A&M University, Tallahassee
Florida Atlantic University, Boca Raton
Florida Gulf Coast University, Ft. Myers
Florida International University, Miami
Florida State University, Tallahassee
University of Central Florida, Orlando
University of Florida, Gainesville
University of North Florida, Jacksonville
University of South Florida, Tampa
University of West Florida, Pensacola

The Chivalric Epic in Medieval Italy

Juliann Vitullo

University Press of Florida
Gainesville · Tallahassee · Tampa · Boca Raton
Pensacola · Orlando · Miami · Jacksonville · Ft. Myers

Copyright 2000 by the Board of Regents of the State of Florida
Printed in the United States of America on acid-free paper
All rights reserved
05 04 03 02 01 00 6 5 4 3 2 1

ISBN 0-8130-1815-3
Library of Congress Cataloging-in-Publication Data are available.

The University Press of Florida is the scholarly publishing agency for the State University System of Florida, comprising Florida A&M University, Florida Atlantic University, Florida Gulf Coast University, Florida International University, Florida State University, University of Central Florida, University of Florida, University of North Florida, University of South Florida, and University of West Florida.

University Press of Florida
15 Northwest 15th Street
Gainesville, FL 32611-2079
http://www.upf.com

*For my own little virago
of the mind and the heart,
Natalia*

Contents

Preface ix

Introduction xi

I. The Chivalric Epic in Communal Italy

1. A Hybrid Genre: The Italian Chanson de Geste 3
2. The Conflicting "Family Values" of the *Marciano XIII* Manuscript 30

II. Cultural Cross-Dressing

3. Hybrid Identities: Monsters, Wild Men, and Warrior Women 51
4. Masculinity, Sexuality, and Orientalism in the Medieval Italian Epic 74

III. Discursive Rivalries: The Case of *Ugo d'Alvernia*

5. Orality, Literacy, and the Prose Epic 93
6. Chivalry and Classicism 114

Epilogue: The Pleasure of Reading and the Power of the Text 128

Appendix 135

Notes 137

Bibliography 149

Index 165

Preface

My interest in the medieval epic tradition began with my study of Old French at Indiana University. I owe a large debt of gratitude to Emanuel Mickel for both introducing me to the chanson de geste and also providing me with the necessary skills to read the epics on my own. It was in his survey of Old French literature that I first became interested in the generic link between the Old French Carolingian epics and the Renaissance Italian epic poems. After a little research, I was surprised to discover what a rich and largely unstudied epic tradition thrived in Italy before the works of Luigi Pulci, Ludovico Ariosto, and Mattea Maria Boiardo.

From the beginning of this project I was intrigued by how writers used the epic narratives that they had inherited from previous generations and other societies to deal with the cultural and political questions of their own day. The other aspect of the genre that immediately caught my attention was the way in which the authors of late Carolingian epics combined different literary and cultural traditions to create not only hybrid texts but also hybrid characters such as the woman warrior and the wild man.

The explicit way in which these texts play with ethnic, class, and gender identities encouraged me to investigate how I could apply a cultural studies approach to these medieval texts. My participation for several years in an interdisciplinary medieval studies reading group at Indiana University helped me develop such an interpretive strategy, and I wish to acknowledge my debt to all the members of that group, especially the late Cliff Flannigan, who organized it and led the discussions with great intellect and passion.

The scholarship I admire most in medieval studies combines new archival sources with contemporary approaches to the study of culture. These kinds of texts offer new information to specialists and also engage in larger interdisciplinary debates. I have tried to follow that model in my book, but it never would have been possible without the financial assistance that I received to search for and study Carolingian epics in Italy. I would like to thank both Indiana University and Arizona State University for the generous grants that have allowed me to spend valuable time in the libraries of Florence and Padua.

Many colleagues in both medieval and Italian studies have improved my work through their questions, suggestions, and critiques. In particular, I want to thank Leslie Morgan for providing me so much information and insightful analysis about the *Marciano XIII* narratives, Gloria Allaire for sharing her vast knowledge of Andrea da Barberino and his texts, and Zyg Baranski for helping me to improve my argument about the ideological importance of orality and literacy in the medieval epics. Both Bob Bjork and Christopher Kleinhenz read the prospectus for this project and gave helpful suggestions about how to structure my work.

I have also benefited from the intellectual, emotional, and practical support of many colleagues, especially Susan Braidi, Piero Baldini, Bob Clark, Julia Douthwaithe, Letticia Galindo, Chiara Lage, Deborah Losse, Dhira Mahoney, Helene Meyers, Guy Raffa, Corine Schleif, Debora Schwartz, and Diane Wolfthal. These academic allies have helped me in numerous ways, from stimulating conversations to childcare, and I greatly appreciate their support.

I also wish to thank the three readers of my manuscript who all gave detailed comments and suggestions. Their work improved not only this text but also my skills as a scholar.

My biggest debt of gratitude goes to the two people who offer me continuous support in everyday life: my husband, Aaron Baker, and my daughter, Natalia Vitullo Baker. Aaron has always read my work and offered invaluable insights. Although not yet old enough to read my work, Natalia helps me in other ways. Listening to her use of stories to investigate adult culture reminds me continually of the important role narrative plays in all of our lives. Most of all, the enthusiasm that my little virago has for her "work" encourages me to keep focused on my own, and I hope in return that my love of books and study will inspire her in the future, just as the passion my father, Vincent Vitullo, has for reading and discussion has always stimulated me.

Introduction

This study analyzes the role of the chivalric epic in northern and central Italian culture during the late Middle Ages. Its tales of Emperor Charlemagne, his valorous nephew Roland, the rebellious vassal Renaud/Rinaldo, and the faithful counterpart Huon/Ugo d'Alvernia circulated throughout the Italian peninsula, but most of the extant manuscripts derive from two distinct areas and time periods: the Venetian Trevisan March of the late thirteenth and fourteenth centuries and fifteenth-century Tuscany.[1] The chapters follow the genre's historical development beginning with an early-fourteenth-century codex from the Veneto and ending with an analysis of a Florentine text written in the middle of the Quattrocento. The *comuni* or city-states that developed in these regions of the Italian peninsula fought for independence from traditional powers such as kings, emperors, and the Church; yet, they also adopted and pieced together elements of the myths which supported these established authorities to create a version of history that validated their own political power.[2]

The Italian Carolingian epic borrowed many of its narratives and even its early lexicon from the Old French chanson de geste. Because of nationalistic concerns, however, several nineteenth-century medievalists sought to identify specific Italian characteristics in the Carolingian epics and established one of several dichotomies (Italian/French), which have structured the study of this genre. Other important oppositions that this book will discuss include: feudal vs. bourgeois ideology, orality vs. literacy, and chivalry vs. humanism, all of which could be subsumed under the well-known dichotomy of tradition vs. modernity. As Brian Stock points out, seventeenth- and eighteenth-century historians classified medieval culture as "traditional," and for the last century many medievalists have reacted against that categorization by trying to prove the "modernity" of various epochs or social groups in the Middle Ages (160). Descriptions of the Carolingian epic in Italy have not escaped that tendency. Scholars have searched for modernity in the Italian romance epic in the form of new bourgeois values.

This study reevaluates these oppositions by applying different notions of tradition and genre to the Italian chivalric epics. Instead of focusing on tradition as a monolithic whole, the following interpretation of the Carolingian material in Italy describes how the urban elite of certain Italian city-states such as Padua in the Veneto and Florence in Tuscany (itself a hybrid group of titled nobles, merchants, judges, and artisans) employed various traditions in order to produce its own mythological bricolage. The Italian versions of the Carolingian legends are not seamless ideological wholes that mirror the values of a more modern society, but rather dialogic texts which incorporate several different competing traditions.

Martin Krygier lists four characteristics of all traditions: (1) each tradition belongs, or at least is believed to belong, to a remote past; (2) each tradition has a present meaning for those who inherited it; (3) each tradition is perceived as being passed down through generations; and (4) each tradition is by nature social (224). The second characteristic of Krygier's list has the most relevance for this study because it emphasizes the *present* meaning of tradition. Though perceived as belonging to the past, traditions would not persist if they no longer had meaning for the social groups that use them. Thus, the adoption of the Carolingian tradition implies that Italian authors did not entirely reject its chivalric mythology but rather chose to employ the genre because they found the values associated with it meaningful.

Scholars such as Stock and Gerald L. Bruns have dismissed the notion of tradition as a monolithic whole, instead focusing on its dynamic use and polyvalent nature (Bruns 1–21). Social groups, in their view, constantly combine both the traditional and the modern in different ways so that they cannot be described as exclusively one or the other. While communities may change a tradition they employ, they can not efface it by simply claiming its modernity. As Gadamer points out, even societies that undergo revolutions preserve a great deal of tradition and blend it with the modern to create new values (281).

Stock makes a distinction between what he labels as "traditional" and "traditionalistic" norms. Traditional actions consist of inherited behavior that social groups simply accept as their norm, while traditionalistic action is the self-conscious endorsement of a traditional norm. Stock states that the contrast between the two types of behavior consists of the difference "between habitual activity that merely continues past practices without reflecting on them and self-conscious innovation based on the recovery of an allegedly authentic tradition" (165). In a traditionalistic culture, norms are consciously chosen from a pool of traditional behaviors. After a process of reflection, codification, and abstraction, the traditionalistic culture calls its own modified norms modernity and the norms it inherited tradition (166).

The Carolingian material in Italy contributes to a larger chivalric discourse that helped fashion social identities in late medieval Italian city-states. Urban patricians in search of ways to define their status and to create their own traditionalistic norms adopted the legends surrounding French knights. The self-conscious use of traditions marks an important characteristic of this mixed social group. Rather than labelling these texts traditional or modern—feudal or bourgeois—this study analyzes how one traditionalistic discourse, chivalry, combined with others in the Carolingian epics to help shape new ideals of nobility and masculinity.

The manner in which traditions are transmitted also affects their meaning. As Stock states, "The type of transmission is not neutral: it is rooted in politics and institutions, and it helps to shape the message it transmits" (162). This study will therefore look at the translation of Carolingian epics from verse into prose by Italian authors as a formal change that combined the new literary discourse of humanism aimed at individual readers with the chivalric epics which—even though they were written—were at times transmitted orally in Italy during the late Middle Ages. The different forms of transmission also suggest that these texts were enjoyed by members of several social groups who could identify in different ways with the epic's interplay of chivalric, Christian, and republican discourses. While we have evidence that Carolingian narratives were performed for large groups in piazzas, we also know that these texts were collected and read by seigneurial families who catalogued them in their libraries.[3]

The definition of genre adopted for this study relates directly to the notion of tradition described above. A literary genre is a pragmatic "explanatory tool" that one uses to compare and contrast individual texts (Rosmarin 50). Authors employ certain formal elements associated with a particular group of texts, or genre, as one of many signifying codes that can transmit meaning to their readers. The markers which identify a text as belonging to a certain genre change according to the needs of the communities that adopt them. All characteristics of a genre such as the epic, therefore, are historical, not essential.

Krygier's notion of traditions applies particularly well to one literary genre, the epic. Most texts labelled by modern scholars as epics take place in the past, yet, this does not preclude a present meaning. Bakhtin defines the epic past as "walled off absolutely from all subsequent times" (*Dialogic Imagination* 15). This epic boundary, according to Bakhtin, precludes change: "its reliance on impersonal and sacrosanct tradition, on a commonly held evaluation and point of view . . . excludes any possibility of another approach" (16). Yet, epics, like traditions, are adopted and used in various ways by different social groups precisely because they have a present, and perhaps even personal, meaning.

This understanding is further validated in the work of Hans Robert Jauss who defines genre in historical rather than essential terms by looking at it from both a synchronic and a diachronic perspective (81–82). My study therefore compares the Carolingian epic in Italy to both the preceding and contemporary Old French chansons de geste and to other late medieval Italian genres. In a divergence from Jauss's method, however, the Italian epics will be analyzed not only to see how Italian writers altered their Old French models, but also to see how the chanson de geste—largely unchanged—contributed directly to the formation of a horizon of expectations. Although I adopt Jauss's strategy of analyzing genres from both a synchronic and diachronic perspective, I disagree with his notion that a text's value depends upon its author's "alteration of the horizon of the genre" (94). I find the Italian chivalric epics interesting because of, not despite, their conventionality. My argument, in fact, is that the chanson de geste's "rules of the game" change very little even though they are being produced for a different audience. If Italian authors chose to imitate the Old French genre because they found it meaningful, the question then arises why their so-called bourgeois culture adopted a genre associated with chivalry and a rigid, social hierarchy.

The first part of *The Chivalric Epic in Medieval Italy* analyzes the eight Carolingian narratives of the Franco-Italian manuscript, the *Marciano XIII*, in order to demonstrate the hybrid nature of the late medieval Italian epic and examine how critics have attempted to read these texts as the depiction of a bourgeois Italian worldview, which stands in opposition to the earlier feudal ideology of the French chanson de geste. The first chapter focuses on how competing discourses about nobility and chivalry diminish the status of the king without questioning the chanson de geste's representation of a universal social hierarchy. Moreover, I argue that many of the modifications that have been labelled Italian or bourgeois also occurred in the late Carolingian epics produced in France and that these generic changes had more to do with socioeconomic developments in European urban centers than with an Italian mentality. In the second chapter, I examine how the representation of other identities, in particular clan affiliation and gender roles, contributes to the epic discourse on social class examined in the first chapter. Once again, the Italian texts are not the only late medieval Carolingian epics that focus on the relationship between clan and empire. Like Padua and Florence, many urban centers throughout Europe became battlegrounds for two competing notions of power: local factions who controlled cities through violence and regional or state governments that tried to rule through administrative and legal bureaucracies. The late Carolingian epics deal directly with this issue and suggest that often regional and state governments did not overcome the factional violence of local clans, but instead became absorbed in it.

In order to understand how the chivalric epic contributed to discourses of social power in late medieval Italy, the second part of the book analyzes the representation of marginalized groups in the epic narratives. Chapter three delineates the connections between three forms of alterity in late medieval epics: the monster from the East, the worker as wild man, and the woman as Amazonian warrior. After describing the similarities in the portrayal of these exotic races, I examine the cultural forces that destabilized traditional dichotomies in Italian urban centers and produced such a fertile breeding ground for hybrid figures in the chivalric epic. Chapter four argues that Carolingian epic writers used Orientalism to help refigure ideal heterosexual masculinity that had been challenged by the socioeconomic changes described in the previous chapter. I discuss how the Orient served as an imaginary space in which questions about sexuality and ethnicity could be examined at a safe distance.

The last part of the book traces the development of one chivalric epic, *Ugo d'Alvernia*, from several Franco-Italian versions in the poetic form of *lasse* to a Tuscan narrative written both in prose and in a different poetic form—the *cantare*. Chapter five describes the competition between the various forms of the epic in Italy and how that rivalry relates to the self-definition of social groups through orality and literacy. In chapter six I use the narratives of *Ugo d'Alvernia* to analyze the ideological tensions that arose within fifteenth-century chivalric epics between textual references to the oral transmission of verse chansons de geste and other formal elements which belonged to historical prose traditions. The genre of the chanson de geste was associated with both public performance and the discourse of chivalry just as prose genres were connected to individual readers and the humanist discourse of the new administrative elite. The book concludes, then, with an example of how the stable social hierarchy of the chansons de geste still had a great influence on Italian epic writers who tried to ground new elements of their culture in the secure world of an epic past. *The Chivalric Epic in Medieval Italy* also shows that despite these efforts, the epic's popularity among different social groups confirms its role as a forum for examining competing and often contradictory notions of ethnic, class, gender, and sexual identities.

Part I

*The Chivalric Epic
in Communal Italy*

I

A Hybrid Genre

The Italian Chanson de Geste

Latin, French, Provençal, and various Italian dialects competed for linguistic and cultural hegemony in the Italian peninsula during the thirteenth and fourteenth centuries. Each of these languages had a cluster of ascribed characteristics, a personality, to which northern and central Italians would refer; the communal authors such as Brunetto Latini wrote in French both for its status as a prestigious language shared by many literate people and for its association with the pleasurable tales of knights' adventures. In his explanation of why he wrote in a language other than his native tongue, Latini claimed that French was "plus delitable" (more delightful) and "plus commune a tous langages" (more common among all the languages) (*Li livres* 18). The most popular literary vehicle for the diffusion of French cultural models in Italy was the chanson de geste, whose appeal surpassed that of other French genres, including yet another tradition devoted to the adventures of knights—the courtly romance (Grendler, *Schooling* 292).

Ruggero Ruggieri coined the term *umanesimo cavalleresco* (chivalric humanism) to describe the tendency among northern and central Italian writers of associating the diffusion of French with chivalry. This expression not only communicates that the late medieval translation of French texts in Italy paralleled (and often overlapped) the absorption of Latin ones, but it also suggests that while Italians connected Latin with a republican ethos, they identified French with a chivalric cultural model. Although the juxtaposing of republican and imperialist/monarchic ideologies may seem contradictory, Italian communal authors such as Latini worked hard to make these traditions compatible.

Just as the writers of northern and central Italian communes adopted various languages for the production of literary or historical texts, they also grafted together the mythological traditions associated with those languages. The commune was an amorphous form of government with an ambivalent relationship to traditional sources of authority, such as the Church, the emperor, and titled nobility. In creating their own mythic tales, communal writers and artists often combined elements from several traditions. One example of this process is the *Nine Worthies* model, which appears in fourteenth-century Italian art. This historical paradigm juxtaposes heroes of the "three laws": three biblical leaders (Joshua, David, and Judas Maccabeus), three classical heroes (Hector, Alexander, and Julius Caesar), and three medieval knights (Arthur, Charlemagne, and Godfrey de Bouillon). While the prophets and classical heroes prefigure the medieval knights, the chivalric acts recreate biblical truths in the recent past.[1] This common medieval conception of allegory is developed within a chivalric framework as all of the exemplary men are depicted as exceptional knights. The *Nine Worthies* is just one instance of the Italian commune's practice of mythological bricolage, but it stands out in how it exemplifies the power of the chivalric archetype to organize other competing discourses in the imagination of late medieval Italians.

While the Carolingian material appealed to different social groups throughout the Italian peninsula, the chivalric epic gained its greatest popularity in two communal regions of late medieval Italy: first in the cities of the Trevisan March such as Padua in the early fourteenth century, and second in Tuscany at the turn of the same century.[2] This chronology of the chivalric epic's success in late medieval Italy, however, should be considered approximate at best since we know that Tuscans enjoyed Carolingian narratives before they produced their own written versions, and that northern Italians continued to produce manuscripts containing chivalric epics into the fifteenth century.[3] Economic and political networks between French and Italian cities, as well as the oral transmission of these narratives by singers, produced multiple channels of circulation for the chivalric epic. Therefore, it is best to avoid analyzing the Tuscan tradition as if it descended directly from the earlier northern Italian epics.

Although we do not have extant Italian epics from the twelfth century, scholars agree that narratives of French chansons de geste were already circulating in Veneto's Trevisan March, either in written or oral form, at the beginning of that century. Evidence of this early diffusion includes the figures of Roland and Olivier on the Duomo of Verona from 1139 and archival records showing that Italians had begun naming their progeny after the Carolingian heroes.[4]

5 · A Hybrid Genre: The Italian Chanson de Geste

The first chansons de geste produced in northern Italy, or what was known as Lombardia, date from the late thirteenth or fourteenth centuries and are best known for their unique linguistic traits. These texts were written in a hybrid language containing elements of both Old French and local Lombard or Venetian dialects.[5] Whereas the nineteenth-century scholars who rediscovered the manuscripts assumed that the *assauvagie* (savage) language of these texts was the product of jongleurs who did not know how to write French correctly, contemporary linguists no longer analyze the linguistic hybridity of the early Italian epic as a sign of the genre's decadence, but as an interesting and complex sociological occurrence.[6] These scholars also point out that a writer's knowledge of the languages is not the only factor in the production of such code-switching (Wunderli and Holtus 11). Noting that each Franco-Italian author uses the mixed language in a slightly different form, Lorenzo Renzi has divided the texts into two general categories (570). In texts like the *Marciano XIII* manuscript, the writer alternated between the two codes in order to retain the prestige of the French tradition, but still communicate with local audiences and readers. The second group of texts includes works like the *Entrée d'Espagne,* which are written in French but with numerous Italian interferences; in other words, these epics were written by Italians for whom French was a second but well-studied language (573).

The *Marciano XIII* and the *Entrée d'Espagne* have received the most scholarly attention of the Franco-Italian epics because they are perceived as representative of two types of epic narratives with different intended audiences. They not only differ linguistically but also at a broader cultural level. While the *Marciano XIII* deals with concrete topics in a clear but unsophisticated manner, the *Entrée d'Espagne* contains references to learned traditions and philosophical debates. Scholars have hypothesized that the *Marciano XIII* texts were written to be recited to a largely uneducated audience, whereas the *Entrée d'Espagne* was produced either in a courtly or clerical environment.[7] Because of its form and content, then, the *Marciano XIII* compilation in particular has been interpreted as reflecting Italian popular or communal values, which celebrated the family and promoted an antifeudal "bourgeois" ideology. The dating of these texts to the late thirteenth or the first half of the fourteenth century has also encouraged scholars to view it as a textual mirror of the new values that emerged in the northern and central Italian communes before the rise of *signorie* in the fourteenth century. Although several scholars have proposed that the manuscript was produced towards the middle of the fourteenth century, which would place it outside of the communal period for most of northern Italy, the *Marciano XIII* continues to be read as a testament to the new "modern" values unique to Italy.[8]

In analyzing the narratives contained in the *Marciano XIII,* I question two of the dichotomies that have shaped the study of this compilation and of the medieval chivalric epic in general: French/Italian and feudal/bourgeois. This chapter focuses on how *Marciano XIII* narratives retain elements of the French chanson de geste, while accommodating new elements to the genre's model and thereby creating a hybrid text, both linguistically and ideologically. Moreover, I will argue that many of the modifications that have been labelled Italian innovations also occurred in the late epics produced in France. In the next chapter, I examine how the representation of other identities, in particular clan affiliation and gender roles, contributes to the epic discourse on social class explored in this chapter. Before I begin my analysis of the *Marciano XIII* narratives, let me first briefly survey the critical reception of the genre and analyze how questions of social identity have been implicated in interpretations of the late medieval epic.

Genre and Gender: Epic or Italian Melodrama?

Epics have always played an important role in the creation of gender and ethnic identities, but this is particularly true of the chanson de geste since it was first defined during the fervent nationalism of the late nineteenth century. At the time, French historians dealt with the rising power of a unified Germany and the ideological subordination of their own culture by their eastern neighbor, by stressing France's Germanic, hence "masculine," roots (Hayes). Literary scholars followed suit using the Carolingian epic, and in particular the *Chanson de Roland,* to weld an ideological link between modern France and a warrior culture of the country's origins. The early chanson de geste in *laisses,* with its connection to orality and a militaristic culture, served as a symbol of France's virile roots.[9] In contrast, scholars such as Léon Gautier viewed the late chanson de geste of the thirteenth and fourteenth centuries, in particular prose versions, as the product of a more literate, but nonetheless weaker and more effeminate culture. In describing the late epics Gautier claims that "the historical element had, in effect, disappeared for all time. Everything that, in our ancient poems was fierce, coarse, Germanic, but also everything that was truly epic, was erased, with dutiful care, by our new writers of *romans.*"[10]

Gautier not only connects the genre's decadence with the prose epics of his own country, but also with the reworkings of the tradition in Italy. The hypercivilization and effeminate nature of the Italian Renaissance castrates France's once manly epics: "makes feeble everything that is strong and makes effeminate everything that is male" (366). In his comments about the *Marciano XIII*, Gautier suggests that generic modifications in the manuscript's narratives reflect the culture of the "joyous Paduans and Trevisans" whose civilization he describes as "delicate, artistic, and charming" (352–53). While France's chanson de geste revealed a society of warriors, Franco-Italian epics mirrored northern Italians' quest for the good life of parties, food, jousts, and women. When he then describes the Italian Renaissance epic, Gautier portrays Italians in a similar but more exaggerated fashion. In the following quotation, the French scholar makes clear that the Italian Carolingian epic is a literary genre in drag:

> Between these crude barons of the eleventh century, weighted down with double coats of mail and their heads hidden by helmets covering their noses, very brusque, very straightforward, very religious, who dreamed only of their large fortresses and reconquering the Holy Sepulcher; between these primitive men and the beautiful Italian courts at the beginning of the sixteenth century, very refined and more than halfway corrupt, these women magnificently dressed . . . between these two societies, these two worlds, there is nothing or almost nothing in common (381).

Ironically, Gautier's scholarly goal was very similar to the goals of the thirteenth- and fourteenth-century French and Italian epic writers he despised. Both the nineteenth-century scholar and the late medieval authors attempted to systematize the literature they had inherited into large, comprehensive, and orderly volumes. In fact, the eight narratives of the *Marciano XIII* are a good example of this tendency. Like Gautier, the turn-of-the-century Italian scholar Pio Rajna also tried to bring order to literary studies by transforming his discipline into a science:

> The Nineteenth Century, which has done and continues to do so much for the progress of the experimental sciences, was also able to give a new and vigorous impulse to literary studies. . . . To it alone belongs, in fact, the glory of having put in place the foundation for a true and proper science of literature. ("Rinaldo" 213)

As Gautier had, Rajna catalogued the late Italian epics in prose and verse as part of a "scientific" endeavor. And like his French counterpart, Rajna also did not identify the similarities between his project to discover "the laws of popular literatures" and the attempts of late medieval writers to order and elevate the popular traditions that they had inherited. Instead, Rajna shares Gautier's opinion that the French compositions of the earlier age were more robust and pure:

> Without doubt, the *Chanson de Roland* and other *cantari* of the first age are more pure, severe, noble and strong; but these epics could not bring as much pleasure as they merited, after the customs had been weakened. ("Rinaldo" 108)

While Rajna accepts the description of the Italian epics as "weak," he recasts that national characteristic in positive terms: Italian writers focused on passions in their epics because they desired "delight" rather than a "national poetry." According to Rajna, his compatriots preferred the emotionally charged stories of rebellious vassals because they loved freedom and could not tolerate the haughtiness of princes (109). By comparing the epic narratives to nineteenth-century melodrama, Rajna perceptively notes that the medieval texts might have served as a vehicle with which men could explore and question their own relationships in a socially acceptable form. Yet by doing so, he supports the notion that national and gender identities are binary opposites.

The characteristics that Rajna associates with Italy's emotional epics, the excessive evil of Ganelon's clan and its passionate desire to destroy the Chiaramonte lineage as well as the corrupt king who is in constant conflict with innocent and faithful vassals, exist in late Old French Carolingian epics as well. Moreover, despite its "freedom-loving" public, the fourteenth- and fifteenth-century Italian epic (like its French equivalents) usually focuses on the exploits of a hero from noble stock. In his quest to justify Italy's less than pure and unmanly literary origins, Rajna gives a positive connotation to traits that had been traditionally associated with the feminine: pleasure and emotion. He even claims that scholars should accept and investigate the late Carolingian epic's stylistic transgressions—its lack of generic purity—as a quality of "popular" literature (122–24). Ultimately, however, Rajna repositions the late Carolingian epic with its troubling heterogeneity in a rigid, positivist framework. As he seeks to explain the evolution of Italian literature, the epic of the fourteenth and fifteenth centuries is depicted as a primitive form of the uniformly literary chivalric romances of the Renaissance. Despite the obvious pleasure Rajna found in the melodramatic narratives, he insists that the only reason to study such texts is to understand the "laws" of popular culture and how they reflect national and gender identities.

9 · A Hybrid Genre: The Italian Chanson de Geste

Pio Rajna's notion that Italians modified the Carolingian epic to reflect their love of freedom has been reiterated by several recent scholars in a slightly different form. The writings of Antonio Viscardi, Alberto Limentani and Marco Infurna, and Henning Krauss all express the idea that the Carolingian epics produced in Italy represent a coherent worldview which can be clearly distinguished from that of the Old French analogues.[11] Both this chapter and the following one offer an alternative reading of the *Marciano XIII*, a manuscript that all four of the above-mentioned critics have analyzed.

Krauss's arguments are the most recent and thorough example of the dominant critical view of the genre, which emphasizes national traits within the northern Italian Carolingian epics and often simplifies the complex historical context in which they were produced. Krauss adopts from Lucien Goldmann a concept of literary genre as reflecting the "worldview" of one particular social class. Like Goldmann, Krauss believes that social classes play the most important role in the construction of self. In Goldmann's view, other forms of identity such as national, generational, family, gender, and sexual, are "peripheral elements," while social classes constitute the only human groups "whose consciousness tends to an overall vision of man."[12] This concept of a worldview influences Krauss's description of the Carolingian epic in two important ways: Krauss uses it to interpret the genre as a mirror of the values associated with the rising bourgeoisie in Italy, and it also allows him to avoid analyzing the effects of other identities on the production and reception of this genre.

Critics such as Krauss have adopted an evolutionary model, which focuses on the ways that authors of northern and central Italy modified (and modernized) elements of the traditional chanson de geste; they examine texts as "input" or as a reflection of contemporary social models, but minimize the text's role as "output" or its contribution to and, construction of those same discourses.[13] For the most part scholars have avoided dealing with the problem of why Italian authors chose the generic structure of the Carolingian epic and how traditional components of the late chansons de geste conflict with alterations produced by the Italian authors. Rather than using such an evolutionary model, I study the history of the Italian epic as a contested process, a dialectic of both incorporation and resistance. Fredric Jameson theorizes a dialectical model for the study of literary texts that includes both a diachronic and synchronic analysis of genre. He uses the term "formal sedimentation" in referring to generic elements and their ideologies that persist beyond the time of their origin and therefore coexist "either as a contradiction or, on the other hand, as a mediatory or harmonizing mechanism—with elements from later stages" (141).

Approaching a genre from such a diachronic perspective allows one to analyze formal sedimentation as it manifests itself in a particular text or group of texts. Certain tensions delineate the "early" chanson de geste of twelfth- and thirteenth-century France as well as the late epic of fourteenth- and fifteenth-century France and Italy. The most apparent conflict is the holy war, but this masks the more troublesome question of whether the West's greatest enemy lies within its own boundaries or beyond them. A second polemic is the efficacy and fairness of the feudal hierarchy of which Charlemagne is the ideal leader. This debate is tied to yet another dialectical opposition between the welfare of an individual and his family on the one hand, and the well-being of the greater community on the other. Whether or not a hero can protect his own interests and at the same time respect the social order also leads to doubts about the definition of heroism: should a hero worry more about his own reputation or the survival of his people? should he defeat the enemy at any cost or always play by the rules? does he use his extraordinary skills to free himself from the social order or to defend it? do intellectual and spiritual qualities moderate or undermine the aggression necessary for warfare? and, finally, can a knight function both as a military and spiritual leader?

In the Oxford *Chanson de Roland*, the struggle between Christians and Saracens is interrupted by the conflict between Roland and Ganelon. That confrontation is shaped by the tensions between individual interests and those of the community. In addition, Ganelon's treason sets the stage for the questioning of heroism. When Roland refuses to call for reinforcement, thereby condemning his men to death, does he mistakenly value his own reputation over the survival of the other knights, or does he sacrifice his own life for the Christian community as did Christ? These issues not only appear in the paradigmatic Oxford *Chanson de Roland,* but continue to shape the late Carolingian epics produced both in France and in Italy. It also explains why northern Italians reproduced that narrative and expanded it in works like the *Entrée d'Espagne*.[14]

According to the most common critical model outlined above, the bourgeois authors of Carolingian epics in Italy displaced feudal values with their own ideology of liberty, efficiency, and equality (Krauss, *L'Epica feudale* 213–15). This type of analysis assumes that a text expresses a harmonious and unified system of values and that the ideology of each social class is seamless and pure, uncontaminated by the values of other social classes or other forms of identity. It also ignores the genre's formal sedimentation. Rather than describing the late Carolingian epics in Italy as overturning the traditional qualities of the chanson de geste, I prefer to analyze how these narratives depict and attempt to resolve the oppositions that had always defined the boundaries of the genre's contested terrain.

Marciano XIII: (Re)writing an Urban Mythology

The eight Carolingian epics in the *Marciano XIII* have attracted the attention of medievalists for several reasons: the curious Franco-Italian language in which the scribe wrote, the variety of narratives within one codex, the apparent originality of a few of the stories, and the relationship of these works to later Italian epics. In search of national Italian traits which would separate the Franco-Italian texts from their Old French analogues, Viscardi, Limentani and Infurna, and Krauss proposed that the narratives within this manuscript offered a new perspective on the chivalric epic. They perceived these texts as a critique of the feudal world in which the French chansons de geste were originally written.

As I outlined above, starting with Pio Rajna's work on the Carolingian epic, scholars have associated an Italian bourgeois personality with two aspects of the Franco-Italian epic: a questioning of aristocratic privilege, especially the emperor's status, and a new focus on the intimate details of domestic life rather than on international warfare. I would like to consider first whether the diminished role of the emperor should be read as indicative of an antifeudal ideology.

In his article on the metamorphosis of Charlemagne in the Franco-Italian epics, Karl Bender begins by posing a question: "How was the image of Charlemagne's inherited royalty from the French chansons de geste transformed in the first Franco-Italian epics, considering that the audience was not living in a feudal world?" (164). Although the question that shapes Bender's analysis of the Carolingian epic assumes that Italian communes had erased all vestiges of a feudal hierarchy, he later corrects this vision of Italian communes by noting, as many historians have, that both feudal and communal values coexisted in late medieval northern Italy.

Paradoxically, in order to fight for independence from princes and the Church as well as motivate the men who defended their sovereignty, citizens of Italian communes recycled mythologies that supported the same traditional sources of authority; the writings of Dante illustrate that imperialist ideas and imperialist claimants remained attractive to the communal aristocracy as tools of self-legitimization at the same time that they battled against them. Historian John Larner points out that "in the age of Dante, every citizen was expected to fight for his commune.... [T]hey, as well as those many who lived as professional soldiers, needed . . . a sustaining myth, an ethic to assert their own value in the eyes of the world and of themselves" ("Chivalric Culture" 128).

The classical reconstruction of late-thirteenth- and fourteenth-century Italy derives from the assumption that the communes developed as a means to combat the power of the landed aristocracy (Krauss, *L'Epica feudale* 18). According to this model, a concept of collective self-determination developed together with a new consciousness of individual self-determination. Following this historical paradigm, Krauss assumes that "liberty, efficiency, and equality" were the new ideals of the "protocapitalist" society in which money and goods circulate freely. He cites communal authors such as Brunetto Latini and Bono Giamboni as examples of a new politicized bourgeoisie; this type of writer, according to Krauss, could only exist in a more democratic society "because the feudal hierarchy reduces to the minimum autonomous and responsible activity by those who follow orders: because it needs men who faithfully follow orders and are not political" (24).

To support the notion of a new, politicized bourgeoisie replacing a rigid feudal hierarchy, Krauss quotes Brunetto Latini's statement that an individual owes his first allegiance to his family (particularly his father) and then to the commune:

> ogn'om ch'al mondo vene:
> nasce prim[er]amente
>
> al padre e a' parenti,
> e poi al suo Comuno.
>
> (Latini, *Il Tesoretto* ll. 166–69)
>
> [Everyman who comes into the world is born first to his father and to his relatives, and then to his Commune.]

Although a first reading of this quotation might seem to support the description of Latini as a politicized bourgeois, on the contrary, this statement privileges allegiance to one's family over loyalty to one's city. Such an assertion suggests that groups other than social classes played a large role in the ideological formation of communal authors. Latini also dedicates his text to a king and spends a considerable amount of time defining aristocratic terms such as *cortesia*. Like most of his contemporaries, Latini writes that moral virtue rather than bloodline should determine nobility; yet, he goes on to say that if one must compare two people of equally virtuous character, then naturally the nobler of the two is the person with the most illustrious genealogy (ll. 1733<n.38). Such a text forces us to question whether bourgeois and feudal ideologies can be easily distinguished in this period.

While some medievalists have perceived the early commune as an antifeudal association created to fight the power of the emperor and of the landed aristocracy, other historians have stressed that communes also assimilated pro-imperial and feudal ideologies. Gino Luzzatto, for example, believes that many of the smaller and some of the larger communes such as Padua might have been organized initially by groups of lesser feudal vassals who took over part of the lord's land around a castle or urban center (410–19). As Luzzatto says, the rise of the communes should be considered an internal transformation of the feudal world rather than an antifeudal revolution (411). Another historian, Philip Jones, echoes the opinion of Luzzatto, saying that the landowning feudal class used cities to consolidate its own interests against the sovereign (15). Jones calls this process the "feudalization" of urban spaces, and reminds us that the most distinguishing mark of Italian medieval cities, the towers, graphically represent the partition of the city by aristocratic families (83).

Almost all historians agree that with the rise of communes in northern Italy, the separation between the city and countryside practically disappeared. As communal government grew, landed nobles inevitably moved to the city and assumed an important role in its political life (Luzzatto 413–14). As J. K. Hyde says, "The entire ruling class [of Padua] supported itself primarily by the exploitation of the contado, either directly through the ownership of rights over the land or its products, or indirectly through the administration of the state" (*Padua* 194). In Carol Lansing's book on thirteenth-century Florence, she states that the "medieval Florentine patriciate . . . enjoyed a complex mixture of financial ties and associations, combining interests in banking or merchant enterprise with both urban and rural rents" (147). The seigneurial towers and the armed followers of these aristocratic families provided strong instruments of defense as well as offensive weapons in the fights for familial or factional dominance within the city. Along with an *imborghesimento* of the aristocracy, there is an *aristocratizzazione* of merchants and artisans as these new social groups seek to imitate the traditional nobility by returning to the country as landowners (Hiestand 32).

Although a critic like Krauss emphasizes that the strife between the various Guelph and Ghibelline parties divided the landed aristocracy leaving them open to attacks from the *popolo,* the *popolani* gained effective control over the city-state government in only a few communes.[15] In most towns where a popolo formed, the association did manage to broaden the base of government and contain the violence of the magnate or patrician class, but most political offices fell into the hands of *popolani grassi* who were easily assimilated into the oligarchy. As John Larner summarizes, "The real virtue of the movement perhaps was, outside centres like Florence, mainly symbolic. It gave to the independent communes the traditional theoretical role of a king in his kingdom . . . or at least . . . the idea that they ruled in the interest of the governed classes" (*Italy* 125). Thus, just as the patricians attempted to justify their standing from above by presenting themselves as imperial vassals, they also proved their status from below by presenting themselves as the citizens' protectors.

Many Trecento authors portray a political reality in which the parties attempted to manipulate the popolo in their fight for hegemony. In 1314 a tailor in a lawsuit in Treviso was asked to define *pars* or faction, which he described as "when some of the 'popolani' or other persons look to and hold with one magnate, and some with another" (Hyde, "Contemporary Views" 297). A dominican friar, Remigio Girolami, who preached at the turn of the fourteenth century in Florence read a sermon in which he listed three kinds of civil strife: (1) between clergy and laity, (2) between artisans and great men, and (3) between the Guelphs and Ghibellines. Girolami's analysis of the violence within his commune includes but extends beyond class conflict; he distinguishes class conflict from factional violence realizing that the two were related but not equivalent ("Contemporary Views" 283–84). When a contemporary of Remigio, Dino Compagni, writes about the split between the black and white Guelphs in his city, he reports that the party division affected all social classes: the wealthy and important whom he calls *uomini grandi,* a middle-class or *mezani,* and those with the smallest social standing—the *piccolini* (54).

This type of commentary has encouraged many contemporary historians to question the notion that the Ghibellines represented the interests of the old landed aristocracy while the Guelphs consisted of *la gente nuova* or rising bourgeoisie. Hyde notes that the association of the Guelphs with the papal cause and the Ghibellines with the emperor proves somewhat accurate during the factions' formative years, 1227–1268, when the Hohenstaufen and Papacy continuously fought; yet, for the years that followed "the normal situation was for the pope and the imperial claimant to be an uneasy and ineffective alliance, to the confusion of those who continued to think along traditional lines" ("Contemporary Views" 295). The parties seemed to have remained strong, precisely because their appeal superseded class boundaries.

The aristocratic families or *consorterie* who led the communal factions came from different social backgrounds. The development of sophisticated economies and administrations allowed certain non-aristocratic families to gain enough money and prestige to mix and marry with the old nobility. Lauro Martines proposes, however, that the most important social division was not between the nobles and non-nobles of the communal elite, but rather between the poorest and wealthy popolani: "As we move from city to city in search of the popolo's structural difficulties, we continually encounter one decisive cleavage: the social and psychological distance that divided the artisans and small shopkeepers from the bankers and wealthy long-distance merchants" (68). In a similar fashion, Hyde suggests that one must not place too much value on social distinctions among the ruling class; as he and other historians argue, the most powerful families created a lifestyle and a system of values that were not exclusively mercantile, professional, or feudal but rather a composite of all of these qualities (*Society and Politics* 170). Lansing echoes Hyde's opinion by emphasizing the importance given to knighthood as a cultural model among thirteenth-century urban nobles, including the nouveau riche merchants (159). Several historians of late medieval Florence, including Lansing, also emphasize the continuing importance of lineage in that commune's patronage system.[16]

Even though the emperor was—with a few exceptions—physically absent from the Italian peninsula after 1250 and the pope followed his lead in 1305, imperial and papal symbols continued to influence northern Italy in various ways. For instance, the emperor and the pope were the only figures who had the power to confer the authority to produce legal deeds; in fact, notaries were called *auctoritate imperiali notarius*. More important, the aristocratic leaders or signori often attempted to justify their own power by becoming an imperial vicar or vassal of the emperor (Hiestand 42). Likewise, the lord would request that his own citizens take an oath of loyalty. Rather than resisting the feudal model, many communes modified it to their own needs paving the way for the signoria, a microcosm of the imperial model (47). Feudal customs had not died with the rebirth of cities and a money economy, but rather had left a profound imprint on northern Italian communes, particularly in the Trevisan March.

I am not claiming that the Italian chivalric epic mirrored the complex institutions of Italian communes. Each commune had a unique history in which different institutions (Guelf party, Ghibelline party, Popolo, Comune, Podestariato) played different roles at different times. What I do wish to emphasize is that both the communes and the epic narratives contain conflicting ideologies, which do not reflect directly the values of one social group.

Franco-Italian epics do not overturn imperial or feudal ideology, but rather modify it in different ways. The king is no longer described as the exclusive source of power for the lords, as he was in early epics such as the Oxford *Chanson de Roland*. Epic heroes, such as Bovo d'Antona, still fear and respect the king, but they derive their power primarily from their own family inheritance and skill. Leaders of clans composed of both friends and relatives fight for power amongst themselves, and the king's support becomes only one factor in determining which side wins the conflict. The king's power diminishes as a result, and he is often satirized in the *Marciano XIII* narratives.

Despite these changes, the manuscript does not represent important groups within the new urban culture such as bankers, lawyers, and artisans, instead concentrating almost exclusively on the nobility. The focus of the narratives does change, however, from conflicts between the king's needs and those of his vassals to a conflict between aristocratic families or clans over the political control of urban spaces. Heroes such as Bovo d'Antona no longer simply inherit, but also earn the right to rule a city because of their actions. Yet, nevertheless, the possible contenders for that civic power remain exclusively aristocratic. Fear of betrayal from a member of the clan becomes an essential element in many of the narratives, and female characters are not excluded; the anonymous author pays special attention to the role women play in consolidating the power of a clan. These modifications of the generic model are not antifeudal. Instead, they depict a flattening of the social pyramid that forces noble families to seek their power not only from the king at the top of the social hierarchy but also from the families who constitute their base of support. Moreover, these modifications do not represent a strictly Italian character since the same changes develop in late French chansons de geste as well.

Several examples of the king's diminished role in this refashioning of the social model appear in the *Marciano XIII*, including the tales about Bovo d'Antona and Uggeri. The protagonists in these stories are two rebellious vassals from the Old French epic tradition: Bueve de Hantone and Ogier the Dane. While the other *Marciano XIII* texts focus more on the private and domestic lives of the epic heroes than on their battlefield triumphs, the narratives about Bovo and Uggeri retain the militaristic character of the early chanson de geste.[17] This difference occurs because the other texts center on the internal conflicts within powerful families, while the tales of Bovo and the Dane highlight battles between different lineages. Bovo and the Dane both represent noble families whose interests conflict with those of the king, and whose military prowess contrasts with the monarch's physical and political weakness.

The three continental versions of *Bueve de Hantone* date from the second half of the thirteenth century.[18] In all of these French narratives, Bueve is the son of an English vassal Guion who is assassinated by Doon de Maience. Doon then marries his accomplice, Guion's wife, and takes over the victim's city, Hantone. Bueve, meanwhile, is sold to merchants who trade him to a pagan king. Bueve goes through trials and tribulations in the East and falls in love with a pagan princess, Yosiane. Accompanied by Yosiane and a benevolent monster, Açophart, Bueve eventually returns to Hantone to claim his rights as Guion's heir. Doon finds himself losing battles against Bueve and bribes the king in order to win him to his side. In all three versions, Doon offers money to the king in exchange for his help against Bueve, but only in the second version does the king accept Doon's gifts, after constant prodding from the latter's relatives, Amauris and Rohars. The authors of all three versions emphasize that Doon's relatives appear at the king's court to support his plea for aid. Although the Maience clan convinces the king to accept its bribe only in the second version, the family members appear as important characters in all three Old French texts.[19]

One important difference between the Old French and Franco-Italian texts is the resolution of the battle between Bueve/Bovo and the Maience/Maganza clan (Krauss, *L'Epica feudale* 29.) In the Old French versions, both Bueve and Doon present their stories to the king, who must decide how to resolve their conflict. In two of the versions the king himself proclaims Doon's punishment, and in the other version the king's peers decide Doon's fate. The writers of the Old French versions present the king as a seigneur or lord and Doon and Bueve as competitive vassals.

The conflict in the Franco-Italian text resolves itself in a different manner. Dodo and the entire Maganza clan run to the king for help and bribe him with gifts and money. The king, portrayed as a greedy fool, accepts the bribe and pledges to support the Maganza clan's battle against Bovo and his followers. This decision angers the king's respected advisors, Aquilon de Baivere and Morando de Rivere, who perceive Doon as an evil man. Moreover, the king's peers believe that he is meddling unnecessarily in a conflict between two nobles; the king's right to arbitrate problems among other nobles is not supported even by his closest allies. Aquilon warns the king not to interfere in the affairs of the two men:

> El dist à li rois: "Guarda qe vu façé.
> Bovo è prodon e de bon parenté.
>
> . . . .
>
> Ne'[n] cel ovra ne vos trometeré."
>
> (ll. 3001–6)

[And he said to the king: watch what you do. Bovo is a noble man and from a good family. . . . Don't interfere in this affair.]

Bovo recognizes the king as a powerful lord whom he must fear, but not a sovereign from whom he receives the rights to control the city of Antona. At one point before the fighting begins, Bovo, with a patronizing tone, tells the king to behave wisely and return home, for he will not allow Charlemagne to negotiate a deal with Dodo on his behalf:

> Çentil rois sire, faites le saçamant;
> Torneç en França con tota vestre jant,
> Da mo à Dodo partirò li convant.
>
> (ll. 3279–81)

[Noble king, Lord, behave wisely; return to France with all your people. Now I will divide the territory with Dodo.]

The two nobles fight for the city in an open battle. After killing Dodo, Bovo takes the king and his peers as prisoners. At this point, both Aquilon and Morando tell Bovo that they had warned the king not to take sides in the conflict.

The different resolutions of the conflict between Bueve/Bovo and Doon/Dodo in the Old French and Franco-Italian versions have been interpreted as representations of two different worldviews. According to this reading, the Old French texts focus on feudal law, while the new bourgeois world vision in the Franco-Italian version emphasizes moral questions (Krauss, *L'Epica feudale* 35). Yet, one must consider the continuities between the texts as well as their discontinuities.

In all the narratives, Doon/Dodo is portrayed as surrounded by family members who protect him and help him plead his case in front of the king. All the authors stress the fact that Bueve/Bovo is not only fighting Doon/Dodo but his entire clan; all the texts illustrate a conflict for the political control of the city of Hantone/Antona between two factions grouped loosely around two aristocratic families. In the Old French versions, the authors place the king in the role of arbitrator of these fights, and thus the families are described as competitors for his approval. In the Franco-Italian version, the king does not play such a role; the author of this narrative describes him as a powerful lord who plays a part in determining which faction will control the city but does not have the power to enforce all his preferences. An important element in all the texts is the fact that the two factions are fighting over the control of an urban space, a city.

The word *bourgeois* appears several times in the Old French texts because the authors refer to the groups of citizens whose support Bueve must earn. One of the clearest examples appears in the first version. After Bueve has obtained control of the city, he is forced by the king to take a pilgrimage and leaves the city in charge of his allies. Before his departure, he meets with city administrators, who pledge their support to his family and express their regrets. The writer specifically lists the citizens who meet with their lord and take an oath of loyalty: *eskevins* or judges, *maiors* or city officials, and *jurés* or guild leaders:

> Les saintuaires lor a on aportés,
> Tous les *bourgois* de la vile a mandés,
> Les *eskievins*, les *maieurs*, les *jurés*;
> De par la dame prist Sobaus fëutés:
> Premierement les reçut des fievés,
> Des *eskevins*, des *maiors*, des *jurés*,
> Puis le jura l'autre communités.
>
> (ll. 6919–25; emphasis added)
>
> [The holy relics were carried to them; he sent for all the *bourgois* of the city, the *judges*, the *city officials*, and the *guild leaders*. On behalf of the lady (Bueve's wife) Sobaut pledged his loyalty: first he received it from the vassals, the *judges*, the *city officials*, the *guild leaders*, then the other groups swore it.]

In the second version, when Bueve returns from exile to his native city he is met outside the walls by both *chevaliers* and *bourgeois* who greet him with thanks and kisses:

Li *bourgois* l'öent si l'en ont mercié,
Des *chevaliers* i ot de cel regné
Qui ont Buevon baisié et acolé.

(ll. 8574–77; emphasis added)

[The *bourgeois* having heard it thus they thanked him; some *knights* of that land were there who kissed and hugged Bueve.]

These two quotations describe a sophisticated city government in which men could gain a certain status because of their profession or their lineage. From studying the Bueve/Bovo narratives it becomes apparent that both communal and chivalric ideologies were important in the late medieval French as well as the Italian chivalric epics.

Just as Italian historians have reassessed the model of fourteenth-century communal society as a conflict between the feudal aristocracy and the rising bourgeoisie, French historians have also revised their understanding of urban development in the Middle Ages. Traditionally, the king and the rising bourgeoisie were viewed as allies in a fight for political hegemony against the feudal lords; historians perceived chivalry as an extra-urban phenomenon. Jacques Le Goff, however, has stated that the seigneurial and bourgeois classes shared many of the same economic interests in French medieval cities: "in the end the cities adapted to the lords' form of production and reciprocally the lords accepted the cities" (2:243). The cities integrated themselves into the feudal system creating a "feudo-bourgeois" culture (244).

The feudal system was based on the pledge between lord and vassal, and similarly the citizens of emerging cities took oaths promising mutual economic and military cooperation. Yet, in many of these *serments* the citizen swore faithfulness not only to the city but to its seigneur as well. Even when the lord is not mentioned in the oath, his permission had to be granted before the citizens could make such a pledge to the city (265).

In Italy, medieval writers often divided the emerging bourgeoisie into the *popolo grasso* and the *popolo minuto*. The term *grasso* referred to those non-noble citizens who had enough economic and political prestige to assimilate easily into the landed aristocracy. Similar terms were used in French texts as writers divided non-noble citizens into two groups, the *gros* and the *menus*. Although Le Goff points out that these groups were never as well organized and self-conscious as their contemporaries in large Italian city-states such as Florence, he refers to the *gros* as the patricians who comprised the oligarchical leadership (326). This group forms an urban aristocracy whose "golden age" is the thirteenth and early fourteenth centuries (332). Like their Italian counterparts, powerful clans seeking political hegemony within a city's oligarchy often dragged the entire population into their conflicts (330).

All the Bueve/Bovo narratives depict a similar social structure in which leaders of urban aristocratic families struggle in order to win the support of both the citizens and the king. Although it left less of a mark on French cities than on Italian communes, the landed aristocracy influenced the development of these growing municipalities. In both late medieval France and Italy the chanson de geste served as a vehicle for spreading chivalric mythology in urban societies as the new feudo-bourgeois aristocracies searched for traditions to legitimize their power and glorify their bloody factional conflicts.

Another pair of texts in the *Marciano XIII*, *Enfances Ogier* and the *Chevalerie Ogier*, also describe a conflict between the king and a rebellious vassal from the Old French epic tradition, Ogier. In the Old French versions of the *Chevalerie Ogier*, which date from the late thirteenth through the fifteenth centuries, the great hero represents an entire class of noble vassals who are fighting to retain rights in a feudal system that the king wishes to control; the other barons collectively defend Ogier's position to the emperor (Krauss, *L'Epica feudale* 164).[20] The Franco-Italian text, however, focuses on the struggle between two great dynasties rather than on a conflict between social classes. The author of the Italian version introduces Ogier when Charlemagne, preparing to drive the Saracens from Rome, declares him leader of the squires. Ogier proves his valor by entering the battle to save the Christian standard from the cowardly knight, Aleris, who was dragging it behind him.[21] Since Ogier is still a *baçaler* and not yet old enough to become a knight, he is unarmed and must fight with an apple tree branch as if he were a woodsman. Ogier then runs to meet Aleris, calling his fellow Christian an evil traitor:

> Donc li Dainos prist un baston de pomer
> E grant e groso, merveloso e plener;
> O el vi Aleris, ven davanti à l'incontrer.
> Elo li scrie: "Estes malvasio liçer!"

(ll. 9993–96)

[Then the Dane took a big and thick apple branch, marvelous and full; when he saw Aleris, he came ahead to meet him. He yelled at him: "You are an evil traitor!"]

The woodsman figure, or *boscher*, ties together three of the texts within the *Marciano XIII*. In separate stories, the author represents two different nobles, first Ogier and later Milon, who are forced to fight without the proper chivalric weapons. Like Ogier who defends the French standard with an apple tree branch, Milon uses the same rustic weapon to defend himself from robbers. Milon's characterization as a woodsman is developed even further because he is forced to flee Charlemagne's court and hide in the woods after he impregnated the king's unwed sister. Having no other means to support his family, he uses his physical strength to labor as a *boscher*. While Ogier and Milon come from noble lineages, the last narrative of the manuscript relates the transformation of a humble woodsman, Varocher, into a knight who has earned his new status by proving his prowess in battle using only a tree branch.

The success of each of these characters, both as workers and knights, depends to a great extent on their exceptional physical power. While the author depicts the two extremes of the social scale (*vilains* and knights), the upwardly mobile members of the northern Italian communes (the merchant and professional classes) hardly appear in these narratives. The role of the woodsman ascribed to nobles in the manuscript emphasizes that such men have earned their social position because of their strength and courage; this characterization does not question the notion of a noble caste, but rather pokes fun at the upwardly mobile urban social groups by defining their pursuit of chivalric feats and titles in sylvan terms.

Even when social mobility is endorsed, it is qualified by feudal values. In the *Chevalerie Ogier* text Charlemagne sends Ogier to request a tribute from the Saracen lord of Marmore (Verona), Maximo Çudé, who had repeatedly murdered the king's messengers for having made the same demand.[22] Upon arriving at a hostelry in Brescia, the innkeeper, Baldoin, warns Ogier of Maximo's cruelty and offers to help him kill the tyrant by organizing friends and relatives. The group manages to kill the powerful Saracen and rescue the city. When Ogier returns to Paris he leaves Baldoin in charge. The innkeeper sends his son with an enormous tribute to Charlemagne as proof of his loyalty. On Ogier's recommendation, the king dubs the son of the *cortois hoster* or noble innkeeper. Contrary to the events in *Chevalerie Ogier*, woodsmen, like innkeepers, did not gain a great deal of prestige in communal Italy. The author continues to omit any mention of the new social groups that shared real power in the urban aristocracy. Moreover, Baldoin becomes a knight by supporting the noble, Ogier. The innkeeper's gain in social status, therefore, still derives from feudal practices—his loyalty to a lord.

Although Ogier is a *baçaler* and thus of noble origin, he receives the title of knight because he earns it. When the king announces that Ogier will be dubbed he tells the hero that he is receiving the honor because he had performed well: "Dist li rois: 'vu avi ben ovré'" [The king said: "you have done well"] (l. 10076). Charlemagne's son, Carloto, on the other hand, lacks Ogier's qualities. In fact, the entire family embodies egotism, and its presence establishes the text as a battle between evil leaders who seek to protect their own interests and good leaders who seek to defend God's interests. At one point Carloto even threatens to flee the Christian side, strike a deal with the Sultan, and help the Saracens attack the French, if he does not get his own way. Despite such threats, Charlemagne continues to support his son's weaknesses to the detriment of the entire community. After Carloto murders Ogier's son and threatens to kill Ogier himself, the Dane finally slays him. The king then angers all the nobles by imprisoning Ogier, whom they regard as the best knight in Christendom.

Near the end of *Chevalerie Ogier*, the king must put aside his hate for Ogier—the man who killed his son—and plead with him to fight in yet another battle for the survival of the Christian world. Ogier agrees to forgive Charlemagne and enter the combat only if the king allows the knight to hit him three times with his sword. The narrator describes this scene in comical terms as Ogier clearly shames the Christian leader. The emperor, fearful of Ogier's strength, not only protects himself with arms, but even wears two helmets! When Ogier sees Charlemagne, he cannot help but laugh:

> Adoncha li Danois fo de la carçer ravie,
> E l'inperer fo d'armes ben guarnie;
> En çevo se mis dos elmi de Pavie.
> Li Danois le vi, nen po muer nen rie.

(ll. 12994–97)

[Then the Dane was taken from the prison, and the emperor was well protected with armor. On his head he put two Pavian helmets. The Dane saw him—and he could not help but laugh.]

Like Bovo, the Ogier of the *Marciano XIII* earns his status not only because of his family but also because of his virtuousness and skills. Krauss states that this emphasis on "moral" issues rather than on the intricacies of feudal law reflects the values of the northern Italian bourgeoisie. A transformation occurred between Raimbert's text and the Franco-Italian version of the Ogier story: in the first text, Ogier fights for his rights as a feudal vassal; while in the second, he fights as a knight who realizes that he is at least Charlemagne's equal, if not his superior. The defense of the Christian world rests on his shoulders, not on those of Charlemagne. Ogier, however, is a noble, and his qualities, like the faults of Charlemagne, seem determined largely by lineage. While the author describes Charlemagne's son as insolent and haughty, Ogier's son has extraordinary beauty and a gentle manner. Moreover, when the king dubs Ogier a knight, he states that the distinction applies to the entire *masné*, or household, not just to the individual who earned it. This attitude undermines any attempt to interpret Ogier's feats as an antifeudal statement.

The anti-imperial sentiment expressed in the tales of both Bovo and Ogier reveals their origin in the predominantly Guelf Trevisan March—the cradle of the powerful Lombard League—which fought to limit Frederick II's control of northern Italy. Such a political leaning, however, does not necessarily mean that these texts indicate an antifeudal perspective. Although they present the king of France as corrupt and selfish, there is always an alternative, a "real" leader, who comes from a noble family but displays more virtue and skill than the emperor. Neither the methods nor the goals of the Carolingian epic hero change drastically in their transplantation to northern Italy.

Several scholars, most notably Karl Bender, have suggested that the Franco-Italian epics depict the metamorphosis of Charlemagne from a *personage mythique* (mythical character) into a *personage romanesque* (burlesque character).[23] In this transformation the emperor remains the supreme ruler of the West, but is open to ridicule and disdain because he is no longer portrayed as a sovereign by divine right or the sacred head of a feudal hierarchy. As the emperor's standing as a divine ruler diminishes, therefore, authors feel free to portray the once ideal leader with very human faults such as the frailty of old age, uncontrollable anger, and avarice. Although Bender noted that the Old French epics of rebellious vassals such as the *Chanson de Renaut de Montauban* also depict a flawed and unjust emperor, he argues that the Franco-Italian texts are the first to transfer this portrayal of the emperor to the *gestes des rois* or Carolingian epics (166).

The description of two homogenous, yet oppositional Old French traditions—the ideal emperor of the *gestes des rois* and the anti-ideal of the rebellious vassal epic—does not take into account several early Carolingian texts that portray the king in conflicting ways. One of the most famous is *Le Pèlerinage de Charlemagne,* which was probably written in the second half of the twelfth century. This text must have circulated in the Veneto because its comic episodes clearly influenced a prose epic, *Li fatti de Spagna,* produced in that region during the middle of the fourteenth century (see Ruggieri *Li Fatti*; Fassò, "La materia" 65). At the beginning of this poem the queen jokingly suggests to Charlemagne that she has heard of a king who is even more handsome than her husband. The king interprets his wife's teasing as a challenge, and forces the queen to confess that King Hugo, the emperor of Greece and Constantinople, has the reputation of being the world's finest knight. The king then decides to find his eastern counterpart in order to verify the queen's assertion and to compare his appearance to that of the other ruler. The emperor, however, does not reveal the original impetus for his voyage to his knights, but rather tells them that he has decided to take a pilgrimage to Jerusalem. These opening scenes establish an ambivalent image of the king that reappears throughout the text; he is at once a foolish, self-indulgent figure, as well as a sacred ruler. In fact, despite the initial portrayal of the emperor as frivolous, when he arrives in Jerusalem the patriarch greets him as the divinely elected ruler of the world, and Charlemagne becomes the first man to sit in a chair that Christ had used.

At the end of the narrative, Charlemagne defends the venerable status of his title by defeating King Hugo. Although the two monarchs compete, Charlemagne does not prove his superiority on the battlefield, but instead with words and help from the Heavens. The emperor's twelve peers drink too much and recklessly make exaggerated boasts or *gabs* about their own virility and power. For example, Oliver asserts that he would be able to have sex with King Hugo's daughter a hundred times in one night, and Ogier contends that he could topple King Hugo's palace by pulling down one of its support columns with his own hands. The eastern king then challenges the western knights to fulfill those claims. The only way that such feats can be realized, though, is through divine intervention; the emperor and his knights defeat King Hugo not because of their own prowess or character but because of miracles. Thus, although Charlemagne and the twelve peers are made to look ridiculous, the emperor's office retains its sacred authority. The text's parodic tone encourages readers to laugh at the heroes of the chanson de geste tradition who can not achieve the ideal rather than at the model of imperial authority, which the Carolingian epic had helped to construct:[24]

Mult fu liéd e joius Carlemaines li ber,
Ki tel rei ad cunquis sanz bataille campel.

(ll. 858–59)

[Charlemagne the Brave was filled with joy to have overcome such a king without a pitched battle.][25]

In the passage above, the conventional coupling of the epic hero's name with the adjective *ber* or brave—a description of an ideal knight's character—is comically juxtaposed with Charlemagne's delight at having successfully avoided military conflict. This text, which was probably produced a century before the *Marciano XIII*, demonstrates that hybrid narratives containing both humorous and reverent images of the emperor appeared in the Carolingian narratives before Italian authors ever joined the tradition.

Although the *Pèlegrinage* is a unique Carolingian text that does not focus on the battles characteristic of the traditional chanson de geste, other early Old French epics also combine the sacred with the comic. One scholar, Nicolò Pasero, identifies several early epics that contain different cultural discourses. In his Bakhtinian analysis of the genre, he argues that dichotomous categorizations such as ideal/anti-ideal, high/low, or aristocratic/popular cannot adequately describe the chanson de geste (4–5). Instead he suggests that even "classical" Old French epics contain carnivalesque elements like disguises, role inversion, and the grotesque body, but that these dialogical tendencies are usually subsumed into the monological, as the chanson de geste ultimately supports the notion of one sacred, universal hierarchy (16–17).[26] An example of the carnivalesque in the twelfth-century epic *Le couronnement de Louis* is the deformed nose of Guillaume d'Orange, which the epic hero himself describes as *accorcié* or shortened.[27] The grotesque body is also used to deflate a heroic character in the *Marciano XIII* when the emperor laments his own small stature, but Pasero proposes that such ambivalent descriptions were not just characteristic of the late epics, but instead had always been a part of the chanson de geste's structure.

While the chanson de geste's tendency to first represent and then suppress different voices is evident in the classical narratives, it becomes even more apparent in the "hybrid" Old French epics of the late twelfth and thirteenth centuries. These texts are defined as hybrid because they modify the chanson de geste by combining it with elements from other genres including romance, hagiography, and folktales.[28]

One such early hybrid epic is *Hervis de Mes* of the *geste des Loherains* in which the hero's love for a lady inspires his bravery as it would in a romance, whereas in the traditional chanson de geste such prowess is usually motivated by a warrior's love for his lord. In describing *Hervis de Mes*, however, Catherine M. Jones suggests that this twelfth-century text also differs from other thirteenth-century hybrid epics because the marvelous does not play such a significant role as it does in later Carolingian narratives (65). Instead *Hervis de Mes* depicts "daily life" including details about transactions with money and the procurement of necessities such as bread. The text's concern for such quotidian affairs derives from Hervis's mixed ancestry as the son of a rich bourgeois and a noble woman.

In the first part of the narrative Hervis's father attempts to raise a son who will be a merchant as well as a knight—who will fulfill the bourgeois function of accumulation as well as the aristocratic function of distribution. Hervis, though, eventually distances himself from his father's profession, and instead seeks to protect his matrilineal nobility as a warrior. Jones describes the differences between the two parts of the narrative: "Part One opposes two social value systems only to bring them into harmony; although the bourgeoisie definitely suffers in the balance. . . . Part Two, on the other hand, no longer acknowledges the resourcefulness or even the necessity of the merchant; only the noble warrior can succeed in this battle of feudal rights" (93). Thus, *Hervis de Mes* does not mirror historical transformations, but rather tries to contain their ideological significance.

Jones's analysis of *Hervis de Mes* suggests that the text illustrates in a more dramatic fashion the narrative structure that Pasero finds constitutive of even the classical chanson de geste, that is, a tendency to express but then suppress different voices. It is also important to note that although the narratives of the *Marciano XIII* strengthen this generic tendency, they never illustrate a mixed lineage of merchants and nobles. Although *Hervis de Mes* was produced more than a century earlier, and in France rather than Italy, it offers a more striking example of how epic writers attempted to anchor the flux of urban life in a static representation of an ideal social order.

Recent scholarship of the once neglected late chanson de geste of the thirteenth century also challenges the assumption that Charlemagne remained an ideal leader in the French tradition. Two French chansons de geste of the thirteenth century, *Huon de Bordeaux* and *Gaydon*, contain many of the generic modifications usually described as part of a late medieval Italian worldview. In both these texts the heroes must earn their status by overcoming obstacles created by an unjust emperor. While the Charlemagne portrayed in *Huon de Bordeaux* is a weak ruler who lacks good judgement, the emperor in *Gaydon* is very similar to the sovereign depicted in the *Marciano XIII*. Gaydon, like Bovo, must not only fight a group of traitors (once again descendants of Ganelon), but also the emperor who has allied with the evil clan out of greed. The text makes clear that the ruler's actions are antithetical to the traditional image of the ideal leader presented in the *Chanson de Roland;* after the emperor accepts the traitors' bribes, one of his men reminds the sovereign that he is betraying Roland's memory by selling out to the clan responsible for his nephew's death:

> La mort Rollant vostre neveu vendez,
> Quant les avoirs des traïtors prennez.
>
> (Guessard and Luce 163, ll. 5393–94)
>
> [You are selling the death of your nephew, Roland, when you take the traitors' possessions.]

In *Gaydon,* just as in the *Marciano XIII,* the conflict between the king and his vassal has less to do with feudal law than with broader moral issues. Just as in the Franco-Italian *Bovo* narrative, the emperor is not criticized for violating the lord/vassal relationship but for his avarice. Moreover, even though Charlemagne's character is questioned, the vassal continues to respect the emperor's office and eventually reintegrates himself into the social order by negotiating a peace with his sovereign. Both heroes of the *Marciano XIII* discussed above, Bovo and Ogier, recognize the necessity of reconciling their differences with the emperor, and the author repeatedly reminds the audience of Charlemagne's unquestionable reputation, labelling him *le milor rois* or the best king (l. 10898).

Another link between the late French epics and the *Marciano XIII* narratives, particularly *Bovo,* is that the traitors use money to cloud the emperor's judgement. This negative portrayal of the most important tool of social mobility in the late Middle Ages is as evident in the Italian "bourgeois" epics as in the French "feudal" texts. The nobles who use money for political advantage, who have adopted the habits of mercantile patricians, are portrayed as the spiritual descendants of Judas. All the late epics analyzed in this chapter, those produced both in Italy and in France, do not question the feudal hierarchy by depicting an emperor who is physically and morally weak; rather the epics support the notion of a universal social hierarchy, which can negotiate the conflicts among local patrician families in a fair and honest fashion. The clash between the interests of the individual/clan and those of the larger community had been an integral part of the chanson de geste tradition since its inception. In the *Chanson de Roland* it is exemplified by Ganelon's feud with Roland, which causes him to betray Charlemagne and the social order the emperor represents.

The thirteenth-century French epics discussed above, *Huon de Bor-*

deaux and *Gaydon,* both portray Charlemagne in diminished terms, but only the first text was produced in a region with strong communal institutions. While *Huon de Bordeaux* derives from the province of Arras, an area in which mercantile, patrician families dominated through the thirteenth century and which is often compared to late medieval Italian communes, *Gaydon* derives from Anjou where local nobility had to subjugate itself to the French king early in the same century.[29] It would be particularly difficult to see this text as a reflection of a communal, antifeudal ideology. In fact, one scholar has suggested that *Gaydon* encouraged Angevins to accept their new submissive relationship with the king of France (Subrenat 51).

Both the communal governments and the French king, however, did share the same dilemma of how to implement a larger regional or national system of justice that could negotiate and suppress the violence of local factions. The epics represent a society in which these two levels of authority continue to contaminate each other—a society in which nobles, even the emperor, are unable or unwilling to place the interests of the greater community above those of their family. The late Carolingian tales present the notion of a universal empire free from the political interests of local politics as an unrealistic utopian ideal. The clan, then, replaces the empire as the most important institution for determining social order (or chaos). This discursive move pushes late epic writers to integrate the domestic, the quotidian, even the feminine into the once sacred and exclusively male social hierarchy of the chanson de geste. The next chapter examines how gender roles and notions of social identity in general change as the genre shifts its focus from the battlefield to the bedroom.

2

The Conflicting "Family Values" of the *Marciano XIII* Manuscript

> The foreigner is within us. And when we flee from our struggle against the foreigner, we are fighting . . . that "improper" facet of our impossible "own and proper."
>
> *Strangers to Ourselves,* Julia Kristeva

Strife within and between clans is clearly the most prominent element of the eight narratives that make up the *Marciano XIII*.[1] These stories consistently portray familial struggles that quickly escalate into regional or international warfare. Although the epics included in the *Marciano XIII* do not limit themselves to what Viscardi calls *"vicende tutte private, intime, famigliari"* [private, intimate, familial affairs], all the battles begin with an act of familial betrayal or vendetta (24). This notion of family conflict as the source of international warfare was not unique to the Carolingian epic, but had many supporters among other communal writers. Dino Compagni, for example, retells in his *Cronica* the legendary origins about how the bloody conflict between the Guelph and Ghibelline parties arose over a marriage dispute: Buondalmonte de' Buondalmonti had promised to marry a woman of the Uberti clan but broke off the engagement after having seen the beautiful daughter of Forteguerra Donati. To avenge the dishonor, the Uberti clan arranged for the murder of Buondalmonte on his wedding day. This incident, according to the legend, sparked the spiral of violence between the two political factions (7–9).

As Italian epic writers foreground familial conflicts in their narratives, wives, daughters, and sisters take on new importance in a genre that had traditionally left women in the wings while their men fought battles on the main stage. The emphasis on clan places the spotlight not only on women, but also on more general issues of gender identification. Women are portrayed as having an enormous influence on the survival of their "house," and that power is portrayed as disturbing the traditional male/female dichotomy.

In addition, clan leaders need skills other than martial prowess to succeed in negotiating political struggles between clans and amongst their own followers as well. Together with moderation and reason, rhetorical skills were considered essential attributes for patriarchs to succeed as merchants and administrators, but these qualities were depicted ambivalently because they also functioned as a restraint on the aggression conventionally associated with the ideal masculinity of the chanson de geste. While Roland's courage stands as the outstanding characteristic of masculine heroism in the *Chanson de Roland,* the *Marciano XIII* and other Italian epics are just as likely to associate physical strength and martial bravery with non-noble supporters as with the noble lords themselves. The destabilizing of ideal masculinity also appears in other late medieval writings about chivalry, as more Italians gained the title of knight because of the power they acquired through the intellectual accomplishments of mercantile and administrative careers rather than through military feats on the battlefield. In other words, as the growing prominence of new urban social groups prompted authors to reexamine both gender and class identities, the Carolingian epics participated in a larger late medieval debate about what it means to be a man and to be noble.

Discussions of clan identification and chivalric titles often overlapped in late medieval Italian texts because urban patrician families used the rank of knighthood to affirm their status and define their "house." One problem that faced the ruling class of Italy's city-states was how to define their power. While the old nobility claimed that it had received its power to rule from various emperors or from the Church, many members of the *la gente nuova* or newcomers felt anxious about carrying the title *Messer.* Dante's dubious explanation of his own "noble" ancestry offers a good example of this need to justify one's social status. In canto 15 of *Paradiso,* Dante's great-great-grandfather appears and describes how he was dubbed by the Emperor Conrad. This attribution of noble lineage to his family allows Dante to separate himself from *la gente nuova* and condemn their immoral behavior.

Another option existed, however, for the patriarchs of wealthy families who could not piece together a noble heritage: if they gained enough money and fame, they might in effect "buy" knighthood from the commune. Such knights were known as *cavalieri popolari* (knights of the popolo), and although there existed a distinction between these knights and the so-called *cavalieri nobili* (noble knights), their title still brought them prestige and privileges (Salvemini 361). As the historian Carol Lansing says, "For Italian urban nobles, chivalry and knighthood were a means of self-definition. A man spent lavishly to have his son dubbed a knight not to justify the young man's status but rather to define it" (160).

From the 1260s on, there is evidence of great ceremonies in the communes when a knight was dubbed. Although it was more prestigious to be awarded knighthood by men of royal or imperial blood in the way Dante describes his ancestor receiving a title, the communes increasingly usurped this function (Larner, "Chivalric Culture" 120–21). The uncle of Frederick Barbarossa, Otto of Freising, describes the creation of knights by communal authority as far back as the middle of the twelfth century. Yet, Salvemini and other historians write about a drastic increase in the number of knights created by the communes in the second half of the thirteenth century. A Florentine preacher at the end of the thirteenth century described four kinds of knights: *cavalieri di natura* (knights of nature), or descendants of a noble family; *cavalieri di ventura* (knights of fortune), who received the title because of their wealth, friendships, or virtuousness; *cavalieri di sciagura* (knights of misfortune), who are derided because they do not have enough money to maintain their position; and *cavalieri di grazia* (knights of grace), or defenders of the Church. Girolami makes it clear that the knights who "earned" their position deserve more praise than those who inherited it (Salvemini 119–20).

Most *cavalieri di ventura* came from two social groups: the wealthy mercantile and the administrative classes. Enrico Scrovegni, the wealthy Paduan usurer, became a knight to solidify his ties to the landed aristocracy with whom he often did business (Hyde, *Padua* 101). Notaries and judges needed to become knights in order to hold certain key positions, such as *podestà,* within the communal structure (Salvemini 121). The writer Franco Sacchetti pokes fun at the notaries, judges, and lawyers who abuse the privileges of what he scatologically labels *cacalería* for their own personal and political gain (*Il Trecentonovelle* 421). One of the most intriguing legal debates of the Trecento centered around the question of whether *dottori* or *cavalieri* should lead communal processions (Salvemini 130–35). While this symbolic tug-of-war might illustrate a growing class consciousness among the administrative professionals, it also demonstrates their desire to share the prestige that the traditionally noble *cavalleria* represented.

Some communal writers did make ideological distinctions among knights, but it is important to remember that Italian city-states were not "closed social containers," but dynamic communities; their urban aristocracies derived from different backgrounds and cannot easily be divided into distinct groups of nobles and bourgeois.[2] Powerful families did use chivalric rituals, however, to try and solidify those fluid social boundaries and distinguish themselves as part of the "true and proper nobility" (Gasparri 11).

Dubbings usually occurred alongside *magna curia* or grandiose celebrations such as the weddings and anniversaries of the communal elite. Activities at these festivities included jousts, tournaments, feasts, and entertainment by *giullari* or minstrels (Larner, "Chivalric Culture" 123). In several descriptions of these events, members of important, new social groups, such as judges, are specifically mentioned.[3] Therefore, the giullari did not just recite their texts to large uneducated crowds, as some scholars have suggested, but also for the ruling urban aristocracy including its administrative professionals.

One example of how chivalry was used to help define the status of families is the genealogical writings of a Paduan judge, Giovanni da Nono.[4] He was an educated man whose knowledge of Carolingian epics becomes quite evident in his *Liber de generatione aliquorum civium urbis Paduae, tam nobilium quam ignobilium.* Da Nono came from a noble family that had already lost much of its money and prestige (Hyde, *Padua* 67); therefore, in his history he is concerned with trying to anchor the relative nobility and virtuousness of families such as his own in a mythological past so that the character and distinction of these clans cannot be challenged by political and social changes. For instance, he despises the powerful Este family and traces their lineage back to the bad seed of Ganelon, whereas the clans that Giovanni admires he rewards with a heroic ancestor, such as the legendary King Desiderio of Lombardy (Rajna, "Le origini" 169–71). While discussing the Buzacarini family, Giovanni mentions in disparaging terms that one member of the clan was a giullare. Interestingly enough, Giovanni mentions other members of this family who belong to the new administrative class and were even worthy of the title of knight. Thus, by giullare, Giovanni probably meant an educated man who both wrote and performed literary works (163). Giovanni's work sheds light on the use of Carolingian epics by the communal aristocracy to develop its own mythology at the same time that it illustrates the importance of clan structures within the city-states' oligarchy.

Historians in recent years have taken a new look at the importance of clans in the political and social structures of late medieval urban societies. One of the most extensive studies on this subject is *Le clan familial* in which the author, Jacques Heers, concentrates on the importance of the clan in Italian communes and particularly in the city of Genoa. Heers questions the idea that the Italian city-states can be labelled bourgeois or protocapitalist (43). Instead, Heers believes that large, artificial "families" led by powerful nobles transported feudal models from the countryside to the city. These clans were either powerful aristocratic families who recruited lesser families to join their ranks, or families of equal social ranking who agreed to give up their ancient ancestral names and coats of arms to create a new, artificial familial group. Merchants and other popolani not only joined the already existing aristocratic clans, but followed the example of the nobles by creating their own collectives based on the same model (93–94).

These clans contributed to the placement and construction of a commune's architecture as well as its political and economic structures. Heers argues that the needs and desires of the leaders of powerful clans determined the building of fortresses, towers, and secure neighborhoods in Italian cities. Neighborhoods were not divided by social class, but rather by clan; the allies and dependents of clan leaders lived close to their patriarch for his protection as well as their own (175).

Due to geographical and social factors, the feudal nobility retained more power in Genoa than in other city-states (Martines 131). Yet, despite this difference a similar pattern of neighborhoods uniting around powerful families developed in other communes such as Florence. In Florence patrician families or *consorterie* not only tended to group themselves together in specific neighborhoods, but also in distinct areas of the surrounding countryside. Such proximity helped them to develop informal kinship networks that offered the clans' members both social and economic benefits (F. W. Kent 227–52).

The desire to consolidate and to build larger and more powerful clans among families was contradicted by an equally strong drive towards fragmentation within the clans. When these superfamilial structures grew too large, internal conflicts and the fears of the commune often caused division (Heers 97). In particular, the legal and social power invested in the patriarch left adult sons with very little legal and economic power and could lead to intense generational conflict (Kuehn, "Il diritto" 112).[5] Just as violence between clans, especially the vendetta, became a source of great pride, the possibility of internal strife and betrayal was a cause for anxiety and fear.

The *Marciano XIII* tale of Charlemagne's childhood, *Karleto,* describes how clan violence can threaten the entire social structure of the Christian world. In this text, the young Charlemagne grows up in exile among the Saracens in Spain after his half brothers, Lanfroi and Landris of the evil

Maganza clan, kill their father, Pepin, and their stepmother, Berta. Charlemagne triumphs in the conflict with his half brothers when he returns to the Christian world as a young man and regains his title of Holy Roman Emperor with the help of his grandfather, the king of Hungary, and a Saracen army. The struggle for the imperial crown first takes place in Rome, where a Maganza pope plots to choose a Holy Roman Emperor from his own clan. The author describes how the pope attempts to rig the election of a new sovereign, emphasizing the importance of the clan in fourteenth-century European politics:

> Cel apostoile fu de male rason,
> Si fu del parenté de qui de Gainelon.
> Mesaçer mande entorno et inviron:
> A principi e à dux, à marchisi et à con
> Et à li rois e altri baron,
> Qe à Rome vegna sença demorason,
> Qe de l'inperer vol fair l'alecion.
> Ben cuita faire un de soa mason.

(ll. 7760–67)

[This pope was of evil mind, as he was a relative of Ganelon. He sends messengers all around: to princes and to dukes, to marquises and to counts, and to other kings and other barons, so that they might come without delay to Rome, since he wants to have an election for emperor. He plans to elect one (a pope) from his own house.]

After Charlemagne wins the battle for control of the Empire, he names a cardinal from his own clan the new pope. While the narrator states that the Maganza pope is of evil mind or *de male rason*, Charlemagne's hand-picked choice for head of the Church is *saço e valant* or wise and valorous (l. 8186). Thus, the clan that gains control of both the Empire and the Church earns its authority through its goodness and wisdom. As in the stories of Bovo and Ogier analyzed in the last chapter, the *Karleto* narrative portrays a society in which familial conflicts define international politics. Moreover, the clan violence disrupts the most important structural opposition of the chanson de geste. Since Charlemagne cannot trust his own family, he must turn to Saracens for support. He is raised by the wise eastern king Galafro, marries Galafrio's daughter Belisant (although only after she has converted to Christianity), and eventually is aided by the Saracen army when he reconquers his territory. The *Marciano XIII* and the *Karleto* narrative in particular, then, represent clan violence as disrupting the Christian/Saracen dichotomy. While Charlemagne's Christian half brothers betray him, his pagan father-in-law remains faithful, even to the point of banishing his owns sons for plotting against the Christian upstart. The royal French family transforms from a pure "house" into a hybrid one in which the influence of the East cannot be clearly separated.

In these clan-centered texts, betrayal by a family member, even a wife, sister, or daughter, is a common fear. In the narratives of *Berta da li pe grandi*, *Berta e Milon*, and *Rolandin*, all the female protagonists are women who deceive their clans. In the first tale, the female lead is Berta Big-Foot, the wife of Pepin, and in the other narratives she is Charlemagne's half sister, Berta. The story of Berta Big-Foot precedes *Karleto* and explains why the young Charlemagne was forced into exile and raised by noble Saracens. Although women, following the archetypal example of Eve, spark the evil spiral of clan violence, they cannot betray families in the same way that men do because they lack economic and political power. They simply refuse or ignore their familial responsibilities as defined by the patriarch, either by neglecting their spousal duties or by choosing an inappropriate partner who has not been sanctioned by the clan. In other words, betrayal by a female character means an attempt to subvert the power of the patriarch over her body. Women were often expected to consolidate and expand the power of a clan through marriage to an ally; refusal to fulfill such a responsibility had both personal and political repercussions.[6]

Because she is exhausted after the long journey from her native Hungary, Pepin's wife, Berta Big-Foot, allows someone from outside the clan, a member of the Maganza family, to take her place in her husband's bed on their wedding night. This action is a betrayal; Berta Big-Foot fails her husband. The imposter usurps Berta's place and hires an assassin to kill her, but the hired killer takes pity on the queen and lets her go free in the woods, thinking that she will be killed by wild animals. Eventually the queen and Pepin are reunited, and the false Berta is burnt at the stake. While the Maganza pretended to be Berta Big-Foot, she gave birth to three children: Lanfroi, Landris, and Little Berta. Lanfroi and Landris will eventually poison their father and stepmother and wrest the kingdom of France from their baby brother, Karleto, the rightful heir. Charlemagne's half sister, Little Berta, will also betray him by having sex out of wedlock with the son of one of his barons. As Leslie Morgan states: "The two Bertas . . . offer an object lesson in two parts: against avoiding sex (Berta, Pipin's wife) and against overdoing it (the younger Berta, mother of Roland)" ("Berta" 45–46). Because of their transgressions, particularly Berta Big-Foot's decision not to sleep with Charlemagne's father, Pepin, on their wedding night, conflicts erupt not only in the French territory, but throughout Christendom.

Another version of the Berta Big-Foot story was written by the French courtier Adenet le Roi in the late thirteenth century at roughly the same time as the *Marciano XIII*. In his narrative, Berta is replaced in Pepin's bed by a servant rather than a woman from another aristocratic family. While scholars still debate whether the author of *Berta da li pe grandi* used Adenet's version as a model, it is clear that the Franco-Italian compiler chose a version of the Berta Big-Foot story that emphasized the conflict between two powerful families rather than between two social classes as in Adenet's rendering of the tale.[7]

The Franco-Italian *Berta Big-Foot* also differs from earlier versions by stressing the strength of Berta and her mother, the queen of Hungary. One critic describes the queen as both a "matriarch and a fish wife" (Adler, "Structural Meaning" 107). When Pepin's barons arrive in Hungary to ask the king if he would give his daughter to the emperor in marriage, the queen plays an active role in the negotiations, reminding her daughter that their family has enough wealth for Berta to decline Pepin's proposal if she would prefer not to marry him. She asserts Berta's independence just at the point in the narrative where her daughter is treated like merchandise when Pepin's advisor Aquilone inspects both "front and back" (l. 1805) to assure that Pepin is acquiring a wife with only one small defect.

Krauss has analyzed this scene as a reflection of the new Italian worldview because of its attention to the details of the marriage negotiations and to the "material aspect of the contract" (Berta's body) (*L'Epica feudale* 93). Yet as we saw in the last chapter, several late Old French epics also emphasize the importance of money in urban culture, even among the nobles. For instance, in the late-twelfth-century epic, *Hervis de Me*, the narrator tells us the exact amount that the hero pays to purchase his love interest from a band of squires who had kidnapped her (Herbin 63). Catherine M. Jones has commented on the text's "curious admixture of amorous and commercial ties," which she believes undermines "the lofty ideals of courtly love" (50–51). In a similar vein, the "inspection" of Berta's grotesque body in the *Marciano XIII* narrative diminishes the aura usually associated with the women of aristocratic families. Once again we see that the juxtaposition of contradictory views about nobles—the dialogic aspect of the Carolingian epic—is not unique to Italian texts, but instead is accentuated in the late narratives of both France and Italy.

The exceptional power of women in this tale is also represented on a symbolic level. In the French version of the story mentioned above, Berta's big feet serve a primarily narrative function by allowing the real queen to be distinguished from her imposter (Morgan, "Berta" 38). In the Franco-Italian version, however, Berta's fetishized feet represent both the queen's extraordinary strength as well as the emperor's fears and desires. When the courtly jongleur suggests that Pepin take Berta as his bride, Pepin laughs at the mention of the princess's distinguishing feature:

> "Plu bella dame non è in Oriant,
> Nian plus saçe, se la mer no me mant;
> Una colsa oit qe tegno por niant:
> Ela oit li pe asa plus grant
> Qe nulle autre dame qe soit de son convant:
> Berta da li pe grant, si l'apella la jant,
> E soa mer oit nome Belisant;
> Plu francha rayne no è à li segle vivant.
> Son per estoit rois d'Ongarie la grant."
> Li rois l'intent, si s'en rise bellement.
>
> (ll. 1297–1306)

["There is neither a more beautiful woman in the Orient, nor a wiser one, if her mother is not lying to me; she has one thing, which I don't consider important. She has feet that are somewhat larger than other women of her condition. Berta Big-Foot the people call her, and her mother is called Belisant, a more noble queen never lived. Her father was king of the great land of Hungary." The king listened to him and then laughed heartily.]

Besides Berta's big feet, the other characteristics ascribed to the princess and her mother, wisdom *(saçe)* and nobility *(francha),* were traits that epic writers usually bestowed on aristocratic men. Berta's gender-bending becomes even more obvious in a later fifteenth-century Italian version of this legend when she dons armor, enters battle, and successfully kills a knight.[8] The protagonist's difference, however, is more understandable if one remembers that she is from Hungary, which although a Christian country, is still considered part of the *Orient*. Authors of chansons de geste had always represented eastern women as transgressing the male/female dichotomy that structured western marriages. The importance of Berta's big feet becomes evident when Pepin explains that he is particularly interested in the Hungarian queen because of his own slight physical defect, which has prevented him from marrying in the past. After having described his future bride to the French barons, Pepin reacts to his vassals' laughter by noting his own small stature:

> Li baron s'en rist, si s'en oit gabé.
> Dist li rois: "Nel teneç à vilté;
> Se Deo me dona gracia no m'aç à refué,
> Por qe eo sui petit e desformé,
> Altament eo serò marié."
>
> (ll. 1401–5)
>
> [The barons laughed, and then joked about it. The king said: "Don't consider her vile, if God gives me the good grace that she does not refuse me because I am small and deformed, I will be well married."]

Not only does the juxtaposition of *petit* (not to mention *desformé*) with the emperor and *grant* with the princess overturn the traditional gender hierarchy, but the Franco-Italian author depicts a Holy Roman Emperor fearful of sexual rejection. Berta's unfeminine large feet clearly represent the unusually virile traits in the women of the Hungarian royal family.

Berta's mother, Belisant, also displays "masculine" strength, proving that she has great power or, as the text states, *gran segnorie* (l. 2380). She refuses to back down to her husband, and even the emperor, when she feels her daughter's life is in danger. After discovering the imposter and helping to recover her daughter, Belisant tells Pepin that she would have stabbed him to death if he had not found Berta:

> "Deo vos óit secoru e la Maesté sant;
> Car por cel Deo qe naque en Oriant
> Se mia filla trovea nen aumes al presant,
> Morto v'aeroie à un coltel trençant,
> Ne da le mi man nen ausés guarant."
> Li rois l'olde, s'en rise bellemant.
>
> (ll. 2747–52)
>
> ["God and her holy Majesty helped you, for that God who was born in the Orient, if we had not found my daughter immediately, I would have killed you with a sharp knife, you would have had no defense from my hands." The king heard her, and laughed heartily.]

Just as with the earlier mention of Berta's large feet, Belisant's large voice is contained by male laughter, as humor distinguishes masculine traits that an authentic knight embodies from those which women attempt to imitate. The most obvious critique of Belisant's and Berta's autonomy, though, is the chain of events caused by the princess's decision to control her own sexuality by resting after a long journey rather than making love with her new *petit* husband. Because of this lack of *loialté* to her husband, Berta and Pepin will be killed by the imposter's sons; civil war will divide the Western world; and Berta's son, Charlemagne, will be forced to unify the Empire by seeking refuge and aid from the Saracens! At the beginning of the epic, the Franco-Italian author entices his audience to listen to the Berta Big-Foot story by explaining that the tale will describe how one woman caused great battles and bloodshed:

> E por una dame el cresè tel tençon
> Donde ne morì plus de .X.mil baron,
> E França tota fu en tel tençon.

(ll. 1195–97)

[And because of one lady grew such conflict that more than ten thousand barons died, and all of France was involved in the battle.]

Although the author underlines the disruption caused by a woman who transgresses her gender role, he also describes the emperor, the traditional model of ideal masculinity, as a man of both small physical and intellectual stature.

In the two other *Marciano XIII* texts that center on betrayal by a woman, *Berta e Milon* and *Rolandin*, Charlemagne's half sister, Berta, the daughter of Pepin and the false Berta, falls in love with Milon, gets pregnant out of wedlock, and flees with her lover. Once again it is a descendant of the Maganza family who upsets the harmony of the royal family. The lovers escape to northern Italy where their son, Roland, is born. The author establishes Italy as the birthplace of Roland, whose role in Italian chivalric epics will overshadow that of his uncle, Charlemagne, throughout the fourteenth, fifteenth, and sixteenth centuries. Milon, who is of noble stock, is forced to work as a humble woodsman while his son, Roland, endowed with miraculous strength and talents, matures quickly. Charlemagne on his way home from Rome happens to pass through the area where Berta, Milon, and Roland are living. The emperor meets Roland and is charmed by the child's bravado. Recognizing that Roland must be the child of noble parents, Charlemagne insists on meeting Milon and Berta. When the emperor first recognizes the lovers, he wants to kill them, but Roland stops him. Once again, the child's courage impresses Charlemagne, and for his nephew's sake he forgives the boy's parents. Reunited, the entire family returns to Paris.

Berta causes familial conflict by choosing her own partner rather than marrying the man her brother, the emperor, would have selected as a family ally. The text makes explicit that Charlemagne would have enhanced the status of the entire family with his half sister's marriage. Berta's relationship with Milon disrupts those plans and thus is interpreted as a form of family betrayal:

> D'ele cuitoit far un gran parenté,
> Donerla à rois, à cons o amiré;
> Contra d'ele non avoit mal pensé.
> Mais li amor tanto oit ovré
> Qe anbidos oit fraito castité.
> Se li rois li aust ni saplu ni esmé,
> Milon fust à dos fors apiçé
> Et ella fust e arsa e brusé.
>
> (ll. 9087–94)

[He thought of marrying her to a great family, giving her to a king, a count, or an admiral; he had never thought badly of her. But Love had worked so hard that they both broke their chastity. If the king had either known or imagined, Milon would have been hung, and she (Berta) would have been burnt at the stake.]

Berta and Milon pay a price for their familial betrayal through a loss of status and their banishment to the margins of western society where Milon must make a living through hard physical labor. The once courtly couple are reduced to a bestial state. The suffering and manual labor, however, are represented in an ambivalent fashion. The humble nature of Roland's birth and childhood is compared to that of Christ, establishing the miraculous origin of an epic hero who becomes famous on the Italian peninsula as much for his intellectual and spiritual qualities as for his martial prowess:

> Là o R[oland] fo né no le fo pavilon
> Ni çanbra depinte, ni palés, ni mason,
> Ni leito grande como à lui convenon;
> Coltra ni lenço, ni altra guar[n]ison.
> Se nu de lu volen ben far rason,

A Jesu Christo nu li asomilon,
Qe naque en un presepio, cun dist li sermon,
En una stable cun bois e con molton.

(ll. 9386–93)

[Where Roland was born, there was neither a tent, nor a painted room, nor a palace, nor a house, not even a large bed as suited him; neither was there a blanket, nor sheets, nor any other kind of protection. If we want to talk well of him, we will compare him to Jesus Christ who was born in a manger, as the sermon said, in a stable with wood and sheep.]

Roland's upbringing in the woods conveys a set of opposing values. His parents send him to school in the city where he surpasses all others in wisdom and learning. At the same time he is described as a feral child whose raw aggression even allows him to overpower the emperor. While the narrator praises Roland's intellect, the emperor and the knights laud his ferocity. Paradoxically, it is the child's outlaw spirit and his brutish behavior that the tale represents as revealing Roland's noble heritage to his uncle's court. When Roland first visits the French camp, he heads to the knights' table and goes immediately to Charlemagne's plate because he sees that it is full of meat. He then begins to take food from the emperor like a hound:

El non va mie à li altri tajer
Se no à quelo de K[arle] l'inperer,
Qe de çarne le vi tuto plener.
Quando le fu q'el se le pote aprosmer,
Jamais non fu ni bracho ni levrer
Cun R[olandin] pris la carne à mançer.
Molto li guarda dux N[aime] de Baiver.

(ll. 10950–56)

[He does not go to the other plates, but to the one that belongs to Charlemagne the emperor, which he saw was full of meat. When he could get close to it, never was there a hound or a greyhound that began to eat meat like Rolandin. Naime de Baiver looked at him intently.]

The comedy of this passage clashes with the hagiographic attitude of the earlier description of Roland's humble birth. Other critics have noticed these variations of tone in the *Marciano XIII* and have explained that they represent the gradual infiltration of a *spirito novellistico* (popular spirit) into the traditional epic structures (Zambon 63). As mentioned in the last chapter, this generic hybridity is a general tendency of the late epic, not just of the Italian tradition, and has important social implications since the comedic element often deals with issues of gender and class. The *Marciano XIII*, therefore, like other late epics, served as contested terrain for competing notions of masculinity and nobility, which were difficult to combine into a unified text without obvious contradictions.

In several epics of the *Marciano XIII* issues of gender and class coalesce, as the tales portray differing, and at times, contradictory qualities of the ideal knight. The eighth text of the manuscript, *Macaire,* is perhaps the best example. In this tale, a female character serves again as the target of the nasty Maganza clan, and once again the emperor does not properly defend her. Macaire, the representative of the evil faction in this tale, falsely accuses Charlemagne's wife, Biancofiore, of adultery with a dwarf. Charlemagne eventually realizes that Biancofiore is innocent of the charges and has Macaire quartered. By this time, however, the pregnant queen, exiled by the emperor, has already been abandoned in the forest. She meets a woodsman, Varocher, who helps her return to her father, the king of Hungary. Upon learning of the injustice against his daughter, the king of Hungary declares war on Charlemagne. During the ensuing battle, the queen's father dubs the woodsman a knight and eventually Varocher and Ogier reconcile the two sides.

What was implied in the tale of Roland is made explicit in the last story of the manuscript. The physical force and aggressive behavior associated with the *vilain,* or rustic peasant, are also considered attributes for honorable knights. When the queen first meets Varocher he is described as a hairy wild man with a club. All the strategies that he uses to defend the queen and her family prove successful, but can hardly be defined as chivalrous acts. For instance, since Varocher is not equipped to ride with the knights, he decides to infiltrate the emperor's tent while Charlemagne is sleeping to steal the enemy's best horses:

Qe vos diroie de le pro Varocher?
Elo savoit le vie e li senter
E de Paris e l'insir e l'int[r]er
E le mason de alti çivaler;
Elo aloit la noit avanti l'aube cler,
E si se ficoit en l'oste l'inperer,
E si aloit à modo de scuer,

Si se ficoit in la tenda l'inperer,
Là o il savoit qe estoit li bon destrer.

(ll. 15790–98)

[What was I saying to you about the noble Varocher? He knew the roads and the paths and how to enter and exit Paris and the houses of the noble knights; he went at night before sunrise and sneaked into the Emperor's camp, and dressed as a squire sneaked into the Emperor's tent, there where he knew were the good steeds.]

Because of his loyalty and heroic thievery, the king of Hungary rewards Varocher by dubbing the wild man a knight. Even after his transformation, however, he continues to make a name for himself by stealing from the enemy camp while Charlemagne and his knights are asleep. The only aspect of Varocher's portrayal that changes is that now he carries a sword, rather than a club:

Varocher s'en torne quando il oit robé
Tota la tende de K[arlon] l'inperé,
. . . .
No s'en percoit homo de mer né,
De cella colse no s'avoit doté,
Nen cuitoit qe *lairon* fust là dens entré
Por la paure d'eser apiçé.
E Varocher cun tota sa masné
S'en retornò tuti çoiant e lé
A la soa oste avanti li jor sclaré.

(ll. 16063–78; emphasis added)

[Varocher returned after he had robbed the Emperor Charlemagne's entire tent. . . . No man alive would have thought, no one would have suspected such a thing, no one would have thought that a thief would have entered there out of fear of being hanged. And Varocher with his entire company all returned joyous and happy to their army before daybreak.]

In this passage Varocher, the knight, is labelled a thief *(lairon)*, albeit a brave one. The epic describes very similar behavior for Varocher the loyal wild man, and Varocher the knight, collapsing the traditional dichotomy between the uncivilized vilain and the courtly knight who defends widows and orphans.

As Eugene Vance has pointed out, debates about wildness and domesticity were common in early vernacular literature as authors tried to resolve the "conflicting messages of antiquity" about whether heroes need to overcome animalistic passions and desires, or rather harness them "as the raw material of responsible human action" (*From Topic to Tale* 61, 63). In his analysis of Chrétien de Troyes's *Yvain*, Vance reads the meeting of the knight, Calogrenant, with a vilain as a symbolic step in the hero's development, one in which Chrétien questions the traditional dichotomy between nature and culture or forest and court by depicting the wood as "a place where a man's elementary, passional self is first summoned forth in its fullest range of expression, and this aspect of a man's nature as *potency* is indispensable to that ultimate perfection of his being in the arts of chivalric warfare and courteous love" (64).

The *Marciano XIII* establishes the same type of opposition between forest and court in several of its narratives, but the author resolves the question in a different manner. Rather than illustrating the evolution of a hero who recognizes but learns to control his passions, Ogier and Varocher remain aggressive and coarse figures even after they are dubbed. In fact, it is their ability to act without restraint and to break the rules of chivalric practice that establishes their heroic status. As in *Yvain,* this text plays with the traditional opposition between vilain and knight, but rather than placing these two figures along a philosophical continuum, the *Marciano XIII* collapses the dichotomy and highlights the contradictions that had always existed in the notion of a *cavaliere di Dio* (knight of God)—that is, of a powerful and often brutal warrior, who also follows Christ's example of humility and service. It is striking that the two most aggressive and coarse heroic figures of the *Marciano XIII,* Ogier and Varocher, are the ones responsible for ending the war and reinstating order in the Christian world. Like the heroes of the Old French "epic of revolt," Ogier and Varocher do not rebel against the traditional social hierarchy, but simply against the weakness and corruption of the emperor and his lineage.[9]

The tales of the rebellious vassal Renaut de Montauban, which enjoyed great success in Italy, including an early Franco-Italian version, also depict a clan leader who recognizes that it is in his family's best interest to make peace with the emperor, despite the sovereign's flaws.[10] Even fifteenth-century Italian versions of this legend retain the traditional ending of the tale, which supports the social status quo.[11] The outlaw makes peace with the emperor, gives up his possessions, and travels as a barefoot pilgrim to Cologne where he joins workers in the construction of a church. While his extraordinary strength and diligence shame the other laborers, his refusal to accept the normal compensation angers them. Out of concern for their livelihood, the workers decide to kill the saintly Renaut/ Rinaldo. Even though the hero had spent most of his adult life fighting the emperor, the hagiographic ending of his tale reestablishes the ontological nature of aristocratic privilege. The stories of Bovo, Ogier, and Varocher in the *Marciano XIII* follow this same pattern; the unconventional heroes begin as outlaws, but their extraordinary strength and uncourtly behavior eventually support the social hierarchy rather than undermine it. Yet, the transformation itself raises questions about the universal hierarchy and the notion of natural identities.

In each of the *Marciano XIII* epics, clan violence creates a chaotic environment in which figures are forced to change their identities. Bovo d'Antona disguises himself as a doctor in order to trick his enemy and regain his father's city; his wife Druxiana is separated from her husband but makes a living travelling as a minstrel; Berta Big-Foot takes on the identity of a merchant's wife when she is discovered in the woods by a knight; both Charlemagne and Roland hide their noble lineage while they are in exile; Ogier and Milon are portrayed as fighting like wild men with clubs rather than proper weapons; and finally, Varocher, the wild man, transforms into a knight. The divisions that occur in clans, therefore, lead to cracks in other forms of identity that the chanson de geste had always upheld as part of a universal, unchanging hierarchy.

R. Howard Bloch has described the early French epic as "deeply implicated in the strategy of linguistic and familial origins" (93). He goes on to explain that the genre "can be situated precisely at the point of convergence between a model of the noble family, whose legitimacy is rooted in the soil and is perceived to be part of an immutable social order, and a model of representation implicit to early medieval grammar and according to which language is assumed to be grounded in an original order of things" (99). The linear logic of the chanson de geste is modified, however, in the late Carolingian epics because the most important form of identity in this epic genre, that of the noble family or clan, is represented as fragmented and impure. In the world of the late Carolingian epic, Charlemagne can marry a Saracen princess and a wild man can become a knight. While the author of the *Marciano XIII* affirms the traditional dichotomies that structured the chanson de geste, the narratives themselves continue to disrupt those same oppositions.

The most important opposition in these epics is the good Chiaramonte lineage vs. the evil Maganza lineage. Yet, Berta Big-Foot's substitution by the Maganza imposter in the emperor's bed means that the two clans merge. Moreover, the product of this union between good and evil is Charlemagne's half sister, Berta, who then gives birth to the ideal hero of the entire Italian tradition—Roland. With the false Berta as his grandmother, even the exemplary knight has an impure heritage, which will continue to haunt him throughout the Italian epic tradition.[12] His mixed ancestry also raises the troubling question of whether it is even possible to identify the enemy—the stranger amongst us.

Part II

Cultural Cross-Dressing

3

Hybrid Identities

Monsters, Wild Men, and Warrior Women

The conflicting ideologies of the late Carolingian epic take on concrete form in the genre's numerous hybrid characters. Although all the marvelous figures that appear in the late chivalric epic derive from earlier classical and medieval legends, the Carolingian texts are distinctive in the way they combine figures from different traditions and give them important roles in the narratives.

One such tradition is the portrayal of monstrous races from the East, which appeared both in written and figural texts throughout antiquity and the Middle Ages. From the fifth century B.C., when Herodotus first reported stories of fabulous populations in India, western writers became fascinated with the depiction and analysis of the exotic peoples whom they believed to exist in the East (Wittkower 159). Church fathers debated the status of these races, attempting to decide whether or not the hybrid monsters should be considered part of God's creation or *contra naturam*. St. Augustine set a precedent when he stated that if such populations did exist and were truly human, then they must derive from Adam. He even hypothesized that God might have created such monsters to dissuade us from interpreting abnormal births as a failure of his divine plan (Wittkower 168). Thus, St. Augustine both collapsed and sustained the opposition of western man/eastern monster by claiming that such diversity contributes to the beauty of the whole—to the unity of the creator's plan. Many late medieval writers followed St. Augustine's model and accepted the existence of eastern monsters while absorbing them into a Christian framework.

In the early Middle Ages a text known as the *Marvels of the East* spread images of wild races such as pygmies, giants, creatures with a single large foot used as an umbrella, and a hybrid race—half-human/half-dog—known as cynocephali. These collective fantasies made their way into various types of written texts including philosophical treatises, bestiaries, and chivalric epics (Husband 5–7).

During the twelfth and thirteenth centuries, the wild man, with his characteristic hairiness, gigantic stature, and club or tree branch for a weapon, emerged as a new monstrous race (Husband 7). His particular identifying traits combined features of earlier monstrous races but also differentiated him from those eastern counterparts. Artists and writers often ignored these subtleties and simply placed the western wild man within the textual framework of the *Marvels of the East* (Husband 42). In the late Middle Ages and Renaissance, according to John Friedman, wild men "by metonymy . . . [came] to represent all of the races, or at least the memory of all the others" (200).

Represented as both feared and desired, the wild man became a common figure in late medieval literature and art. He was feared because he symbolized temptation and chaos—all that was free of religious and social control. The wild man's club also suggested violence, and some authors, following St. Jerome's choice of the word *pilosi* to describe demons, interpreted his hairiness as a sign of immorality, especially lustfulness (Husband 11). The depiction of the wild man living in the woods, however, also elicited desire because he symbolized a source of power seemingly untainted by social and political corruption.[1] As a result, European explorers and scholars would later use the prototype of the idealized wild man to interpret their encounters with the "noble savage" of the New World (Friedman 1997). Medieval epic writers adopted this same figure to represent a second idealized form of alterity whose difference was based on class rather than on ethnicity: the faithful peasant, or vilain.

The wild man was not the only monstrous race described as noble in medieval art and thought (Friedman 164). The Amazons were another fabulous population considered praiseworthy; for example, Jacques de Vitry celebrated their military skills as well as their chastity (170–71). Authors of the early Italian epic often exalt a similar figure, the warrior woman, for those very same traits.

This chapter examines the connections in medieval Italian epics amongst the three hybrid figures described above: the monster from the East, the worker as wild man, and the woman as Amazonian warrior. The focus is on the *cultural cross-dressers* who seem to proliferate in this genre[2]—rational monsters, wild men, female knights, knights in drag, Christian knights posing as Saracens, Saracens who are secret Christians, knights dressed as vilains or merchants, vilains who transform into knights, and even monkeys that raise epic heroes—because they are examples of what Carolyn Dinshaw has called the *queer touches* of medieval texts.³ These hybrid figures question the borders of northern and central Italy's social topography in the late Middle Ages and help us to study the intersecting discourses of Orientalism, class, and sexuality. As Dinshaw states: "Around the queer it's . . . harder to keep the categories that underwrite oppressive control invisible. Around the queer what is natural and what is unnatural tend to lose their distinctive differences" (92).

The Italian epic genre is a fertile breeding ground for hybrid figures. In her book on transvestism, Marjorie Garber suggests that the appearance of cross-dressers in texts that do not focus on gender difference "indicates a *category crisis elsewhere*, an irresolvable conflict or epistemological crux that destabilizes comfortable binarity, and displaces the resulting discomfort onto a figure that already inhabits, indeed incarnates, the margin" (17). Following Garber's lead, I will examine the cultural forces that destabilized traditional dichotomies in fourteenth- and fifteenth-century Italy, which led to a "crisis of category itself."

The Monster from the East

The authors of late medieval epics in Italy worked hard to order the unwieldy material that they had inherited from the long oral and written tradition of Carolingian narratives. They sifted through various narrative possibilities to write encyclopedic texts that they perceived as the most authoritative and verisimilar version of a particular hero's story (Vitullo 29–45). Epic writers had the opportunity to systematize Asia and Africa as well because many of the heroes travel East reproducing a narrative pattern established by chansons de geste such as *Bueve de Hantone* and *Renaut de Montauban*. Even the otherworld enters the Italian epic cosmos; knights, following Dante's model, map out Hell, Purgatory, and Paradise. It is precisely this attempt to render the epic's imaginary universe whole and coherent that allows the queer to flourish. Like St. Augustine, who viewed the monstrous as an important part of God's plan because it helped reveal the cosmic order, the epic authors used hybrid figures to reinforce the notion of a naturalized and universal model.

The first figure I will examine, Pulicane, comes from the story of *Buovo d'Antona*, and exemplifies how Italian epic writers adopted the images of monstrous races from the East—in this case the cynocephalus with a human body and the head of a dog.⁴ Critics such as Daniela Delcorno Branca and Henning Krauss have interpreted these monstrous epic characters as symbols of a new democratized concept of chivalry, which developed in late-thirteenth-century Italian communes (Delcorno Branca, "Fortuna" 304; *L'Epica feudale* 202). According to these readings, monsters like Pulicane represent a new bourgeois concept of society in which every man, even if he has the head of a dog, may "earn" the status of signore or lord.

In her article on the history of the *Buovo* narrative, Delcorno Branca describes the popularity of the *Bueve de Hantone* chanson de geste in Italy during the fourteenth and early fifteenth centuries. After observing that the Saracen giant of the Old French epic, Açopart, transforms into the dog-headed figure of Pulicane in the Italian versions of the story, Delcorno Branca focuses on an early-fifteenth-century version of the tale by the Tuscan writer Andrea da Barberino, who expands the function of the hybrid creature by embellishing his role with a theological discussion, dating back to St. Augustine, about whether monstrous races have souls ("Fortuna" 304). In fact, the cynocephali had been the focus of this debate among theologians for centuries because many of their mythical behaviors were considered rational (D. G. White 60–67).

While I agree with Delcorno Branca that this ethical discussion attempts to humanize that which is fantastic and monstrous about Pulicane, such an inclusive and egalitarian notion contradicts the text's equally strong support of aristocratic privilege and a rigid social order. A scene that illustrates these contrasting tendencies occurs when Buovo and his wife Drusiana escape from the Saracen king Marcabruno who wants to marry Drusiana against her will. Pulicane is sent by Marcabruno to capture the couple. When he catches up with them, however, Drusiana reminds Pulicane that she had once saved his life by claiming his status as a rational being, and she asks in return that he take Buovo as his lord and adopt the Christian faith:

> "O, Pulicane, è questo il merito che tu mi rendi del servigio che io ti feci, quando io ero d'età di nove anni, che tu fusti menato per essere arso nel fuoco ardente, e dicevano che tu eri nato di mortale peccato, e generato d'animale inrazionale, come era uno mastino, in una femina razionale, e io ti domandai di grazia al padre mio, e scampa'ti dalla morte? E ora tu mi vuoi fare morire me e 'l mio signore? ché sai che Buovo è primo mio marito. O franco Pulicane, quando mi renderai merito di quello ch'io t'ho allevato e nodrito, se tu non mi meriti a questo punto? Or non credi tu che Buovo ti possa fare gran signore? E faratti battezzare in acqua santa, e sarai fedele cristiano." (Da Barberino, *I Reali* 343–44)

["Oh, Pulicane, is this the reward you give me for the service I rendered you, when I was nine years of age, when you were sent to be burned in a blazing fire, and they were saying that you had been born from mortal sin, and begot from an irrational animal (since he was a dog) in a rational woman, and I asked my father to take mercy on you and to save you from death? And now you want to kill me and my lord? Because you know that Buovo is first of all my husband. O courageous Pulicane, when will you give me a reward for having raised and fed you, if you do not reward me at this point? Now, don't you believe that Buovo can make you a great lord? And he will have you baptized in holy water, and you will be a faithful Christian."]

In this passage, the author Andrea da Barberino uses terms from a tradition of philosophical texts such as *animale inrazionale* and *femina razionale*. Yet, Andrea has placed the scholastic debate about the status of monsters within the context of a feudal pledge; Pulicane's status as a rational being with a soul depends on his fealty to a noble, Buovo. The "bourgeois" philosophical discussion uses the terms of a feudal discourse so that God's grace can only be obtained by this hybrid figure through the agency of a signore.

The Wild Man as Worker

Unlike Pulicane, whose alterity derives not only from his subordinate class status but also from his pagan religion, the woodsman Varocher in the Franco-Italian *Marciano XIII* narrative *Macaire* has no religious characterization. At the turn of the fifteenth century, Andrea da Barberino retold the early-fourteenth-century tale of *Macaire* in his text *Le Storie Nerbonesi,* changing Varocher's name to Ispinardo and his profession to that of a charcoal burner. Varocher and Ispinardo performed jobs on the margins of urban culture, but despite the low status accorded such workers in late medieval Italian communes, both the anonymous writer of the *Macaire* text and Andrea da Barberino represent their character as a wild man whom the nobility seems to accept. Just as cynocephali lived on the edges of the known world in Africa and in Asia, wild men inhabited the margins of urban culture in Europe (D. G. White 68).

In order to illustrate the role of the wild man in the Italian chivalric epic of the late Middle Ages, I would like to digress briefly and look at Hayden White's analysis of the representation of the noble savage in eighteenth-century Europe. In his article on the noble savage as fetish, White explains how such a figure fulfilled the ideological needs of the rising bourgeoisie:

> The rising classes needed a concept to express their simultaneous rejection of the nobility's claims to privilege and desire for similar privileges for themselves. The concept of the Noble Savage served their ideological needs perfectly, for it at once undermined the nobility's claim to a special human status and extended that status to the whole of humanity. But this extension was done only *in principle*. (194)

White stresses in this passage that the equal status extended in theory to all of humanity in reality only empowered the bourgeoisie. While the noble savage of the eighteenth-century bourgeoisie is distinguished from the medieval wild man in that his or her difference derives from ethnic identity rather than lower class status, these two figures resemble each other in that the extension of equal rights which they represented occurred only in a token manner, demonstrating that these egalitarian ideals remained abstract.

To illustrate this point let me return to the *Macaire* narrative first discussed in chapter two. Varocher earns the status of a knight by saving the queen of France from an attack by the wicked Maganza clan and protecting her in a long journey. Macaire, representing this evil faction in the tale, falsely accuses Charlemagne's wife, Biancofiore, of adultery with a dwarf. The queen flees for her life and hides in the forest where Varocher offers her refuge and protection. With the help of the benevolent woodsman, Biancofiore is able to return home to her father, the king of Hungary. Angered by Charlemagne's false accusations, the king of Hungary declares war on the emperor. Varocher remains a loyal supporter of Biancofiore's family, fighting with such abandon that the king of Hungary rewards the woodsman by dubbing him a knight.

Despite his eventual success, when the *Macaire* narrator first introduces Varocher he uses less than complimentary terms, adopting instead the stereotypical description of a vilain as a hybrid creature whose nature is often both bestial and human:

> En soa man oit un gran baston prendu;
> Grant fu e groso e quaré e menbru,
> La teste oit grose, le çavi borfolu:
> Si strançes hon no fo unches veu.

(ll. 14773–76)

[In his hand he carried a big club; he was big, large, square, and strong. He has a big head and dishevelled hair: such a strange man has never been seen.]

Later, Varocher will be labelled *velu* (hairy) and a *homo salvaço* (wild man).[5] Although his appearance is first described as strange, his brutish qualities prove useful when defending the queen and her father. As soon as Biancofiore runs across the woodsman in the forest, the narrative emphasizes the queen's largesse and the mercenary nature of Varocher's service. During their first conversation, Biancofiore gains the wild man's assistance by offering him a *guierdon* or reward for his protection.

Varocher receives his guierdon during the battle between Biancofiore's father and Charlemagne. Even when the Hungarian king dubs the woodsman a knight, however, his military tactics clearly reveal that chivalry has not completely transformed his wild nature. Instead of fighting the enemy, the woodsman leads a group of men into the emperor's camp where they steal arms, horses, gold, and silver while Charlemagne's knights are sleeping. The narrator describes Varocher as a wild man and a thief, yet this knight is also blindly loyal to the cause of the "just" family with whom his interests are linked even when they are in exile. As reward for both his loyalty and his thievery, Varocher receives immense wealth and prestige.

In *Le Storie Nerbonesi*, the Florentine Andrea da Barberino transforms Varocher into a charcoal burner named Ispinardo. Because of his profession Ispinardo lives in the woods, but unlike Varocher he is never described as brutish. This change in the vilain's character also alters the nature of his subsequent metamorphosis, making it less dramatic. In the earlier Venetian text, Biancofiore calls Varocher strange because his appearance questions the traditional boundaries between animals and humans. In Andrea's version, though, the queen hears Ispinardo sawing wood and immediately recognizes that labor as a sign of human rather than animalistic behavior:

> Ella si dirizzò a quello tagliare, pensando essere segno di persona umana, e trovò uno che tagliava legne, e facia carboni, il quale avia nome Ispinardo. (Da Barberino, *Le Storie Nerbonesi* 1:29)

> [She headed towards the sawing, thinking that it indicated the presence of a human being, and found a man cutting wood and making charcoal, whose name was Ispinardo.]

After the queen explains her plight to Ispinardo he immediately offers her his help. Although Andrea does not change the social standing of Ispinardo, he creates a manual worker who is not only human, but also courteous and generous.

Like his appearance, Ispinardo's ascent in the social hierarchy is not nearly as extraordinary as Varocher's transformation. Varocher becomes a knight who fights and even shames traditional epic heroes. Ispinardo is neither dubbed a knight nor given a chance to prove himself on the battlefield. Following a general trend of the late medieval epic, domestic life plays a larger role in Andrea's text than in the earlier Venetian narrative. The denouement of Ispinardo's narrative occurs in his own home rather than at war. The emperor is in Hungary and hears of the exceptional nobility of a *carbonaia,* and decides to verify for himself how a charcoal burner's daughter could possess such gentility. When he reaches Ispinardo's home, he is astonished by Biancofiore's beauty (he doesn't recognize that she is his wife!), and asks one of his servants to touch her improperly in order to determine whether she is a noble woman or a prostitute. Ispinardo sees the servant's "dishonest action" and uses his club to defend Biancofiore. He gives the emperor's man such a wallop that the servant immediately falls down dead. At this point, the queen reveals her identity and saves the charcoal burner by explaining to the emperor that she owes her life to Ispinardo. Although Ispinardo is virtuous and strong, he never claims the title of knight. Rather the king gives him and his family land and riches, which eventually permit Ispinardo's son to acquire the title of count.

Since the ascent of the charcoal burner's family in Andrea's text is less dramatic than the tale of Varocher, at least one critic has described the later story as an example of the "rearistocratization" of a more egalitarian Franco-Italian tradition (Krauss, "Von Varocher" 204). In my view, however, the fourteenth-century Venetian epic and the fifteenth-century Florentine text do not demonstrate a clear change in ideology, but rather both contain conflicting notions of class identity. Although Varocher becomes a traditional epic hero, embodying the ideal masculine qualities of prowess and courage, as a worker he is described in animalistic terms. Moreover, the military tactics he adopts clearly distinguish him from the traditional knights of aristocratic origin. Andrea da Barberino, on the other hand, restricts Ispinardo to the domestic sphere inhabited by women, but consistently describes him as a virtuous man, even when he is working as a charcoal burner. Also, Andrea's text represents a second, divergent notion of nobility when the emperor refuses to believe that a charcoal burner's daughter could possess great gentility. In the end Varocher and Ispinardo have more similarities than differences: both workers earn a higher social standing through loyal service to aristocratic families.

Varocher and Ispinardo represent a concept of chivalry in which the knight can come from the most humble background if he earns the title. This democratization of chivalric mythology, though, still allowed communes and the aristocracy that controlled them to maintain the polarization of vilain and noble, even while promising that the exceptional vilain, if he were loyal to the right faction, might enter the privileged group. Thus, the wild man or worker warrior did not mirror social changes, but rather functioned as an imaginary construct through which contemporary social categories could be modified and affirmed at the same time.[6]

In several Old French chansons de geste, such as Raimbert's version of the *Chevalerie Ogier*, French epic writers describe Italians as incapable of fulfilling the duties of a knight. Despite the rise of mercantile and administrative classes within their own communes, French authors often represented the Lombards as cowardly warriors whose status as knights depended more on wealth and profession than on bloodline (Ruggieri, "Les Lombards" 37–45; Krauss, "Ritter und Bürger" 209–15).[7] Thus, the French aristocracy's fear of social mobility, of the economic changes that had begun in their own cities as well as in Italy, was displaced onto the foreigners, the Lombards.

So as not to accept the role of scapegoat, the Italians rewrote the Old French epics and in the process seemed to embrace the notion of earned social mobility. In *La Prise de Pampelune*, Lombards take the city of Pampelune for Charlemagne, who rewards them with the fulfillment of their leader's three wishes. The Lombard leader, Desiderio, asks that, first, all Lombards become free men, that, second, all those with enough possessions have the opportunity to become knights even if they are not of noble origin, and that, third, all Lombards can carry a sword in front of the emperor (Mussafia 10). This epic not only exonerates the Lombards from the French accusations of cowardice, but helps to redefine the institution of knighthood. A knight can now earn his title, as evidenced by his possessions rather than his blood lineage. Yet, both Desiderio and Charlemagne are dynastic rulers, and the apparent democratization of chivalry in *La Prise de Pampelune* ignores that many of the men who were wealthy enough to become knights came from or married into noble families.

While this new construction of chivalry empowered the elite of the emerging mercantile, administrative, and artisan classes, it did not usually extend to workers. The difference of the monstrous man in chivalric epics is not only defined in terms of his status as an easterner or foreigner but—

in the case of Pulicane, Varocher, and Ispinardo—by his social class. Despite these textual representations, laborers rarely assimilated into the urban aristocracy but rather remained as alien to communal nobility as the figures in the *Marvels of the East*. The new definition of knighthood, therefore, did not challenge the old one but instead modified it to the needs of a new urban aristocracy dependent on the support of the popolo.[8] The new patricians wanted the kind of autocratic power possessed by the German emperors and French kings without the economic submission required for alliances with such rulers. Democratizing chivalry was one answer to that dilemma.

Another textual model for the wild men of the early Italian epic is the Saracen giant Rainourt, who appears in several different epics of the Old French Guillaume cycle. The chanson de geste that expands and delineates this character, *Aliscans,* enjoyed considerable success both within France and on the Italian peninsula. A Franco-Italian version exists dating from the middle of the fourteenth century, and the narrative is retold in Florentine by Andrea da Barberino towards the beginning of the fifteenth century in his *Le Storie Nerbonesi*.

Rainourt and the wild men of Italian epics share several features: their gigantic stature and power, their preference for a club rather than a sword, their humble professions, and, finally, their generosity and fidelity. Rainourt, however, also shares Pulicane's eastern origins as he is the son of a pagan king and the brother of the Saracen princess, Orable, who marries Guillaume. Even though he is of noble origin, Rainourt descends to the level of a wild man and is forced to work as a kitchen-helper at the court of the French king before he transforms into a knight and later converts to Christianity. Like Varocher, even after Rainourt reintegrates into the social and military elite, he elicits laughter from his fellow knights (and presumably the epic's audience) by confusing the social codes of the vilain with those of a knight: he rides his horse backwards, overindulges in food and drink, and scorns the use of a knight's proper weapon, a sword, for his enormous *tinel* or Herculean club.

In exception to the standard critical view of feudal chansons de geste as less democratic than their bourgeois Italian imitations, Rainourt demonstrates the existence in Old French epics of wild men who move up in social status. Rustic vilains who transform into chivalric heroes appear in several late Old French epics including *Gaufrey, Gaydon,* and *La Chevalerie Doon de Mayence* (Newth xxv). In *Gaydon,* for instance, even though the farm worker Gautier is a loyal supporter of the epic hero and defends his lord bravely, he uses a *massue* or club as a weapon just as the rustic heroes of the Italian epics do (Guessard 191). Like Varocher and Ispinardo, Gautier is also praised for his loyalty and courage even though his rustic manners separate him from the real knights. When the narrator first introduces Gautier, the vilain proudly vows to pummel the emperor with his primitive weapon. Rather than inspiring respect, however, his oath induces the noble barons to laugh heartily (192).

In one of the first studies on the Rainourt figure, written in 1909, the critic Alberto Friscia interprets the Saracen wild man as a metaphor for the new urban population of France's twelfth-century communes, which refused the oppression of the landed aristocracy and the Church. He compares Rainourt to the working people who seem good and charitable in everyday life but if angered might transform into monsters difficult to control (55–56). In a similar but less dramatic fashion, Henning Krauss, in a 1980 analysis of the *Marciano XIII* manuscript, theorizes that the wild man Varocher represents a protobourgeois ideology that promotes equality for everyone and denounces the concept of nobility by birth.[9]

Because laborers become knights in both French and Italian chivalric texts, it no longer seems tenable that their transformation in the early Italian epic represents a bourgeois worldview particular to Italy. Such interpretations perpetuate the notion of a communal social order in which wealthy merchants, artisans, and administrators, the bourgeoisie, ally with the workers to fight the traditional nobility. Instead, the ideologies of new social groups that were able to assimilate into the communal aristocracy often did not openly question the privileges of the elite but rather tried to appropriate them.

THE AMAZONIAN WARRIOR

The Old French Guillaume cycle not only offers a model for the figure of the wild man but for yet another marginal figure in the early Italian epics—the warrior woman. *La Prise d'Orange* relates the early history of Rainourt's unruly sister, Orable, who betrays her own family and faith, converts to Christianity, takes the name Guiborc, and marries the Christian hero Guillaume. This chanson de geste has confounded critics because it mixes narrative elements of two distinct medieval genres: the Carolingian epic and the Roman courtois. Sharon Kinoshita, though, has proposed that the epic's generic hybridity serves to highlight its "congruence of love-as-war, and of war-as-seduction" (267). Guillaume conquers both "the foreign and female Other" in the same military campaign by obtaining the city of Orange and Orable as trophies (267). The epic hero's romance does not distract from his Christian military mission, but instead glamorizes it.

The princess, in both her roles as a Saracen and as a Christian, enjoys more autonomy than most western women in the epic tradition. Kinoshita explains this seemingly contradictory social code for women by reminding readers once again of the chanson de geste's eroticization of Orientalism:

> The very rebelliousness and independence that . . . [is] incongruous if not impossible in a proper Christian heroine is *constitutive* to the story of the enamored Muslim princess. Where the Christian heroine who attempts to exercise agency threatens to disrupt feudal society, the pagan woman who chooses to remake herself as a Christian strongly enhances it, for it is precisely her narrative and ideological function actively to reject husband, family, and religion, and to embrace Christianity—and feudal Christian Society—in their place. (276)

Thus, the epic recontextualizes female behavior that would normally be interpreted as dangerous to the sexual hierarchy so that it appears to sustain rather than question the naturalized social order.

Even though Guiborc does not actually enter battle, in the epic *Aliscans* she does don armor and encourages the other noble women of Orange to follow her lead so that they might defend the city while Guillaume goes to seek aid from the king in Paris. When the pagan forces arrive before Guillaume's return, Guiborc and her female followers keep them at bay by throwing rocks down on the invaders' heads from the towers. This strategy earns them some time and the respect of the narrator. The competence of Guiborc and her rock-throwing ladies quickly comes into question, however, when Guillaume returns in disguise, but his wife does not recognize him and refuses to open the gate for the epic hero.

In both the case of Rainourt and of his sister Guiborc, humor is used to differentiate workers and women who have borrowed the trappings of chivalry from the true knights whose prestige the exploits of these temporary surrogates serve only to enhance. Christian men with titles remain the model of behavior, the paragon of virtue and courage. Although the medieval epics rewrite various hybrid figures (easterner, worker, and woman) in terms of the ideal knight, the authors of such texts add a humorous element to these new characterizations so as to reestablish the social hierarchy. According to Peter Stallybrass and Allon White, "The Other must be transformed into the Same, the savage must be civilized; . . . but at the same time, the Other's mimicry . . . is treated as absurd, the cause of derisive laughter, thus consolidating the sense that the civilized is always-already given" (41).

As *Aliscans* demonstrates, the lady in armor, like the wild man, appears as a figure both in fourteenth-century chansons de geste as well as the Italian epics. In several late French epics such as *Tristan de Nanteuil* women not only dress the part, but even enter the fray. In that epic the lady Aye d'Avignon disguises herself as the knight Gaudion in order to save her husband and two children:

> Mais s'estoit pour aquerre honneur parfaittement
> Que de son seigneur puist fere delivrement
> Et de ses deux enffans qu'elle ama loyaulment.
>
> (ll. 2843–45)[10]

[But it was for acquiring perfect honor so that she might free her lord and her two children whom she loved loyally.]

Although Aye performs as a knight, while Guiborc just dresses the part, paradoxically both characters take on masculine roles only because they are fulfilling their traditional feminine duties of serving husbands and protecting children. We will see that the same type of warrior woman appears in the Italian chivalric epics when we analyze the figure of Galaziella.

The chansons de geste, however, did not serve as the only textual model for such figures. Classical tales about Amazons also contributed to longstanding notions of gender difference and women's essential inferiority.[11] Benoît de Sainte-Maure's twelfth-century reworking of the classical tales of Troy into a French epic, *Le Roman de Troie,* functioned as one of the most important sources of information about Amazon mythology throughout the late Middle Ages. Benoît introduces the Amazons by describing their "great land" somewhere in the East, which he calls *Amazoine* or *Femenie* (12–14, 36). These warrior women live without men most of the year, but from April to June they inhabit an island covered with precious trees and herbs, where the most valiant of the Amazons mate with men from nearby lands. The male children stay with their mothers for only one year before they are given to their fathers to be raised, while the female progeny remain citizens of Amazoine. Benoît emphasizes the women warriors' strength and prowess (14). He also makes clear, however, that the warrior women's ability to defend themselves and their space threatens men; any man who dares to step on their land will be cut to pieces (13–14).

The Norman writer then somewhat softens this picture of the Amazons by describing their leader's retention of feminine qualities. Panthesilée is both beautiful and courageous in battle:

> Proz e hardie e bele e sage,
> De grant valor, de grant parage,
> Mout ert preisiee e honoree.
>
> (ll. 23287–89)

[Courageous, bold, beautiful and wise, of great valor and lineage, she was very esteemed and honored.]

The queen's unique combination of masculine and feminine attributes reappears when Benoît explains her reasons for offering military assistance to the Trojans; she wants to see her love-interest Hector, but also intends to win rewards and booty.[12]

Once Panthesilée arrives in Troy with her legions of Amazons and discovers that Hector has been killed by the Greeks, her yearning to see the Trojan hero transforms into a desire to avenge him. She does so admirably—equalling the Greek hero Pirrus in both arms and words. At one point, Pirrus sees his fellow Greeks fleeing from a battle that they had been losing against the mighty Amazons. He chastises his men for allowing themselves to be overcome by mere females. Panthesilée then responds to Pirrus by claiming that she and her soldiers are not "ordinary" women who are vain and fickle:

> Tu cuides que nos seions taus
> Come autres femmes comunaus,
> Que les cors ont vains e legiers:
> Ço n'est mie nostre mestiers.
> Puceles somes: n'avons cure
> De mauvaistié ne de luxure.
>
> (ll. 23999–24004)

[You believe that we are all like other ordinary women, who have vain and fickle hearts: that is not our calling. We are maidens: we do not pay attention to either evil or lust.]

The queen goes on to say that Amazons carry arms and protect their own land, but above all she defends their extraordinary status by proclaiming that, unlike most women, they are chaste, engaging in sex only for procreative purposes. Thus, Panthesilée upholds the traditional ideal of chastity for women and critiques a feminine role defined by sexual pleasure.

Although she articulates a notion of female sexuality that he favors, Benoît follows ancient models by killing off Panthesilée for her martial hubris. Pirrus and the other Greeks gang up on Panthesilée, hacking her into small pieces. Benoît concludes the description of the Amazon queen by acknowledging her death with a perfunctory comment: "C'est damages" [What a shame] (65). The woman who thought she was as virtuous as a man dies with little dignity.

A thirteenth-century Italian author who frequented the court of Frederick II in Palermo, Guido delle Colonne, used Benoît's text as the basis of his *Historia Destructionis Troiae*, which then became the most popular vehicle for communicating the medieval tales of Troy; there may be close to 150 manuscripts of the various translations of Guido's text into French, German, English, Spanish, Flemish, Bohemian, and Italian (Meek xi). Through both vernacular and Latin texts such as Benoît's and Guido's, the myth of the Amazon warriors contributed to debates about gender difference in Italy as well as the rest of Europe.

Boccaccio's treatise on famous women, *De mulieribus claris*, serves as an important example of the contradictory nature of such classical representations in late medieval Florence. Just as Benoît depicted a queen of the Amazons who described herself as having overcome women's natural moral and physical weakness, Boccaccio praises his Penthesilea for having overcome the "softness" of her female body with virile exercise (730).[13] Boccaccio then goes on to question the whole notion of essential gender qualities by asserting that *usus* or custom can change one's nature (732). He claims that idleness can feminize men's nature just as military exercise had improved Penthesilea's into a virago. Boccaccio contains the threat presented by his admission that gender is defined in cultural terms, however, by continuing to represent masculinity and femininity as binary opposites, with the former as the superior identity.[14] Women receive praise only when they are as virile as men. St. Augustine hypothesized that monsters from the East served as a reminder of the order of God's universe; in a similar fashion, Boccaccio conceived of warrior women as monstrous figures whose discomforting presence actually strengthened the notion of a rigid feminine/masculine dichotomy.

Like Benoît and Boccaccio, the authors of early Italian epics develop strategies of praising yet containing warrior women. The Italian versions of the Carolingian epic *Chanson d'Aspremont* introduce a new warrior woman, Galaziella, who is the daughter of Penthesilea and a Saracen king

Agolante. Andrea da Barberino's fifteenth-century prose rendition of this same story mentions that Galaziella is an illegitimate daughter of the king; from her first appearance in the text her difference is marked by the term *bastarda* (*L'Aspramonte* 44).[15]

Galaziella immediately stands out in yet another way: she does not follow the long-standing literary model of the lady who encourages her beloved as she watches jousting matches from a balcony.[16] Instead the warrior woman sighs in disappointment because she would like to participate and defeat the male contestants whose skills she can surpass. After her brother arms her so that she "seems" a knight, Galaziella overcomes several Saracen opponents.

It is at this point that the narrative reinscribes Galaziella into the proper social order; she makes a deal with her father that she may marry any man who can beat her in a duel. In all the versions, Galaziella's father or brother states that the warrior woman should only marry a man who can control her through physical force. In yet another version of this epic, the fifteenth-century Tuscan *Cantare d'Aspramonte*, it is Galaziella herself who first decides that she should marry a man who can dominate her.

> "Dammi parola, padre, per tu' onore,
> che ss'io truovo uomo di me più possente
> il qual m'abatta per suo gran valore
> in piana terra del destriere corrente,
> ched io il prenda per marito e signore."

(Fassò 37, 6:13)

[Give me your word, father, on your honor, that if I find a man stronger than I, who knocks me down from a running horse on even ground through great valor, that I may take him as my husband and lord.]

Once again, the threat to established notions of gender provoked by the appearance of the warrior woman is contained by the naturalized social dichotomy of masculinity/femininity. The woman who has defied the binary construction of gender states that her father must honor this essential social order. The Christian knight, Riccieri, defeats Galaziella and she immediately insists on converting to Christianity and marrying her former opponent. Galaziella the warrior woman quickly transforms into Galaziella the wife and mother.

Furthermore, in Andrea da Barberino's prose version of the story, the narrator parallels the threat of Galaziella to patriarchal rule with the

Saracen threat to Christian supremacy.[17] Before the description of Galaziella's masculine behavior, a Saracen king, Galafro, who wants to make peace with the princess's father, Agolante, offers her a gift. Galafro gives the warrior woman a sword—in fact, the world's most famous sword, Durindarda, which had once belonged to the emperor Charlemagne. After this exchange in which the imperial symbol of power has been passed to a woman, Andrea da Barberino states that Galaziella took pity on the Saracen king because of her *cuore feminile* or feminine heart (*L'Aspramonte* 46).

The term *feminile* is used only one other time in the epic, when Andrea da Barberino berates *buffoni* or jesters. In an aside to the audience, the narrator claims that minstrels tend towards a feminine soul, which makes them cowardly and envious (39).[18] For Andrea to assert that Galaziella's nature is feminine, or in other words, weak and envious, suggests that she should not be the bearer of this sword as it is a symbol of patriarchal power. The rest of the epic deals with how to restore Durindarda to its rightful owner, the Christian emperor. Just as Galaziella must accept the authority of her husband, the Saracens must accept their subordination to the Christians.

Unfortunately, Galaziella's domestic bliss ends very quickly when she and her husband are attacked by Saracens allied with Riccieri's jealous brother. Riccieri is killed and Galaziella is condemned to die by her Saracen father, who had opposed his daughter's marriage to a Christian knight. At this point, Andrea da Barberino informs us that his unreliable oral sources differ as to subsequent events. Some say that the pregnant Galaziella was burned at the stake, while others claim that her brother imprisoned her in Africa, and still others maintain that she gave birth to twins.

The fifteenth-century Laurenziano Palatino manuscript 101, vol. 2, narrates the last of the three versions.[19] Galaziella is on her way to be imprisoned in Africa when she tells the captain that she has a strange craving to put on armor. The captain gives in to the apparent whim of the pregnant princess, only to be overwhelmed by her military skill. Galaziella forces the captain to set her free on an unknown shore where she follows a road into a city. On her journey she just happens to run into an enormous, threatening snake, which she kills with her sword. She then becomes the hero of the African *signoria* where she finds herself, and which is ruled by a female lord—the queen Frolisetta.

This version of the Galaziella story then employs another common strategy used to contain the warrior woman: it kills her off by having her die in childbirth. Galaziella's story does not end, however, because before dying she gives birth to twins, who each continue the mother's trait of contained difference. Her son, Aquilante, after a series of adventures, is abandoned in the woods, raised by a female monkey, and becomes a wild man. He is hairy, gigantic, very strong, and carries a club. The other twin, a daughter, Formosa, is raised by the Amazon queen Frolisetta, and grows to be an even more skilled fighter than her biological mother. The narrative describes how both Formosa and her wild man brother are eventually reinscribed into the proper social order and learn to use their force to support Charlemagne.

Continuing in her mother's footsteps, Formosa fights and defeats several Saracen and Christian knights, even giants. The only one she cannot defeat, Roland, she wants to marry (fol. 37v). Since Roland is already taken, however, she pledges a vow of chastity and converts to Christianity (fol. 159v).[20] The story ends when Formosa is knifed to death in bed by a Saracen knight whom she had defeated in battle and rejected in love (fol. 162v). Just as Galaziella learns to use her military skill to defend her husband and the Christian cause, Formosa's final scene illustrates not her exceptional military skill but the ultimate feminine virtue—chastity. The beautiful warrior woman becomes a metaphor for the entire Christian cause; she dies defending her body's boundaries from the threat of pagan contamination. The author first marks the character's difference—her femininity—with the name Formosa, and then systematically denies her each of the three ways by which she attempts self-assertion: Formosa's physical skills are subordinated to romance, her only alternative to a monogamous relationship with a man is chastity, and even her self-definition through sexual abstinence is punished by a violent death.

Another famous warrior woman, Braidamonte, appears in several anonymous fourteenth- and fifteenth-century versions of the rebellious vassal story, *Rinaldo da Montalbano*. Like Galaziella, she too is a bastarda since her father is the French Duke Amone who had an affair with the pagan queen Belialta and left her pregnant when he returned to France.[21] While Formosa shares some of her exploits with her brother the wild man, Braidamonte's partner-in-arms is another warrior woman Dama Roenza. Gloria Allaire notes that this "early example of a female 'buddy' story" explicitly links the two women's military careers and develops their relationship with a good deal of detail ("Warrior Woman" 38). In one fifteenth-century version of the story, the narrator introduces both Amazonian fighters in the same chapter; they each arrive with troops to reinforce the Saracen cause during a cease-fire in the midst of a bitter struggle with the Christians.²² Although the women are portrayed as unusually strong and courageous, the narrator suggests that Dama Roenza is the more fearsome of the two. Unlike Braidamonte, Dama Roenza usually runs rather than rides a horse and carries a sickle instead of a sword. Despite her wild nature, Dama Roenza nurtures Braidamonte, who is only sixteen years old and on her first military campaign. She invites Braidamonte to stay in her tent, treats her with great respect, and enjoys her companion's friendship. Because Dama Roenza loves Braidamonte for both her beauty and military skill, she organizes a tournament to show off her friend's skills and is overjoyed when Braidamonte manages to defeat all the male opponents.

Braidamonte's identification with her female companion does not last. Dama Roenza succeeds in defeating and capturing numerous Christian heroes, including Ulivieri and Braidamonte's father, Amone. Braidamonte soon shifts her loyalty, identifying with her Christian father rather than her Saracen "sister." It is at this point in the story that the narrator distinguishes between the two warrior women. The root of Dama Roenza's power becomes evident: the narrator connects her uncontrollable physical force with women's most well-known vice—lust. Dama Roenza expresses her desire by inviting the Christian knight Ulivieri to sleep with her. He refuses, saying that he could only sleep with a Christian woman and would first need to marry her. The bitter Dama Roenza then pledges to kill Ulivieri for having refused her advances.

Braidamonte decides to switch sides and free the Christian prisoners, including her father. Before revealing her plan, however, she meets her brother Rinaldo on the battlefield. Unaware of her identity, he defeats Braidamonte and removes her helmet to kill her, but the Saracen's appearance surprises him: "Rinaldo . . . si maravigliò che tanta forza fusse in nuna damigella et quasi non sapea s'ell'era femmina o maschio" [Rinaldo . . . marvelled how a young lady might have so much force and almost could not determine if she were a woman or man] (fol. 70v). Braidamonte convinces Rinaldo not to kill her by explaining that she is his sister and that she intends to free their father and the other Christian prisoners. Her image is softened even further when one of the Christian prisoners, Girardo, tells the father that he hopes to marry Braidamonte when she converts to Christianity.

As Braidamonte evolves into a feminine character, Dama Roenza becomes a monster. When she discovers Braidamonte's betrayal, she seems possessed and calls her former companion a *puttana* or whore (fols. 72r–72v). She expresses her evil nature, once again, by trying to seduce

Roland. She asks him to father her children, saying that their offspring would be powerful enough to take over the world. He responds to her advances by claiming his virginity and explains that he is already promised to the most beautiful woman in the world. The narrator then tells us that it is the knight's innocence that upsets the worldly woman warrior:

> Quand'ella gli udì dire ch'era vergine, tutta si turbò e andògli addosso, gridando: "Ai Machometto, or chome sofferi che um tale huomo . . . è nimicho dell'umana natura?" (fol. 73v).

[When she heard him say that he was a virgin, she became very upset and attacked him, screaming: "Oh Muhammad, how can you tolerate that such a man . . . is an enemy of human nature?"]

In the end, Rinaldo saves the desperate Christian forces from the monstrous Dama Roenza by tricking her. He succeeds in lopping off her right leg in a surprise attack after pretending to have died (fols. 77r–77v). Although such a tactic does not seem chivalrous enough for a famous Christian knight, her nearly satanic character justifies his conduct. In fact, a long tradition legitimized less-than-honorable strategies when male heroes needed to conquer unruly Amazons (Wettan Kleinbaum 60). In the meantime, Girardo, who happens to be Braidamonte's uncle, receives a papal disposition to marry his own niece, and the other warrior woman takes on the domestic role of wife and mother (fol. 77v). The confusion over gender that had frightened Rinaldo when he first saw his sister has been resolved. Braidamonte has allowed her identity as a daughter and a wife to take precedence over her role as warrior woman. While the narrator asserts Braidamonte's ultimate femininity (and Christianity), Dama Roenza's gender-bending, her ability to express physical force and sexuality, earns her the status of a monster who needs to be destroyed at any cost. Like most female "buddy" stories, this one has a tragic end.

Despite such strategies to contain the woman warrior, why does this figure, along with her brother the wild man, still occur with great frequency in fourteenth- and fifteenth-century epics? One could interpret them as a reflection of the growing independence of women in the early Renaissance, particularly in Florence.[23] Yet, several studies by historians such as Manlio Bellomo, Judith Brown, and Christiane Klapisch-Zuber suggest just the opposite.[24] In many ways, women's legal and economic status deteriorated rather than progressed during this period.

Instead of interpreting the warrior women, all of whom are Saracens, as a reflection of the status of women in Florence, it might be more fruitful to examine these texts from the perspective of recent theorists in gender studies such as Judith Butler. According to Butler, gender is a performance that must be maintained to retain its normative power (273). Since gender is an identity we construct, it is open to challenge and must be continuously refigured to retain the dichotomy of masculinity and femininity. If this is the case, then what challenge to traditional gender roles might have pushed late medieval Italian to adopt and develop the figure of the warrior woman?

Carolingian epics describe ideal masculinity as embodied in an elite class of knights of noble birth. Yet during the late Middle Ages and early Renaissance, the institution of chivalry in Florence underwent two important changes. In the twelfth and thirteenth centuries, communes had used the title of knight, *miles,* to indicate a man's noble status and the privileges and responsibilities associated with such social rank (Salvemini 116). From the second half of the thirteenth century and throughout the fourteenth century, however, the title of knight was no longer synonymous with the status of a noble. Communes, in particular Florence, began to dub non-noble men knights, especially men from the new mercantile and administrative classes (118–21). Participants in the chivalric rituals of thirteenth-century Italian communes did not come from a static nobility, but rather from a hybrid, urban aristocracy whose membership was constantly changing (Gasparri 8). In fact, knighthood continued to thrive in Italian communal life because of, not despite, this social fluidity; individuals and families often used chivalric practices and titles as a vehicle for "nobilization" (91).

Although the political significance of chivalry remained important, the concrete, military responsibilities of knights diminished during this period. For instance, communal Florence had always expected knights to cover the expenses of maintaining a horse for combat, and throughout the thirteenth century most knights did continue to ride their own horse into battle to defend the city. Only in the fourteenth century did that tradition change, as knights began to pay others to take their place in military conflicts (Cardini 27). By the middle of the fourteenth century, communal writers replaced the term *miles* with *equites* or *equitatores* because the majority of men fighting on horseback were simply mercenaries who did not hold the rank of knight (Salvemini 126).

This substitution of men of lower socioeconomic status for titled patricians in the art of warfare threatened the elite masculine ideal that the knight represented. In a similar fashion, the gender distinction based upon the notion that the man is stronger and must protect the woman was also threatened when the patrician class was no longer defined by its martial skills but by its ability to read, write, and calculate numbers. The fourteenth-century writer of short stories, Franco Sacchetti, describes the anxieties produced by these changes within the institution of chivalry and its masculine ideal. Sacchetti satirizes members of the non-noble mercantile and administrative classes who claim the title of knight even though they express their prowess with a pen rather than a sword: "Ecco bello esercizio cavalleresco! . . . che li notai si fanno cavalieri, e più su; e 'l pennaiuolo si converte in aurea coltellesca" [How wonderful the chivalric practice is! . . . notaries make themselves knights, and take even higher honors; and the pen-case transforms into a golden sheath] (421).

Sacchetti's satire valorizes notions of masculinity and nobility threatened by social changes. For similar reasons, it was common for young men of the urban patrician class to demonstrate their fighting skills in jousts held in Florentine piazzas. At times, readings of epics accompanied these chivalric games.[25] Whether included in this spectacle or not, the epic in fourteenth- and fifteenth-century Florence also affirmed that the leaders of the new urban aristocracy truly were superior to workers and women—even if they no longer defended them with the sword.

Although authors of the early Italian epic used various means to contain the threat posed by the representation of easterners, manual laborers, and women as knights, such strategies were not completely successful. At least one mercenary who worked for the Medici family, Giovanni Mazzuoli known as "lo Stradino," was an avid collector of Carolingian epics (Masaro n.p.). While Stradino's contemporaries described him as if he were a wild man—ugly, ignorant, and strange—and the humanists poked fun at his collection of "popular" texts written in vernacular, his *armadiaccio,* the epics he owned glorified the type of military service that he and other soldiers provided for the elite of Florence (Maracchi Biagiarelli 51).

Just as Stradino enjoyed texts that represented mercenaries as idealized wild men, women writers felt empowered by the literary depictions of the virago. One of the epics explicitly encourages such identification. In the *Storia di Rinaldino da Montalbano,* yet another Saracen warrior woman, Queen Laura, decides to leave immediately to aid her Christian friend, Rinaldino, on the battlefield after she remembers having read about Penthesilea and how the Amazon queen arrived too late to save Hector.[26] The text, therefore, suggests that the woman warrior should serve as a model for aristocratic women. In fact, several female scholars of the fifteenth and sixteenth centuries, such as Laura Cereta and Moderata Fonte, did identify with Amazons, and portrayed themselves as viragoes "of the mind" (Labalme 1–8). Like Penthesilea, Galaziella, Formosa, or Braidamonte, they demonstrated *virtù* in a public forum, defying the strictly domestic role "of chastity and motherhood" prescribed for women by male contemporaries (Kelly [-Gadol] 38).

In order to gain a voice, however, many of the women writers adopted the same strategies of containment that the male epic writers had used to limit the threat posed by the warrior woman. Like Formosa, some female writers sought to embody the important "feminine" virtue of chastity to counteract their threatening "masculine" voice.[27] Still others viewed themselves as having transcended their own "inferior sex"—like Penthesilea who overcame her "natural" moral weakness (Schiesari 81). Women writers might have been able to view the Amazonian warrior as a model who had earned a public role by imitating the actions of aristocratic men; but in doing so, they often needed to deny their own sexuality and their relationships with other women.

As the example of the literary viragoes illustrates, the late chivalric epic provided an imaginary space in which new identities could be constructed across ethnic, class, and gender boundaries. Yet traditional dichotomies still structured the literary wilderness in which the monsters, wild men, and warrior women appeared. Rather than providing real mobility within this mediating space, the epic's cross-dressing reinforced stereotypes, encouraging only a select few to crossover and assume the superior identity.

4

Masculinity, Sexuality, and Orientalism in the Medieval Italian Epic

> The historic assumption that men do the fighting is colliding with modern egalitarian ideals. . . . [W]ill the military be strengthened or emasculated?
>
> *New York Times Magazine*, June 22, 1997

At one point in a debate between Roland, the exemplary knight of the Italian epic, and the Duke of Carthage, his Saracen counterpart, the easterner makes an unusual comparison by equating the Carolingian hero's rhetorical skills to those of Muhammad:

> "Sire de Clermont, se estes tant saze che cum paroles pansés sovertir les homes, lasés les armes e alés predicant por le monde cum fist Macomet!" (1:159).[1]

> [Sir of Clermont, if you are so wise that with words you think you can convert men, drop your arms and go preaching throughout the world as did Muhammad.]

This challenge from a powerful Saracen warrior displays the ideological significance of transforming an epic hero into an orator who often relies on words rather than arms. Although Roland is praised for his rhetorical skills, those same abilities threaten his position as the ideal knight and question traditional notions of both masculinity and ethnicity. How the anxiety over ideal masculinity converges with Orientalism in the medieval Italian epic is the subject of this chapter.[2] While in chapter three I analyzed how the construct of the "wild" was used by Italian epic writers to discuss issues of class and gender, here I will address how the Orient served as an imaginary space in which questions about sexuality and ethnicity could be examined at a safe distance.

Late Carolingian epics, both in France and Italy, redefined ideal heterosexual masculinity to include not only the art of war but also of rhetoric. With long scholastic arguments, Christian knights attempt to prove aspects of their faith, such as St. Mary's virginity and transubstantiation, to their eastern counterparts (Bancourt 1:474–76). In the late thirteenth century a new hero starts to develop in Carolingian epics whom Marguerite Rossi in her analysis of *Huon de Bordeaux* has labelled the *preudome* or gentleman. She describes Huon as a knight who avoids violence whenever possible in an attempt to balance his military prowess with reason and diplomacy (477–81). The epic hero of the late Carolingian epic, then, often embodies the skills necessary to achieve success among the new mercantile and administrative classes, since the epic writer instills the rhetorical talents associated with his own work into the Carolingian paragons of ideal masculinity. Combining the arts of a warrior and of a contemplative rhetorician, however, can create curious contradictions. While critics like François Suard have noticed the uncertainty surrounding the Carolingian heros of the late epics, including the type of cross-dressing discussed in the last chapter, they have not analyzed the role that Orientalism and homophobia play in the changing definitions of heroism.[3]

Florentine Andrea da Barberino is the best known of the late medieval Italian epic writers.[4] Because of his prolific writings, it is easy to compare Andrea's own rhetorical style with the discursive habits of the heroes he creates. Several scholars, most recently Gloria Allaire, have noted how Andrea presents himself as an historian sorting through various sources to present the most rational version to his audience ("Portrayal" 243–44). His epics are also extremely detailed; when heroes such as Guerrino il Meschino travel in the East, Andrea is careful to list the exact names of cities, rivers, and other geographical landmarks.

Telling the story in an orderly fashion, or as the text phrases it, *seguendo per ordine,* is another important part of Andrea's rhetorical strategy.[5] At the beginning of his epic tale, *Guerrino il Meschino,* Andrea explains that although he is of humble origins, he lives better than many of *magore nazione* or greater birth. Andrea then states that we are all created by one maker who gives us more or less of his grace depending on whether we earn it in our particular profession (fol. 1r). In other words, Andrea portrays himself as having earned a certain social station through his own rational and systematized storytelling, as well as by the grace of God.

Andrea also portrays his epic hero, Guerrino, as having earned his status as a Christian knight. Although the son of Mellone, the Prince of Taranto, as a baby Guerrino is kidnapped. He is then sold to and raised by a wealthy merchant from Constantinople, Pidonio, and rebaptized Meschinello because of his poverty. The text mentions that Pidonio has Guerrino learn several different languages so that the Meschinello can aid his master in business dealings: "[Guerrino] inparò turcho e latino anchora gli faceva Pidonio inparare molti linguaggi perché erano utili all'arte della merchatantia per lo navichare" [Guerrino learned Turkish and Latin, and Pidonio still made him learn many languages because they were useful for mercantile shipping] (fol. 5r). Guerrino is of such good character, however, that the son of the emperor befriends him, frees him from slavery, and teaches him the chivalric arts. When Guerrino enters his first tournament he is simply known as *il villano* or the peasant. As a young man, Guerrino decides to leave Constantinople in search of his biological heritage. While travelling he often uses his linguistic skills to gather information that would be of particular interest to merchants; in Africa and Asia he not only describes the exotic populations and monstrous races he encounters, but also catalogs the merchandise they produce or trade. As Guerrino moves closer to discovering his aristocratic genealogy, however, he uses those same skills to defend Christianity against the Saracens, transforming himself from a merchant into God's knight—the *cavaliere di Dio*.

Together with rational thinking and order, Andrea also highlights rhetorical skills in the actions of the epic heroes; reason replaces courage as the most important virtue for the mythic Carolingian knights. It is also what separates western warriors from their Saracen counterparts. Andrea frequently depicts eastern knights as wild men—more bestial than human, more wild than orderly. They are often giant, hairy, and carry crude weapons. He comments on the lack of *ordine* in their appearance, table manners, military operations, and even their battle cries.[6] The epic hero, Guerrino, becomes the captain of both the Persian and Arab armies against the Turks, precisely because they cannot properly organize themselves. The portrayal of easterners, particularly Muslims, as primitive and inept created one of the most consistent sources of humor in the epic, beginning in the Italian tradition with texts like the *Entrée d'Espagne* (Limentani, "Il comico" 63).

Just as reason and order are associated with the great Christian hope Guerrino, so the Saracens—in this case the Persians, Arabs, and Turks—are all labelled lustful sodomites.[7] Like many earlier western writers, Andrea attributes the easterners' unruly sexuality to their dry and sterile climate as well as the influence that the astrological sign Scorpion wields over the regions they inhabit. When Guerrino first enters Persia he describes its citizens as infertile "per la forza dello segno di schorpio" [because of the strength of the sign of Scorpion], which encourages the vice "chontro a'cieli e chontro alla natura humana" [against Heaven and human nature] (fol. 38v). Guerrino then goes on to explain the etymology of the term sodomite, telling the biblical stories of Sodom and Noah's Ark. As soon as Guerrino meets the realm's king, Pantinfero, the ruler notices Guerrino's beauty and questions whether the Christian hero is a man or a woman: "vedendo sì bello il Meschino il domandò s'egl'era maschio o femina, ed egli [Guerrino] molto si vergognò e rispuose, 'io sono più che huomo e non fenmina'" [seeing how beautiful il Meschino was, he asked whether Guerrino was a man or a woman. And Guerrino felt ashamed and responded: "I am more than a man and not a woman"] (fol. 38r).

The reason for the king's interest in Guerrino's gender becomes explicit at the dinner table, when Guerrino is forced to protect himself from his host, who tries to contaminate the epic hero with the *vizio di sozza lussuria* [vice of dirty lust] (fol. 39r). Andrea associates the Persian's sexuality with other Saracen habits that his epic hero had already experienced on his travels and denounced as uncivilized. Like other Saracens Guerrino had encountered, the Persians dine sitting on the floor and eat off a communal plate. The Christian dismisses the easterners with such bizarre table manners as disgusting pigs. He also compares their dining posture to that of tailors as they sew, thereby suggesting that Saracens, like workers, represent less than ideal masculinity.

Andrea then allows Guerrino to show that he is "more than a man." Although the Persian king accepts that Guerrino will not give into his advances, he orders under pain of death that the Christian have sex with his daughter, and as the text states, "perde il Meschino la sua verginità per chanpare da morte" [il Meschino loses his virginity in order to escape death] (fol. 40r). Here Andrea reproduces a narrative situation common to the late medieval epic in which the virginal Christian hero is forced to have sex with a debauched Saracen princess.[8] By assigning traditionally feminine attributes to a male hero, epic authors like Andrea first accentuate and then ease the anxiety created by weakening the bond between ideal masculinity and physical violence. Notwithstanding the threat of death, both Guerrino and the princess enjoy their lovemaking, and the episode ends up underscoring the protagonist's manliness, which earlier had been called into question by the Persian king: "presono insieme grande druderia e piacere perché avea ischosso sei volte in pocho tenpo e poi ella si partì molto allegra" [they enjoyed great passion and pleasure because he had banged her six times in a short period and then she left very happy] (fol. 40r). The Christian hero, therefore, proves his masculinity in bed, yet still remains God's knight, morally superior to the lustful Saracens.

Later in the narrative, Andrea explicitly links the lower body with Islam and reason with Christianity. He makes fun of Muslims for covering their face while praying when he says:

> Egli naschondono a Maomeometto la più bella chosa che Idio facessi al mondo inperò ch'egli naschondono il viso e monstrògli il chulo ch'è la disonesta parte della persona. (fol. 61v)

> [They hide from Muhammad the most beautiful thing that God made in the world, as they hide their face and show him their ass, which is the dishonest part of the person.]

This description creates a concrete image for the theoretical opposition that Christian theologians had already developed: while Christianity was a religion of asceticism and sacrifice, Islam was the religion of physical indulgence. Christians sought spiritual pleasure through reason, whereas Muslims sought pleasure through the flesh (Daniel 135–61). Norman Daniel, in summarizing Jacques de Vitry's notion of Islam, writes that "especially in the hot regions of the East 'rough and lustful' men found the *straight way* . . . intolerable, instead it was the fatal wide and broad way that they chose to follow" (154).

Medieval theological descriptions of Islam's errant path of self-indulgence included numerous other vices, most notably gluttony and greed. Islamic men were often portrayed as a homogeneous group with a distinct lifestyle. In Andrea's depiction of homosocial behavior among Saracens, he describes men aimlessly luxuriating together:

> Lionetto insu uno letto di seta a gacere, e nel padiglone era moltj tappetj in terra e moltj signorj, dove tre e dove quattro a sedere. Chi guchava a uno guocho e chi a uno altro. Non si potre' dire lo scellerato modo chome egli istavano. E Lionetto Meschin avia le ganbe alta e mostrava le disoneste parte della sua persona chosì molti altri. (fol. 182v)

> [Lionetto was lying on a bed of silk, and in the pavilion were many lords, here three and here four, seated on carpets on the ground. Some played one game and some another. One should not mention the disgraceful manner of their positions: Lionetto Meschin had his legs up high and was showing the shameful parts of his person, and so were many others.]

The Muslim's fondness for finery and games in this description points to the important role that misogyny plays in the construction of Orientalism and sodomy. From Andrea's perspective, the idle lifestyle of the Saracens blinds them to reason, encourages the desires of the flesh, and renders them distastefully effeminate in the process.

Like the imaginary Saracens, northern and central Italian men were also described as having an unnatural appetite for sex and money; their queer sexuality was associated with the mercantile economy, or the unnatural accumulation of wealth. Florentines in particular had a reputation for both sodomy and usury. The common practice of pairing these two sins as "unnatural" in theological discourse led to the representation of Florentines as both the paradigmatic usurers and sodomites of the West. One of the most famous examples is in canto 11 of Dante's *Inferno* where usury and sodomy are categorized together as sins of violence against nature, and thus, against God. Dante later places three prominent politicians among the sodomites of cantos 15 and 16. It is not by accident that in 1376 Pope Gregory XI condemned the citizens of Florence for the same "abominable" sins (Rocke 3).

In addition, the leisure time necessary to become *litterati* posed the threat of weakening men, making them passive like women. This popular medieval notion is illustrated in at least one Florentine cantare that narrates the story of Rinaldo da Monte Albano. The followers of the rebellious vassal succeed in stealing Charlemagne's standard and shaming Roland because the great barons had been reading *con diletto* (with delight) a book about the ancient heroic deeds of Trojan and Greek warriors instead of preparing for such feats themselves. After the surprise attack, Rinaldo shows off his trophy by raising Charlemagne's standard on the top of his own tower in Monte Albano. As soon as the king sees the flag flying over his enemy's palace, he wants to know why Roland has not successfully defended an important symbol of power. Roland and the other barons do not dare explain to Charlemagne that they had been reading a book (Melli, *I Cantari* 338–46).

Because of their access to young boys, as well as the association of their work with leisure, clerics and scholars in late medieval Europe were often assumed to be sodomites (Richards 137–38). Dante follows a long textual tradition when he has his old teacher, Brunetto Latini, point out that the sodomites being punished in hell were *cherci e litterati* (clerics and scholars) (*Inferno* 15:ll. 106–7).[9] Since Florentines had a reputation as men who made a living with books and money rather than arms, they were by extension considered sodomites. Moreover, Florentines also condemned their compatriots for sodomitical tendencies and starting in the early fourteenth century enacted laws that transformed it from a sin into a crime with heavy penalties.

Michael Rocke—acknowledging that the repression probably had little to do with the sexual act itself—describes two possible reasons for this late medieval campaign against sodomy: (1) Florence's transformation into a regional state run by a new managerial class, which developed a centralized and efficient administration to control public order as the city-state expanded its territory; and (2) a demographic crisis caused by the plague, which "nourished perceptions that the nonprocreative sins 'against nature' posed a threat to the very foundation of human society" (27–28).[10] I would like to *underscore* that the new wave of polemics and legislation against sodomy had as much to do with discursive patterns as institutional practices. The habit of labelling mercantile, scholarly, and sodomitical activities as "unnatural" or queer forced the Florentines to defend their ability to achieve the ideal of heterosexual masculinity; they did this by both refiguring that ideal and persecuting those who did not or could not live up to the new gender norms.

During the early fifteenth century, when the epics under discussion were written, San Bernardino of Siena, a Franciscan, repeatedly preached in both Siena and Florence against the sin of sodomy. The queer practices he described among the Tuscan youth are quite similar to the behavior attributed to Saracen knights in the epics. San Bernardino chastises wealthy, young Florentines who do not need to earn a living like most men and instead indulge in the *vita oziosa* or idle life.[11] He goes on to explain that this leisure time, which was traditionally associated with women, could easily tempt men to enjoy the pleasures (both natural and unnatural) of the flesh. In order to learn how to live as real men, the Franciscan preacher suggests that listless young Florentines study rhetoric, a discipline which would help them to strengthen the *patria* (Cannarozzi 2:46).

Like San Bernardino, Andrea da Barberino also redefines ideal masculinity to include traits associated with his profession as a writer. One of the ways in which he presents his work as rational and authoritative is by systematizing a great deal of information that he had accumulated from other written sources including travel accounts, bestiaries, astrological manuals, and saints' lives. For instance, he was probably the first western epic writer to describe a mosque (Allaire, "Portrayal" 252–53). Despite the accuracy of the mosque's physical description, Andrea uses it to reinforce the truth of old stereotypes. Inside the mosque Guerrino finds Muhammad's legendary floating coffin. The epic hero proceeds to berate the

Saracens for their ignorance. The Saracens believe that the floating coffin is miraculous, while the rational Christian Guerrino concludes that it levitates because of magnetic force: the top half of the mosque is made of lodestone (fol. 61v).[12] Guerrino's heroic masculinity is assured by his rational argument about the Saracen, while at the same time he uses it to contain Muslims within the "dominating frameworks" of western culture (Said, *Orientalism* 40).

Epic writers not only try to prove the fallacy of Islam through reason, they also attempt to establish the truth of Christian doctrine. Raffaele da Verona, the author of the fifteenth-century Franco-Italian epic *Aquilon de Bavière,* begins his tale with a prologue in which he states that the epic's purpose is to defend the Christian faith against the fraudulent religion of Muhammad. This story narrates the deeds of Aquilon, the son of the Duke of Bavière, who as an infant is kidnapped and raised as a Saracen by the powerful Amirant. The narrator traces Aquilon's adventures in the East and the West as he discovers his true Christian origins and biological father.

Although the narrative centers on Aquilon, the model Christian knight of the story is Roland. Throughout the evolution of the medieval Italian epic, Roland, rather than his uncle Charlemagne, emerges as the ideal secular leader. In this epic he also takes over Archbishop Turpin's role as the ideal religious leader (Wunderli, 759–81). While Roland's part as theologian is more pronounced in this epic, he first uses rhetoric to convert Saracens in the earlier *Entrée d'Espagne,* which was clearly patterned on the theological debates of the *Chronique de Turpin*. In the *Entrée,* the debate of 400 lines (11. 3610–4050) between Roland and the Saracen Ferragu establishes a model followed by several Franco-Italian and Tuscan epics, including *Aquilon*.[13] As mentioned above, this same tendency had also developed in the late epics of medieval France; armed conflict gradually gave way to religious disputations, allowing the writers of late medieval epics to show off their knowledge of theology and raising the cultural capital of these popular adventure tales.

On several occasions in *Aquilon,* it is Roland, rather than Turpin, who explains points of Christian theology to his Saracen opponents. In the one passage where Raffaele da Verona allows Turpin to debate the Saracens, the Archbishop fails miserably. After Turpin and the Christian knight, Astolfo, are taken prisoner by the Africans, their religious leader, the Calif, debates whether Christian doctrine is rational by stating that the belief in Jesus as the son of God, born from a Virgin, is irrational or "contre tout les raixons del mond" [against all reason of the world] (1:268). Instead, he suggests that Jesus was a holy prophet, just as Moses and Muhammad were, and that all three religions have the same God, just different laws. When the Archbishop tries to respond to this relativistic assertion, Astolfo forcefully interrupts him by saying that the Christians have already proven and will prove once again the divinity of Christ by defeating the Muslims on the battlefield. He ends his tirade against the Calif by claiming that warfare will demonstrate that Muhammad was a bawd, so there is no point in discussing theology—especially since it is time to eat:

> Macomet fu un ribaud . . . e baratés est ancor plus chi croit ch'il agie forze ne vertus. Segnor, gi voil manzer, ch'il non est tenp da predicher! (1:269)

> [Muhammad was a bawd . . . and those who still believe he has either power or virtue are deceived. Sir, I want to eat, this is not the time to preach!]

Although Astolfo's words anger the Calif, he responds politely that he will forgive the Christian knight for his outburst:

> Vos avés grand tort a dir mal de Macomet, car gi non ai dit de Yhesu autre che bien. Mes por coi estes prixoner, gi vos pardon. (1:269)

> [You are very wrong to speak badly of Muhammad, for I have said nothing but good things about Jesus. But since you are a prisoner, I forgive you.]

In his analysis of this debate, Peter Wunderli proposes that it not only diminishes Turpin's role in the text, but also portrays both the Calif and Islam in a more favorable light (766). From this point of view, the disputation is an attempt by Raffaele da Verona to gain the readers' sympathy and moderate the traditional notion of a strictly antagonistic relationship between Christians and Muslims. He goes on to suggest that Astolfo represents the most common opinion of Muslims among westerners, while the positive portrayal of the Calif suggests a new, uniquely Italian outlook. According to Wunderli, this evolution of the traditional enmity for Islam occurs as a reaction against the Church, and its prohibition of contact with Muslims. He views the economic and political interests of northern and central Italy's bourgeois society as the key for understanding this new perception of Muslims not as adversaries but rather as partners (780).

Although I agree with Wunderli that this scene helps to reduce Turpin's theological authority, I question whether the Calif's speech indicates a completely new Italian attitude towards Islam, or rather repeats a traditional epic description of Christian/Muslim encounters. The Calif's courteous and humble response to Astolfo's arrogant accusations follow a pattern of epic discourses in which Muslims show deference to Christian knights even when the easterners have the upper hand. These "politeness strategies" are one of many rhetorical tactics that construct Muslim men as feminine since they adopt discursive patterns usually associated with women.[14] On the other hand, the direct aggression of the Christian's speech clearly labels him as a real man who refuses to lose face even as a prisoner. While most of the men present laugh at Astolfo's arrogant behavior, his self-assertiveness clearly marks his point of view as superior to the more open attitude of the Calif. Moreover, Astolfo's angry remarks echo the author's comments in the prologue that he is retelling the story to prove that Islam is false (1:6).

Turpin's attempt to explain Christian doctrine with reason fails, but Roland succeeds at the same task. In each of his explanations of Christian doctrine Roland relies on empirical proofs to demonstrate his religious truths, including the virginity of Mary. The Virgin Mary is a constant presence in *Aquilon*. The author honors her in both the prologue and the epilogue, and she performs many miracles throughout the narrative. In one instance during their eastern adventures, Roland and the Christian army encounter a witch married to a Jew (1:180). The Christians quickly dispose of this evil pair by allying themselves with the couple's only son; he had converted to Christianity after having been visited by the Virgin Mary. In yet another tale, the Virgin Mary helps an African princess, Carsidonie, avoid marriage to a man she despises; in return, the princess promises to convert to Christianity (1:242–43). Throughout the epic, the Virgin Mary continually performs miracles to restore order and reinforce the social norms.

Several of the theological debates in *Aquilon* also center on the Virgin Mary's purity. In one dialogue between Roland and the Duke of Carthage, the Saracen questions Christians' belief in the *immaculata conceptio* and the *parturitio virginalis* on the grounds that these phenomena cannot be observed in nature. Roland then defends Mary's virginity by using *voire sperience*, or empirical evidence for proof.[15] He compares the conception of Christ in Mary's womb to light coming through glass without breaking it. The Duke responds that Roland has explained his faith *por raison* or through reason (1:159). Although this analogy is common in both Latin and vernacular religious poetry, the epic presents it as a fact of empirical science (Warner 44). In his book about the increased anti-Semitism of the late Middle Ages, Gavin Langmuir suggests that the persecution of Jews escalated when Christians tried to explain their nonrational belief system with rational empiricism. He believes that the doubts and conflicts which arose within the Christian world because of the contradictions created between empirical knowledge and religion led to the greater persecution of Jews and other minority groups (Langmuir 127). The irrational fantasies about the dangers of Jews, which were supposedly based on empirical evidence, helped unite the Christian social body fragmented by rational empiricism and the heresies it spawned.

Empirical reason, and its threat to the Christian belief system, clearly plays a similar role in the Orientalism of the late medieval epic. Saracens repeatedly challenge Christian dogma claiming that it is irrational, and Christians respond that Saracens are so self-indulgent that they no longer understand reason because they have subjected themselves to the tyranny of the flesh. For example, in one passage Raffaele da Verona suggests that it is the Saracens' earthly desires that keep them from understanding Christian faith; when talking about Saracen priests and clerics, he says, "che tot le trexor de cist segle non li porent contenter, tan est lor cupidités e lor avaricie" [that all the treasure of the world could not content them, so great is their cupidity and avarice] (1:116). Reason is so closely tied to the Christian cause, that in a moment of divine communication, the greatest epic hero of them all, Roland, learns that the first letter of his name stands for *raixon* or reason (1:398).

In her research on the rise of the eucharistic cult, Miri Rubin has shown how the host was used to symbolize the transcendental unity of the Christian community and to encourage the expulsion of impure elements—Jews, heretics, and witches—from the social body (56–57). Likewise, the Virgin's body, particularly its purity and incorruptibility, is used as a symbol of transcendental unity in the late medieval epic to explain away the variation and diversity of experience.

A community's fear of bodily pollution derives from either an external threat to the social order, or from its own internal conflicts and contradictions. The ubiquitous presence of the Virgin in *Aquilon* not only represents anxiety over the possible blurring of boundaries between West and East, but also between the categories of the West's own social system. Mary Douglas discusses both "a kind of sex pollution which expresses a desire to keep the body (physical and social) intact" and "another kind of sex pollution [that] arises from the desire to keep straight the internal lines of the social system" (140). The real hero of this epic is the Virgin. Her impenetrability is a response to the ambiguity created by the text's multiple hybrid figures and cultural cross-dressers; even Roland disguises himself—first as a merchant and later as a woman—to deceive his enemies. To quote Douglas again: "Purity is the enemy of change, of ambiguity and compromise" (162). It is the role of the Virgin Mary, then, to reestablish the social hierarchies that had been disrupted, making everyone subservient to aristocratic, heterosexual Christian men.

These texts describe ideal masculinity as embodied in an elite class of aristocratic, heterosexual Christian knights. Yet during the late Middle Ages and early Renaissance, the institution of chivalry in Italian communes undergoes important changes. For instance, as mentioned in the previous chapter, although Florence had always expected knights to cover the expenses of maintaining a horse for combat, they did not necessarily need to ride it into battle, but could instead pay someone to fight for them (Cardini 25–26). This substitution of men of lower socioeconomic status for titled patricians in the art of warfare threatened the elite masculine ideal that the knight represented. It also exposed chivalry as a performance of professional cross-dressing that did not necessarily correspond to a coherent, internal identity. Epic writers face this threat by refiguring the characteristics necessary for ideal masculinity. Because they are the talents necessary for the new mercantile and administrative classes, including the epic writers themselves, the rhetorical skills of epic heros such as Roland and Guerrino become external signs of a chivalric identity to which other social groups must submit.

In the late medieval epic the Saracen knights play the pleasure-seeking sodomites to the rational Christians, but the descriptions of queer sexuality in the imaginary East and in contemporary Florence share several tendencies. According to San Bernardino, Tuscan sodomites, like the Saracens depicted in the epic tradition, were also guilty of gambling, drinking, and gluttony. He even tells the druggists that they should stop selling sweets such as marzipan to young men so they will not share in the sin of creating "bad" adolescents (Cannarozzi 2:45–46).

As noted earlier, the Franciscan preacher also argues that Tuscans are famous for sodomy because their culture encourages young men to remain single and idle. He suggests that delaying marriage and a professional career leads to the sodomitical lifestyle.[16] This same explanation of queer sexuality exists in yet another early-fifteenth-century Italian epic that narrates the story of Aquilante, a wild man who transforms into a knight, and his sister, Formosa, an Amazonian warrior.[17] Despite her impressive military and rhetorical skills, Formosa winds up advocating the subordinate status of women in the heterosexual couple. As a young woman, Formosa learns that the Sultan of Babylonia has created *el giardino senza femine* [the garden without women] (fol. 14v). No woman is allowed to enter it under the threat of death. Formosa is clearly outraged by this prohibition and takes it upon herself to open this exclusively masculine space to women. All this seems like a direct threat to the naturalized gender order until Formosa reaches the garden, enters in disguise as a knight, and is propositioned by a dirty old Saracen who, the text explicitly tells us, does not like women and believes Formosa is a man:

> Molti si maravigliavano della sua belleça. . . . Luchanfera, il quale era u[n] saraino che pocho a grado avea il sesso feminile . . . l'andò a vedere e pavegli una bella chosa. . . . Allora, il vechio lusurioso credendo lui fusse maschio lo prese p[er] la mano e menollo alla sua tavola. (fol. 16r)
>
> [Many of the Saracens marvelled at his (Formosa's) beauty. . . . Luchanfera, who had little regard for the feminine sex . . . went to see him (Formosa) and he seemed a beautiful thing. . . . Then the old lustful man, believing that Formosa was a man, took him by the hand and led him to his table.]

This proposition makes clear that Formosa's upcoming battle is not just to support *l'onore delle donne* or the honor of ladies, but also to defend the heterosexual couple threatened by the Saracen sodomites who frequent the garden (fol. 15v). Queer sexuality, therefore, is described as misogynistic; the Saracen sodomites seek out men because they despise women. Such constructions of both sodomy and Islam distract from the misogyny and homophobia of Christianity with its notion that queer sexual or religious practices render men effeminate and weak like women.[18] Sodomites are portrayed as enemies of women, and the heterosexual couple as their liberation. San Bernardino also encourages this antagonism in at least one of his sermons when he compares sodomites to the snake that separated Adam and Eve. He goes on to say:

> "É la natura de le donne, di volere male a' sodomitti, come i sodomitti vogliono male a le donne. Inimicizia è fra loro: l'uno odia l'altro." (Bargellini 910)
>
> [It is woman's nature to dislike sodomites, just as sodomites dislike women. Enmity exists between them; one hates the other.]

He then concludes by encouraging women to help in the purging of sodomites from their homes and city.

As this sermon suggests, San Bernardino often preaches about the importance of marriage, depicting it as the divinely sanctioned institution that bolsters the new mercantile economy. Men should go out and collect *masserizia* or household goods, while women should maintain the home.[19] If men do not marry, not only will they be attracted to the sodomitical lifestyle, but their homes and goods will deteriorate as well.

While San Bernardino describes the heterosexual couple as the base of the new mercantile economy, paradoxically the new socioeconomic order discouraged men from marrying early. Young men living in the city often did not marry until they were between 26 and 30 years of age because they first needed to accumulate a significant amount of capital to establish a household. Research by David Herlihy and Christiane Klapisch-Zuber on the Florentine *catasto* or census of 1427 shows that Tuscan cities had a large population of unattached young men, many of whom seemed happy to be living without the responsibilities of a wife and family (222–23). In addition, Michael Rocke's work on the "Office of the Night"—the court created in fifteenth-century Florence to investigate and punish sodomites—suggests that Florentines did not conceive of homoeroticism as an exclusive orientation but rather as "part of distinct stages in their life course, above all adolescence and the long period of youthful bachelorhood" (121).[20] In a similar vein, Maria Serena Mazzi states that young men in Florence matured in such a homosocial community that they developed a group identity "in which the feminine element appears like something unknown and distant" (130).

Research on sexual practices in Venice illustrates a similar pattern. As in Florence, there existed a large population of unmarried men; nearly half of adult male nobles were bachelors (Chojnacki 78). In the patrician culture of Renaissance Venice, men who did not take on the responsibilities of husband and father could not take on leadership roles, but instead "were locked into the lower echelons of the patriciate's official activity" (81). Although at times young men seem to have chosen to abdicate familial responsibilities in exchange for greater freedom, often they were forced to remain bachelors so that the family's patrimony could be passed on intact to a brother. Thus, these men could never achieve ideal masculinity, but at the same time "the denial (or rejection) of patriarchy could loosen the tethers of conformity to the requirements of mainstream patrician manhood" (83).

The Italian epics analyzed in this chapter depict young unmarried men in search of an identity within a patriarchal hierarchy. These epics follow closely the model established by an Old French subgenre, the *enfances chansons de geste*, which describe the youth of epic heroes. The protagonist of such narratives participates in a series of highly conventionalized adventures: the noble child is exiled from his homeland and raised by non-noble or Saracen parents, he then reveals his true aristocratic character through service to a foreign prince, reunites with his biological parents, and eventually regains control of his homeland (Wolfzettel 325–27). Such biographical tales first became popular in France at the turn of the thirteenth century and then were copied in several countries including Italy (Simpson Shen 182–86). As we saw in the first chapters, four of the *Marciano XIII* tales *(Bovo, Karleto, Enfances Ogier,* and *Rolandino)*— some of the earliest extant chivalric epics written in the Italian peninsula—tell the stories of how youthful heroes lost and regained their noble status.

Besides the exploits described above, many of these heroes also fall in love with a Saracen princess before returning to their native cities. Marriage is often an important event in these narratives because in order to revitalize his lineage, the hero must produce children. In her exhaustive study of this subgenre, Lucia Simpson Shen concludes that enfances epics focus on the success of the family, rather than on just the individual hero: "The social situation is unstable, and the fundamental theme of the action is that the hero must establish a rightful place in society not only for himself but for his family—his parents, on the one hand, and his children, on the other—in a word, for his *lignage*" (201). She hypothesizes that this type of chanson de geste was particularly popular around the turn of the thirteenth century in France because it expressed the anxieties and desires of "a coalition of lesser nobles and those who sought enoblement" (233). These were young warriors who had not inherited land, and, thus, were forced to leave home in order to maintain or acquire a noble status.

Simpson Shen characterizes the enfances epics at the height of their popularity in France as optimistic texts because they represent how young warriors succeed in establishing a lasting lineage. She attributes the happy endings of these tales to their production during a time of great prosperity in France. On the other hand, she finds that the enfances epics of the late thirteenth century and fourteenth century change in character, as the protagonists seem more "helpless" and depend on the supernatural to achieve their goals (265–66). *Aquilon* is a particularly good example of this tendency since both the success of the Christian cause as well as of the title hero depend less on the knights' accomplishments than on divine aid. Despite their different endings, both the early and late enfances narratives in France focus on the obstacles presented to young men as they try to achieve their culture's notion of ideal masculinity. As I mentioned above, like late medieval France, both fifteenth-century Florence and Venice—the areas in which *Guerrino* and *Aquilon* were produced—also had significant populations of young bachelors who faced difficulties in joining the state's patriarchy. The great appeal of enfances narratives in late medieval Italy, therefore, also had to do with how these epics expressed the anxieties created in a culture where young men dream of controlling their own destiny, but know that their future success will be largely determined by their place in the family hierarchy and their clan's status in the community.

Both Guerrino and Aquilon attempt to prove their masculinity with arms and rhetoric while searching for their biological fathers and birthrights. In order to achieve such status, however, they must first free themselves from the queer practices of the decidedly effeminate Saracens and from the homosocial relationships of bachelorhood. While Aquilon renounces his sword, pledges chastity, and decides to join a religious order to expiate the sins he committed against Christianity as a Saracen, Guerrino marries before he takes over his role as family patriarch. Guerrino's destiny is not surprising considering that on several occasions he uses his rhetorical skills to deliver sermons about the importance of family as he searches for his own patrilinear birthright.[21] In each case, the epic hero's ambiguous social status as bachelor ends when he takes his place within the Christian social order.

Both San Bernardino's sermons and the Italian epic suggest that queer sexuality exists because of social forces—young men living in exclusively male spaces—and yet these texts also posit the notion that heterosexuality is natural. The incessant condemnation of sodomy as *contra naturam* reiterated by epic writers, preachers, and even local governments in late medieval Tuscany was a response to socioeconomic conditions that permitted, and at times obligated, young men to spend a great deal of time outside the ideal of heterosexual marriage.[22] The need to continuously redefine sodomy as unnatural emerged because the Tuscan social customs exposed both heterosexuality and sodomy as cultural, rather than natural, practices.

As participants in the "queer" mercantile economy that bore fruit without physical labor, men of northern and central Italy had a reputation as effeminate cowards who could not live up to the masculine ideal of chivalry. By extension, these stereotypical merchants and administrators were also known as sodomites. Boccaccio plays on this stereotype in the famous story of the depraved notary, Ser Cepparello (*Decameron* 1:1). The Italian epic writers responded to these accusations by helping to redefine the traits necessary for ideal masculinity to include not only reason and rhetorical skills, but also marriage to either a religious order or a woman. Orientalism plays a role in this modification of gender roles, since the effeminate and at times queer Saracens provide the contrast needed to highlight the new intellectual and domestic ideal of masculinity embodied in the Christian heroes.

R. I. Moore's book on the "persecuting society" of the late middle ages includes a chapter titled "Power and Reason" in which the historian discusses how the centralization and systemization of legal, administrative, and religious powers not only represented the victory of reason over superstition, truth over custom, or centralization over particularism, but "were also triumphs of the expert, of the clerks over the illiterate" (138–39). He goes on to state that the persecution of oppressed groups which increased in this period stemmed from the *litterati*'s fear of contamination by the *rustici*. At the beginning of his epic tale of Guerrino, Andrea stated that, although of humble origins, he had earned a certain status through his work as a *litterato*. As the new administrative and mercantile classes gained power in both France and the Italian city-states, the myths that had defined and bolstered ideal heterosexual masculinity changed to reflect the characteristics of these new, powerful social groups. The narratives needed to justify some social mobility, while maintaining strict dichotomies between litterati and rustici, real men and sodomites, and Christians and Saracens. Reason and order, what Jacques de Vitry had referred to as the straight path, are the characteristics that sustained each of these ideal dichotomies despite the blurring of their boundaries in the new social structure.

III

Discursive Rivalries:
The Case of Ugo d'Alvernia

5

Orality, Literacy, and the Prose Epic

The Transformation of the Chanson de Geste in Italy

Since the groundbreaking work of Milman Perry on orality and literacy in the 1920s, several medievalists have identified the late Middle Ages in Europe as a transitional period in which a highly oral society became more and more dependent on written texts. D. H. Green has coined the term "intermediate mode of reception" for the widespread practice of producing texts "with an eye to public recital . . . , but also for the occasional private reader" (277). Franz M. Bäuml refers to the same transitional works as "pseudo-oral-formulaic texts" ("Medieval Texts" 44). Even though these texts were produced in written form, they still contain elements of primary orality.

The Old French chanson de geste and its descendant, the Italian Carolingian epic, have received particular attention from these scholars because of the formulae which tie that genre to the world of primary orality. Even when Italian authors of the late Trecento produced epics in writing from written models, they continued to use formulae and other techniques characteristic of oral narratives. Based on the extant manuscripts, the Italian form of the genre flourished among anonymous authors of the Trevisan March in the thirteenth century, and a second center of production developed in Tuscany during the fourteenth century.[1] Concurrent with this transplantation, the Carolingian material gradually lost its Old French veneer as it was translated into the new hegemonic language of Italy—Tuscan. Competing literary forms also developed during this period of transition; communal authors translated the lasse of many of the early Franco-Italian epics into prose and into a new poetic form known as the cantare.

Although several scholars have focused their attention on the cantari, very few have studied the translation of the Italian medieval epic into prose. Why would writers in fourteenth-century Italy feel a need to transform a long tradition of poetic texts? The emergence of a new signifying system, such as prose, generally means that in some ways writers deem the old system inadequate for certain messages and question its authoritative form (Kittay and Godzich 8). Vernacular prose writing emerged together with the development of a more mobile social structure and a new legal bureaucracy. The fragmentation of earlier stable hierarchies that were considered universal into a new social structure of estates such as merchants and administrators occurred along with a transformation of the system of signifying practices which includes the development of prose.[2]

Traditional verse genres such as the roman and the chanson de geste were translated into prose in northern Europe as well as in Italy in a movement known as *mise en prose*, which swept French courts as well as Italian communes (Keller, "Mises en prose" 93). In fact, during the fourteenth and fifteenth centuries the chivalric epic enjoyed a renewed popularity as authors presented Carolingian epics in a new form of voluminous prose cycles (Suard, "La tradition" 100). Two centers of production for this type of manuscript were the Court of Burgundy and Florence. Although the ideologies promoted in these two governments differed, writers like David Aubert, for example, who produced prose compilations for Phillip the Good's court, and Andrea da Barberino, who wrote prose epics in a city that supported republican notions of governance, produced texts with striking similarities. They both created voluminous tomes containing whole cycles of prose epics characterized not only by their length but also by their verisimilitude and didactic tone. These texts also shared certain qualities with their states' growing bureaucracies as the prose epic writers presented their cycles as objective, complete, and truthful versions of heroes' stories or what François Suard calls *une histoire exemplaire* [an exemplary history] ("La tradition" 103). In addition, these epics created fictional genealogies that not only celebrated regional identities but also subverted the authority of the king of France. Heroes like Renaut de Montauban or Rinaldo da Montalbano, who undermine the king's power with their prowess and virtue, are particularly popular in both these regions (Keller, "Mises en prose" 102; Rajna "Rinaldo"). Despite their similarities, the differences between the Burgundian and Florentine prose epics are also important. While the Burgundian cycles appear in illuminated, luxury codices produced for princes and courtiers, the Florentine prose epics tend to be found in "popular" manuscripts characterized by their mercantile scripts and lack of decoration. The Florentine prose epics were not just read by courtiers in a seigneurial library, but rather circulated freely among men of different socioeconomic classes including guild members and nobles (Allaire, "Chivalric 'Histories'" 106–73; Petrucci, *Writers and Readers* 224–25).

The recasting of Carolingian epics in prose provides us with an opportunity to analyze the meaning of this new signifying system in a culture increasingly dominated by written texts, yet also nostalgic for the seemingly stable world that the traditional formulae of orality represented: a culture that simultaneously celebrated both republican and chivalric values. Even after the invention of the printing press, written prose stories continued to imitate the conventions of narratives "told" orally (Ong, *Interfaces* 88–89). This chapter examines both the formal and social functions of orality in the verse and prose versions of one Italian Carolingian epic narrative, *Ugo d'Alvernia*.[3]

Even though Tuscan writers translated romance epics into prose, they did not necessarily stop reading or performing them publicly. The most famous prose translator of Carolingian epics, Andrea da Barberino (1371–1431), is referred to by his contemporaries as a singer (Osella 364). Moreover, a recently discovered cantare attributed to him claims that "Maestro Andrea" performed the text before an aristocratic audience in Piazza della Signoria (Branca, "Notizie di manoscritti" 89–90). The respectful title maestro probably signified that Andrea did not just perform heroic adventure tales, but also wrote them (Allaire, *Andrea da Barberino* 6).

The legendary tales of Carlomagno and his knights, which singers like Andrea da Barberino recited in piazzas, formed part of a larger chivalric discourse. Communes such as Padua and Florence, where Carolingian tales like *Ugo d'Alvernia* circulated, imitated the ceremonies and rituals of French and German nobles at the same time that they fought against such authorities to retain independence. Communal dubbings often occurred alongside the grandiose celebrations for the communal elite, complete with jousts, tournaments, feasts, and entertainment by minstrels (Larner, "Chivalric Culture" 123). Despite its praise of republican values, the Guelf party of Florence continued to bestow the title of knight to members of its political elite throughout the fifteenth century (A. Brown 46).

Although they used Carolingian epics to develop the chivalric mythology that supported their power, many members of the new urban aristocracy in Italy, especially the administrative class or early humanists, shared an ambivalent attitude towards the orality of the genre. They craved the power of the oral tradition with its ability to reach so many people, yet they also felt superior to it because of their training in the written uses of language, which had helped them to earn positions of power within the communal structure. Like the clerical tradition that juxtaposed the mind vs. body dichotomy with the opposition of writing vs. orality, and linked the dangers of the flesh with vocal performance (Nichols 151), the new urban aristocracy attempted to both contain and use the voice. Andrea da Barberino's decision to write in prose the epics that he also recited demonstrates this ambivalence towards the oral tradition. The singer's incorporation of recitative techniques into his prose writing suggests a desire not to be part of the oral epic tradition but rather to master it.

In order to discuss the hybrid narrative strategies by which epic writers such as Andrea da Barberino used orality, it might be helpful to employ the distinction that Franz Bäuml developed for analyzing intermediary texts such as the Carolingian epics. He points out that we must separate a "type" of composition or transmission such as oral performance from a "technique" of composition or transmission such as the use of the formula ("Medieval Texts" 40). By separating type from technique, one can interpret the function of different formal narrative devices within a pseudo-oral-formulaic text. Such a text, though composed in writing, might include quite a few oral narrative techniques so that, to use Bäuml's words again, it contains orality as "an implicit fictional character of literacy."[4]

In the communal culture of Florence, as in other regional and state governments with expansionist tendencies like France, political authority became harder to trace since it no longer descended from one centralized source but instead was dispersed among the numerous judges, notaries, merchants, and nobles who ran the legal and economic apparatus. Prose, like the new bureaucracy, was perceived as natural, objective, and rational. This communal culture's first *auctor,* Dante, refers to prose as a more "natural" form of expression since it is less "adorned" than writings in verse.[5] Although Dante's society was heavily influenced by written texts, he lived in what Walter Ong refers to as the oral-aural culture of manuscripts (*Orality and Literacy* 119). Memorization of texts and mnemonic patterning were encouraged in schools, and individuals often read manuscripts *sotto voce* to themselves.[6] In the first chapter of his philosophical treatise, the *Convivio,* Dante explains his decision to write in vernacular prose by comparing it to a beautiful woman:

> Ché per questo comento la gran bontade del volgare di sì [si vedrà]; però che si vedrà la sua vertù, sì com'è per esso altissimi e novissimi

concetti convenevolemente, sufficientemente e acconciamente, quasi come per esso latino, manifestare; [la quale non si potea bene manifestare] ne le cose rimate, per le accidentali adornezze che quivi sono connesse, cioè la rima e lo numero regolato; sì come non si può bene manifestare la bellezza d'una donna, quando li adornamenti de l'azzimare e de le vestimenta la fanno più [ammi]rare che essa medesima. Onde, chi vuole ben giudicare d'una donna, guardi quella quando solo sua *naturale* bellezza si sta con lei, da tutto accidentale adornamento discompagnata: sì come sarà questo comento, nel quale si vedrà l'agevolezza de le sue sillabe, le proprietadi de le sue co[stru]zioni e le soavi orazioni che di lui si fanno. (1:10, 12–13; emphasis added)

[For by means of this commentary the great goodness of the vernacular of *sì* will be seen, because its virtue will be made evident, namely how it expresses the loftiest and the most unusual conceptions almost as aptly, fully, and gracefully as Latin, something that could not be expressed perfectly in verse, because of the accidental adornments that are tied to it, that is, rhyme and meter, just as the beauty of a woman cannot be perfectly expressed when the adornment of her preparation and apparel do more to make her admired than she does herself. Therefore, if anyone wishes to judge a woman justly, let him look at her when her *natural* beauty alone attends her, unaccompanied by any accidental adornment; so it will be with this commentary, in which the smoothness of the flow of its syllables, the appropriateness of its constructions, and the sweet discourses that it makes will be seen.] (Lansing, *Dante's Il Convivio* 24–25).

Dante clearly recognizes the mnemonic "adornments" of poetry while categorizing the "constructions" of prose writing as representations of "natural beauty."

In order to illustrate a similar change in notions of cognition and language, Jeffrey Kittay and Wlad Godzich, in their book on the emergence of prose in France, contrast the vendette practiced by clans with the later codified law of the state. In the legal system, the lawyer represents himself as distanced and objective: "He [the lawyer] must construct a unique type of relationship, which we will come to know as the subject-object model of cognition, in which he will be the knowing subject of an object, as the latter is *assigned* to him" (202). In a similar fashion, the narrator of the new Italian prose epic "truthfully" reports events that have simply "happened." For example, Andrea da Barberino in his *Ugo d'Alvernia* takes on the first-person voice of the protagonist as if the story had actually been narrated by the eyewitness Ugo.

By combining techniques of the traditional chanson de gestes with those of the new historical prose genres based on classical models, writers of the Italian Carolingian epic referred to two sources of authority. Oral narrative techniques, such as direct address, alluded to the publicly performed chanson de geste, which embodied the community's historical and cultural patrimony with its notion of a stable, hierarchical society led by nobles claiming divine mandate. The epic's use of prose, on the other hand, invoked historical narratives in which "authors" displayed their individual knowledge to achieve their own social and economic advancement. For example, Andrea da Barberino at times directly addresses the audience like a public singer whose narrative belongs to the community while also carefully interjecting his own humanistic knowledge of classical Rome into *Ugo d'Alvernia,* thus asserting his position as a learned member of the emerging administrative class. At a time when Boccaccio employed multiple frames and plurivocal narration to question the role of the narrator, other prose writers, such as Andrea, appropriated certain techniques of oral poetry in order to claim the authority associated with the traditional singer.

Just as Andrea adopted techniques from two traditions to establish his authority, the Carolingian epic in Italy embodied a hybrid model of social organization by modifying the notion of feudal hierarchies to the needs of the new communal aristocracy and its mythology of the *Respublica Romana*. Italian authors of the Carolingian epic, including Andrea, capitalized on the infamous reputation of the Lombards in Old French chansons de geste as "bourgeois," by endorsing, at least in theory, a more egalitarian social structure that condemned traditional concepts of nobility. The Old French texts had portrayed Lombards as merchants who made cowardly and incompetent knights. This disdain for Italian knights derived from the belief that knighthood in Italy was based more on wealth and profession than on bloodline.

In their turn, Italian epic writers helped to redefine the institution of knighthood and valorized earning as much as inheriting the title of knight. As argued in chapter one, the ostensible democratization of chivalry allowed communes and the aristocracy that controlled them to establish a new definition of knighthood, which did not challenge the old one but rather modified it to the needs of a new urban aristocracy that depended on the support of the popolo. The new aristocracy wanted the unquestionable power associated with the French kings without the economic submission necessary for such political alliances. It is against this complex ideological and cultural background that the Italian prose epic needs to be considered.

From Poetry to Prose: *Ugo d'Alvernia*

In the late fourteenth and early fifteenth centuries, Andrea da Barberino wrote several prose epics based on Old French or Franco-Italian models: *I Reali di Francia, L'Aspramonte, La Prima Spagna, La Seconda Spagna, Le Storie Nerbonesi, La Storia di Aiolfo del Barbicone, Guerrino il Meschino, Storie di Rinaldo da Montalbano,* and *La Storia di Ugone d'Alvernia*.[7] I have chosen to analyze the development of the *Ugo* narrative because it clearly documents the struggle in Italy during the fourteenth century for hegemony among competing languages (Latin, Old French, northern dialects, and Florentine) and between means of textual transmission (orality and literacy), literary forms (poetry and prose), and cultural models (chivalry and humanism). The different versions of Ugo's adventures allow us to study the gradual rise of Florentine as the hegemonic language of the Italian peninsula, the translation of verse which had been performed orally into prose for both individual and collective reading, and the appropriation by singers of both classical and Italian medieval literary texts.

Three extant manuscripts contain versions of the *Ugo* story in Franco-Italian lasse.[8] Besides Andrea da Barberino's prose epic, the only other text that treats Ugo's adventures is a late-fifteenth-century cantare by Michelangolo da Volterra. Since I am focusing on the translation of the epic from the traditional lasse into prose, the following analysis will treat the anonymous verse epics and the prose version of Andrea da Barberino.[9]

According to both the Franco-Italian tradition and Andrea da Barberino's translation of the epic, we can easily divide Ugo's adventures into three parts. In the first section, Ugo is at the court of Duke Sanguino and is falsely accused of sexual advances on the Duke's wife, Sofia, who had tried in vain to seduce our saintly hero. The Duke initially believes his wife's accusations and tries to kill Ugo. Ugo flees to his native city, Alvernia, with Sanguino in hot pursuit. Eventually, Sofia's father, King Carlo Martello of France, gets involved in the squabble and discovers that his daughter has lied about Ugo. The king makes the unusually harsh decision to have his daughter killed even though the pious Ugo pleads with Carlo Martello to spare her life.

The second part of the narrative is linked to the first by Ugo's marriage to Honida, whom he had met while fleeing from Sanguino. The blissful happiness of the newlyweds comes to an abrupt end at Carlo Martello's festivities for Pentecost. The king sees Honida and immediately falls in love with her. He soon realizes that Honida is as saintly as her husband and that he must send Ugo on a mission in order to have a chance of seducing his vassal's wife. The king quickly calls a meeting of his advisors, including a *jongleur,* at which he decides to send Ugo to Hell. He instructs Ugo to find Lucifer, to make him a vassal, and to bring back a tribute.

The dutiful Ugo accepts the mission and begins his journey East towards Hell. In this section of the narrative, *Ugo d'Alvernia* follows a pattern common to many late chansons de geste: epic heroes like Roland and Ogier leave their responsibilities in the West (often after a confrontation with the emperor as in the Franco-Italian *Entrée d'Espagne* or after their family had been attacked by traitors as in *Bovo*), and head East to prove themselves in a series of adventures.[10] On all these voyages the marvelous, whether in the form of fairies or divine aid, plays an important role. On Ugo's journey he has numerous exploits: he fights various wild animals, meets with the Pope and the legendary Prester John, faces demons disguised as beautiful young women, and observes exotic peoples. Eventually, with the help of numerous prayers and supplications, Ugo reaches Hell and is guided through an afterlife that shares certain similarities with Dante's *Inferno.* Instead of being led by the poet Virgil, however, Ugo is accompanied by two epic heroes, Enea (Aeneas) and Guglielmo d'Oringa (Guillaume d'Orange). Ultimately, Ugo convinces Lucifer to give him a tribute for his signore, and he magically returns to his homeland, which in his absence has been under siege by the king. Ugo brings Carlo Martello the valuable tribute, but as soon as the king touches it, demons appear and carry him off.

As the third section of the narrative begins, Ugo and most of the other vassals are happy that the king has disappeared, yet they are also left with the problem of choosing a new leader. Everyone supports Ugo, but the humble hero quickly refuses the throne, and eventually Guglielmo Zappetta (William Capet) is elected. Just when the vassals have resolved the leadership problem, a letter arrives from the pope saying that the Saracens are about to conquer the Holy City. Despite the efforts of Guglielmo Zappetta, the barons refuse to mobilize until Ugo intervenes and convinces them of their duty. The Germans, on the other hand, act quickly and make an agreement with the pope that their king will become emperor if they save Rome. By the time the French arrive the Germans have taken over much of the city, and the relationship between the two supposedly allied armies becomes very tense. Eventually the French by themselves conquer the Saracens, but the Germans claim the victory and steal all the booty. Ugo hears a divine voice that tells him to arrange a tournament to decide whether a German or a Frenchman should be emperor. He is also forewarned that he will sacrifice his life and the French will lose the crown for their past sins. Six warriors from each side are chosen and they all kill each other in a brutal contest. A German is the last to die (he outlives Ugo by a short time), so that as the story ends the Germans have prevailed and control the Holy Roman Empire.

All three episodes appear in Andrea da Barberino's prose version of *Ugo d'Alvernia*.[11] The verse manuscript of the story found in Padua (P) contains only the first two parts of the narrative, while the Turin (T) and Berlin (B) manuscripts begin with the second episode. The last page of manuscript P is torn, and, therefore, it is impossible to determine whether its scribe had intended to end the story after the second episode or include the final battle between the French and the Germans. Since there are close similarities between manuscript P and the first part of Andrea's prose epic, I will cite that version of the Franco-Italian narrative in the following analysis.[12]

One sign that Andrea wrote for a more literate audience is the exclusion of many formulaic phrases and repeated plot summaries that appear in earlier versions of *Ugo d'Alvernia* (Vitale-Brovarone, "De la *Chanson de Huon d'Auvergne*" 395–96). For example, the anonymous author of the manuscript P often uses the same formulaic phrases to describe a knight's preparation for combat:

> E luy vesty l'osbergo e calçà le ganbier,
> Alaçà l'elmo çento a lo brando d'açer,
> Do speroni chalçà che fé de fin oro cler,
> Lo bon destrier se fé avanti mener
> De fren e de sella molto ben corer.[13]

[And he wore the breastplate and put on the leg armor, he fastened the handsome helmet to the steel sword, he put on two spurs that were of fine, brilliant gold, the good steed was led forward well-equipped with reins and saddle.]

While Ugo is the knight evoked in this particular portrait, an almost identical description of Sanguino preparing to mount his horse appears only a few pages earlier (fol. 15v) in the manuscript. Although Andrea in the first part of his text followed the manuscript P very closely in terms of the events represented, he omitted many of its oral formulas (Vitale-Brovarone, "De la *Chanson de Huon d'Auvergne*" 397–98).

Andrea also deleted many of the repetitive passages in which either the narrator or a character retells past events. Near the end of the first section of the P manuscript, the narrator three times in a row retells the story of the failed seduction of Ugo by Sanguino's wife Sofia: Ugo explains the truth to his angry friend Sanguino; then, Sanguino has Ugo tell his tale to the king; and finally, the king and Sanguino force the servant who corroborated Sofia's accusations against Ugo to admit that Sofia had tried to seduce Ugo and not the other way around. Andrea's text follows the same sequence of events. Ugo explains his story in full to Sanguino but then Andrea does not have the hero repeat his story to the king; instead the narrator simply says: "Ugo disse a Carlo come aveva detto a Sanguino" [Ugo told Carlo what he had told Sanguino] (1:48). When Andrea next rewrites the scene in which the servant confesses and retells once again the same story, he initially follows the example of manuscript P, but after recounting a good portion of the story Andrea simply states: "così la cameriera ogni cosa contò: e come la Duchessa, poi che Ugone fu fuggito, le fece fasciare il braccio" [and so it was that the servant told everything: how the duchess, as soon as Ugone had fled, made the servant bandage her arm] (1:53).

The repetitive nature of manuscript P implies that the author was more concerned about the performance of the poem than its plot. Andrea da Barberino's prose version, however, demonstrates an impatience with a narrative style that had strong ties to the world of orality. The prose text focuses less on the process of telling the story than on the sequence of events, of "facts": a tension, therefore, exists between the oral narrative model which Andrea follows and the tendency of his prose to organize and systematize the same material in a way that a literate community would find more logical and less redundant.

Another important difference between the anonymous epics and Andrea's translation is that the texts in verse quote no written sources and simply narrate the story as if it were common knowledge, but the prose text makes manifest that it is a written commentary on another written commentary about the oral tradition. Andrea da Barberino utilizes several narrative devices in an attempt to show that he is faithfully recounting the tale from written sources. In the first two books of *Ugo d'Alvernia*, Andrea presents his source as a French epic that he translates into Italian. On several occasions, he even includes some of the original text to convince readers of his fidelity to the source: "E Ugo avea fatto molti remi per remare. E tanto remarono, ch'egli approdarono di là: e attaca i *brais* (in francioso) alla riva" [And Ugo had made many oars for rowing. And they rowed so much, that they landed on the other side: and he clung with his *brais* (in French) to the shore] (1:203).

Andrea uses this same method of narration/compilation in the fourth book of his epic in which he describes Ugo's trip to Hell. Heavily influenced by Dante's *Inferno*, the structure of this book differs from that of the rest of the epic. Andrea begins the book by quoting the first lines of a poem written in terza rima by Giovanni Vincenzio Isterliano, after which he retells in prose the events narrated in the poem. The transitions between Isterliano's passages and Andrea's prose translations not only allow us to juxtapose the two narrative forms but demonstrate shifts in voice that can only be described as acrobatic.

Dante's creation of the terza rima and the immediate success of his *Commedia* among Italian readers provided that rhyme scheme with a great deal of prestige. Andrea certainly viewed Isterliano's poem in terza rima as a text that would lend standing to his writing, and he therefore adopts its authority by merging his own voice with that of Isterliano and the poem's character Ugo. The first example of this appropriation of authority comes with the initial transition from a passage of Isterliano's poem to Andrea's prose version at the beginning of the fourth book. The solid line in the quotation below marks the transition:

Per far l'altrui e la mia voglia sazia:
Secondo Ugo dirò lo scuro entrare
Della città, che li dannati strazia.

Il conte Ugone fa in questa parte menzione, ove san Guglielmo d'Oringa avendolo, per comandamento di Dio, confortato all'albero secco, e dettogli come egli lo menerebbe per tutto lo 'nferno sicuro, si mossono dall'albero, lo spirito di san Guglielmo e Ugo dirieto a lui. (2:84)

[In order to satisfy my own and others' desire: I will retell Ugo's description of the city's dark entrance where the damned agonize. The Count Ugone makes mention in this part where San Gugliemo d'Oringa, having comforted him at the withered tree by God's command, told him that he would lead him through all of Hell safely, they moved from the tree, the spirit of San Guglielmo and Ugo behind him.]

Just as Isterliano's poem claims that the author is narrating the story *secondo Ugo* or according to Ugo, Andrea later refers to Isterliano's Ugo as the narrator of his version as well. Rather than presenting himself as an interpreter of events, Andrea represents the character as simply relating his own experiences to Isterliano as transcriber. To reinforce this idea of an authoritative, eyewitness account, Andrea shifts back and forth from first to third person singular narrative—from Ugo telling his own story to Andrea's describing Isterliano's transcription of that same tale. The first example of this transition in narrative voice occurs in the initial chapter:

> E san Guglielmo segnò la barchetta, e segnò il Conte Ugo, poi entrò nella barchetta, e disse a Ugone: vieni drieto a me. Io mi maravigliai, dice Ugone, che Guglielmo non fè muovere la barchetta, tanto fu leggieri all'entrarvi; ed entrati drento, la barchetta andò tanto giuso, che l'acqua guigneva insino alla sponda a quattro dita; e *io* mi appiccai da ogni banda colle mani, tremando di paura; e Guglielmo *mi* confortò. (2:85–86; emphasis added)

> [And San Guglielmo blessed the boat and blessed Count Ugo, and then he boarded the boat and said to Ugone: come behind me. I marvelled, says Ugone, that Guglielmo did not rock the boat, he was so light in boarding it; having both gotten on board, the boat went so far down, that water came up almost to the edge; *I* grabbed on to each side with my hand, trembling with fear; and Guglielmo comforted *me*.]

Andrea first quotes Ugo ("Io mi maraviglai, dice Ugone") but then shifts the narrative voice to the first person singular, using "io" instead of the character's name for the rest of the chapter. In the same passage, Andrea also uses the first person plural in referring to Ugo and his guide San Guglielmo: "E così sempre andavamo in su" [And thus we were still going up] (2:86).

The Isterliano poem serves as a model for this type of first person narration. Starting with his transcription of its second passage, Andrea narrates all the citations from the poem as if Ugo is speaking:

> Levar *mi* viddi in un porto di mare:
> Da una barca, più ratta che saetta,
> Guglielmo, Enea, e *me* vedea portare. (2:87; emphasis added)

> [I saw myself stand up in a seaport. Faster than an arrow, I saw Guglielmo, Enea, and myself carried by a boat.]

Unlike Dante, who claims to describe his own experiences, Andrea pretends to be transcribing the firsthand experiences of the historical hero, Ugo. Even though Andrea adds a great deal to his prose translations, he continually claims to be simply retelling the story that Ugo had dictated directly to Isterliano. At the end of the first few prose sections, he adds transitions such as "or seguiremo in rima" [now we will follow in verse], indicating that he is faithfully describing the story according to Ugo. This direct access to Ugo's trip to the underworld elevates Andrea's version over the earlier anonymous verse texts whose narrators never claim such firsthand knowledge of Ugo's adventures.

Andrea also uses the oscillation of narrative voice to interject a humanistic quality into the traditional Carolingian epic by referring to classical heroes and authors. In Andrea's version, Ugo becomes the first Carolingian hero with knowledge of fourteenth-century compilations of classical material. At one point in his epic, Andrea quotes Isterliano's list in five tercets of the false gods grouped together in Hell:

> Questi furon gli Dei falsi e bugiardi,
>   Che 'ngannaron le genti: v'è il Re Nino,
>   Che fe' l'idolo al padre; or convien ch'ardi.
> V'è Nabuch, e Leoferne, e Bellaino;
>   V'è Giove, v'è Nettuno; vedi Vestra,
>   Et Mercurio, e Dïana, et Appollino,
> Saturno, e Marte dalla parte destra;
>   Venus, e Vulcano, e vedi qua Junone;
>   Eolo vedi, Vacco e Minerva maestra.
> Vedi Antioco, che mosse quistione
>   Ai Macabei, e facevasi Iddio;
>   Vidi molti altri, e passamo il vallone;
> Giugnémo al lago dispettoso e rio. (2:123)

[These were the false and deceitful Gods who tricked people. . . ; I saw many others, and we crossed the valley; we reached the spiteful and evil lake.]

Andrea in his "translation" then expands on Isterliano's succinct description by having Ugo recite a long treatise on the genealogy of "pagan" gods. Even a short passage from this monologue will illustrate the far greater amount of information contained in this prose pantheon:

> Giove fu figliuolo di Saturno, il quale cacciò il padre Saturno di Creti, e tolseli il Reame, e fue chiamato da' Pagani Iddio del cielo; e

fu il primo che levò il gonfalone dell'aquila nera, e il primo che
trovò il balestro. (2:125)

[Jupiter was the son of Saturn, who drove his father from Crete, and
took away his kingdom, and was called God of the heavens by the
Pagans; and he was the first to raise the banner of the black eagle,
and the first to discover the crossbow.]

Before plunging into his lengthy history of the gods, Andrea explains that
this digression has a moral purpose:

In questa parte *conta il Conte Ugone da Vernia della stolta pazzia
de' Pagani,* che adorarono gli mortali per Iddii: e sotto brevità conta
chi eglino furono, tra' quali fa menzione di certi, per mostrare come
gli truova in inferno, e chi e' furono. (2:124; emphasis added)

[In this part *Count Ugone da Vernia tells about the foolish craziness
of the Pagans,* who worshiped mortals as Gods: briefly telling who
they were, he mentions certain ones in order to explain how he finds
them in Hell, and who they were.]

As this introduction to the list of classical gods shows, even Andrea's "adventures" in classical mythology are attributed to the legendary Ugo. This is only one of many instances in which Andrea instills his knowledge of ancient culture (probably gained through compilations rather than integral classical texts) into his character Ugo.

Kittay and Godzich have shown that catalogs in early Old French verse and prose texts function in very different ways. Verse lists depend on the mnemonic devices of alliteration or rhyme; they usually include only well-known paradigms. List-making in the signifying system of prose, on the other hand, tends to be "inclusive" rather than "exclusive." These "inclusive" prose lists often enlarge the paradigm they draw upon and serve not as an instrument to reinforce common knowledge but rather as a device for authors to go beyond the collective model and display their individual erudition (Kittay and Godzich 51–52). In a similar fashion, Andrea uses the list of "pagan" Gods to inclusively attribute his own knowledge of classical mythology to his narrator/character, Ugo, and thus authorize this learning by placing it within the confines of the Carolingian epic.

Andrea's affinity for such inventories also attests to a respect for a new type of power that arose gradually during the early modern period. The development of what Bruno Latour calls "immutable mobiles" such as currencies, inscriptions, and maps is what allows bureaucracies to dominate with written records and figures rather than with swords. Latour defines immutable mobiles as "objects which have the properties of being *mobile* but also *immutable, presentable, readable,* and *combinable* with one another" (7). The collection of such objects "through space and time is essential for domination on a grand scale" (23). In a society of immutable mobiles a person gains power by collecting and ordering inscriptions and figures. One establishes the validity of a claim or of a point of view by amassing more evidence than others. The legitimacy gained through such documents, however, can be quickly lost; one must continually gather and classify new information in order to prove one's domination over others: "A man is never much more powerful than any other—even from a throne; but a man whose eye dominates records through which some sort of connections are established with millions of others may be said to *dominate*. This domination, however, is not a given but a slow construction and it can be corroded" (29).

In Andrea's age the need to continually collect and reorder information not only helped individuals create and maintain power, but families as well. In both fourteenth- and fifteenth-century Florence, important families kept careful *ricordi* or records of their families' genealogy, patrimony, finances, and morals. These texts helped family patriarchs to protect themselves from the growing power of the city-state and also to support their claim that they deserved to run for positions within the governing oligarchy (Branca, *Mercanti scrittori* xix). Like the leaders of Florence's new administrative and mercantile class, Andrea learned to dominate through the collection and combination of written and oral traces. Just as families created a certain political status by maintaining ricordi, Andrea gains authority as a writer when he asserts superiority over the earlier epic tradition by making continual references to the immobile mobiles he had collected.

The division of the Ugo narrative into chapters with rubrics is yet another sign that Andrea reorganized the Carolingian material for a more literate audience.[14] The manuscripts containing Andrea's epic do not begin with the first line of the narrative, as had many of the verse models, but instead start with a title in an attempt to reify the text as a packaged, fixed object:

AL NOME DI DIO. Questa istoria si chiama *Ugo da Venia,* il quale fu conte di Vernia, et grande amico di Dio; et fue al tempo di Carlo Martello Imperadore di Roma, et Re di Francia; et fu quello Ugone che andò allo Inferno. (1:1)

[IN THE NAME OF GOD. This story is called *Ugo da Venia,* who was the count of Vernia, and a great friend of God; and lived at the time of Carlo Martello Emperor of Rome, and King of France; and was the Ugone who went to Hell.]

The beginning of Andrea's text is also very precise, providing an exact date and place for the narrative:

> Regnando Carlo Martello, Imperadore di Roma, et Re di Francia, negli anni Domini viij. c. lv., avendo avute del Reame di Francia molte guerre, et essendo il Duca Sanguino di Mongrana tornato nella sua signoria, Carlo ebbe di lui gran temenza; et fece parentado con lui, et diegli per moglie una sua figliuola, ch'avea nome Dama Sofia. (1:1)

> [Carlo Martello reigned as Emperor of Rome and King of France in the year of our Lord VIII.C.LV, having had many wars over the Kingdom of France, and the Duke Sanguino di Mongrana having returned to his dominion, Carlo was very scared of him; and he made a marriage alliance with him, and gave him for a wife his daughter, who had the name Lady Sofia.]

This attempt at exactness sets the tone of the entire epic. Although the date is incorrect, its presence seems more important than its accuracy.[15] Andrea begins his epic as if it were a chronicle, a seemingly objective depiction of the life of Ugo d'Alvernia. He anchors his story in a precise time and place, in an extratextual "reality" that he can identify.

The vernacular chronicle was a relatively new but already important genre in fourteenth-century Florence. The two most famous examples are the texts of Dino Compagni and Giovanni Villani, who wrote in the first half of the century. Although both works are divided into chapters like Andrea's texts, Compagni's chronicle focuses on contemporary political problems in Florence, while Villani, closer to Andrea, is more concerned with the mythologies of the city-state. Just as Andrea's *I Reali di Francia* traces the genealogy of the French kings back in time to their supposedly "Italian" origins in Rome, Villani's chronicle asserts that Florence is the legitimate heir to ancient Rome and freely interweaves stories about French kings and Roman heroes. The gradual merging of the chivalric epic and the chronicle was not unique to Florence, but rather a characteristic of the late epic throughout Europe as self-conscious authors attempted either to fit local legends into the providential history provided by the Carolingian tales or create geographical ties between the divine heroes of the chansons de geste and their own cities. The tales about Bernardo del Carpio in Spain are a good example of this tendency: works like *Estoria de Bernaldo* and *Primera Crónica General* present their own histories as more accurate accounts of the earlier Old French "fables" disseminated by unreliable jongleurs (Horrent 144–48). This contradictory attitude towards the chanson de geste not only reveals tensions between local and state cultures but also between oral and written ones.

Chronicles and late epics shared stylistic as well as narrative characteristics. For example, the beginning of Villani's chronicle reveals a desire for precision and neutrality similar to that found in Andrea's epic:

> Questo libro si chiama la nuova cronica, nel quale si tratta di più cose passate, e spezialmente dell'origine e cominciamento della città di Firenze, poi di tutte le mutazioni ch'ha avute e avrà per gli tempi: cominciato a compilare negli anni della incarnazione di Gesù Cristo 1300. Comincia il prolago, e il primo libro. (Villani 15)
>
> [This book is called the new chronicle, which deals with things from the past, especially with the founding and beginnings of the city of Florence, and then with the changes that occurred and will occur with time: I began to compile the chronicle in the year of our Lord 1300. Here begins the prologue, and the first book.]

Like Andrea's version of the Ugo story, the chronicle presents descriptions of historical events as reified objects, which the author did not produce but simply collected. The titles that frame the books in Andrea's text follow a similar pattern: "Finito il primo libro d'Ugone d'Avernia. Comincia il secondo" [The first book of Ugone d'Avernia having ended, the second begins] (1:63). Andrea uses such rubrics to illustrate how he has compiled the chapters of Ugo's story, suggesting that the tales, which seemingly tell themselves, belong to Ugo d'Alvernia, the historical figure, not Andrea da Barberino, the author.

In his prologue, Villani explains his method and reveals two important tendencies of fourteenth-century historical prose found also in Andrea's epics. First, Villani describes himself not as a creator but as an instrument for compiling stories that are accepted as "true." Second, the veracity of these "deeds" is proven by referring to written authorities:

> Io fedelmente narrerò per questo libro in piano volgare . . . e non sanza grande fatica mi travaglierò di ritrarre e di ritrovare di più antichi e diversi libri, e croniche e autori, le geste e' fatti de' Fiorentini compilando in questo. (Villani 17).
>
> [I will faithfully narrate in this book in clear vernacular . . . and not without great labor I will work to reproduce and rediscover from the most ancient and diverse books, and chronicles and authors, the deeds and actions of the Florentines, compiling them in this book.]

In Florence's increasingly literate society, writers of epics and chronicles in vernacular prose appropriated the time-honoured technique of citing earlier written texts for establishing their own literary authority. This technique derived from the commentary tradition that had also recently been used to analyze another epic written in the vernacular, Dante's *Commedia*.[16] Earlier anonymous versions of the *Ugo* narrative had not included such citations since the narrative's authority had derived from its role as part of the community's, not the writer's, patrimony.

Andrea's imitation of Latin prose models also manifests itself in his complex Ciceronian periods, full of gerunds and participles, which form a stark contrast to the fairly simple syntactical constructions of the anonymous verse epics.[17] The following quotations illustrate the stylistic disparities between the P manuscript and Andrea's text:

Carllo Martelo fo a Paris torné.
Ugo e Sanguyn romasse in Viena la çité.

(Manuscript P, fol. 31v.)

[Carllo Martelo returned to Paris. Ugo and Sanguyn remained in the city of Vienne.]

Avendo Carlo Martello fatto morire la sua figliuola, e tornato a Parigi, rimase il Duca Sanguino e Ugo a Vienna. (1:62)

[Having killed his daughter, Carlo Martello returned to Paris, and Duke Sanguino and Ugo remained in Vienne.]

As early humanists uncovered and imitated more and more of Cicero's texts, the ideology of the *Respublica Romana* became associated with prose as a signifying system. The new authority that vernacular prose gained during the fourteenth century made it a popular stylistic choice for other genres. Just as the Carolingian epics were translated into prose during the Trecento, *rifacimenti* or reworkings of Virgil's *Aeneid* appeared as well, especially in Tuscany. Both the reworkings of the classical and Carolingian epics followed two basic principles of the late medieval commentary tradition in Latin: *ordinatio* and *compilatio*.[18] The "reworkers" of the epic traditions, like their Latin predecessors, sought to use the objectivity of prose to organize clearly and rationally what they perceived as fragmentary and contradictory material. The epic writers, in particular, were dissatisfied with reading or hearing different versions of the same narratives; instead they felt a need to organize "historical" events chronologically and concisely in order to write and preserve a definitive account.[19]

One of the reworkings of Virgil's epic has a structure very similar to the fourth book of Andrea's *Ugo d'Alvernia*. Guido da Pisa produced a prose version of the adventures of Aeneas that quotes thirteen passages from the *Commedia* in order to validate his retelling of Virgil's story. Guido often inserts lengthy passages offering moral commentary on the actions of the narrative. He draws on various written sources, but his favorite *auctor* is Dante:

> Ma il traditore Polinestore, sì tosto come ebbe novelle che Troia era presa, e Priamo era morto, affamato dell'oro . . . uccisse Polidoro. E di ciò fa menzione Dante, nel vigesimo canto della sua Commedia, ove, biasimando l'avarizia, pone sette storie di sette antichi avari. (Da Pisa 3)
>
> [But the traitor Polymestor, as soon as he had news that Troy had been taken, and that Priam had been killed, hungry for the gold . . . killed Polydorus. And Dante makes mention of this in the twentieth canto of his Comedy, where, condemning avarice, he puts forward seven stories of seven ancient avaricious men.]

Guido then proceeds to quote five tercets from Dante's *Purgatorio* to further support his interpretation. While Dante is Guido's favorite moral authority, he often cites classical poets, even Virgil himself, comparing them to determine what is *favola* or fiction and what is historical truth. Guido explicitly states that he accepts Virgil's description of Circe but he takes the Roman poet to task for his description of Polydorus's death: "In questa storia si contiene alcuna favola: che le mortelle gittassero sangue, e del sangue uscisse voce, questo è favola" [The story contains some fictions: that myrtle bushes were spouting blood, and that a voice came out of the blood. This is fictitious] (4).

Following the model of commentaries, Andrea and Guido used prose to systematize and analyze epic poems. Guido presented his translation of Virgil's *Aeneid* as a text of historical truths purged of favole. Anything which he considered irrational or immoral was either given an allegorical interpretation or quickly dismissed as false. Andrea appropriated a similar strategy when he explained that Ugo describes the pagan gods only to instruct us about the ignorance and foolishness of those who worshiped them.

Although Andrea da Barberino relies on narrative techniques employed by the increasingly literate culture in which he wrote, aspects of primary orality still survive in his prose (Bäuml, "Medieval Texts" 43). For instance, the narrator of manuscript P often addresses the audience directly:

"De Ugo d'Alvernia ve voio lasere / E del dux Sanguyn ve voio contere" [I want you to leave Ugo d'Alvernia / And I want to tell you about Duke Sanguyn] (manuscript P, fol. 15r). Andrea leaves out most of these direct address transitions, but some still remain in his version, such as when he writes: "Ma lasciamo un poco costoro, e torniamo al Conte Ugone" [But let us leave them for a short time and return to Count Ugone] (1:108).

While both manuscript P and Andrea's *Ugo d'Alvernia* are pseudo-oral-formulaic texts, Andrea more openly acknowledges his debt to written sources. According to Bäuml's terms, then, manuscript P falls into the category of "first-order pseudo-oral-formulaic" texts, while Andrea's narrative could be labelled a "second-order pseudo-oral-formulaic" text ("Medieval Texts" 44). Although Andrea makes it clear to the audience that he employs written sources, the pseudo-oral-formulaic nature of the epic allows him to retain the authority of the singer whether the text is read aloud or silently.

Andrea's continual references to earlier written versions of the narrative, the use of the protagonist's voice, the practice of inclusive list-making, the division of the narrative into chapters with titles in imitation of both the commentaries and the chronicles, and the Latinized syntax are all narrative practices that reveal subtle but meaningful differences between the Franco-Italian tradition and Andrea's translation of the *Ugo d'Alvernia* tale. Andrea asserts his literary authority by showing off a knowledge of Latin textual traditions and his ability to organize "the facts." Like other vernacular writers of his time, however, Andrea plays with the roles of compilator, commentator, and auctor as defined by the commentary tradition; he asserts his own voice in the text at the same time that he uses the roles of compilator and commentator as rhetorical shields of defense (Minnis 160–210). In a similar fashion, Andrea uses certain oral narrative techniques to mask his voice and anchor his text in the authoritative tradition of the chanson de geste.

The tensions created by the juxtaposition of oral and literary techniques also replicate themselves in the *Ugo* narrative, which displays several ideological tendencies common to other late prose epics produced both in French and in Italian. Most noticeably, the king is no longer a terrestrial leader chosen by divine mandate but rather a perverse, hypocritical tyrant inspired by Lucifer.[20] On the other hand, the heroes of these tales remain landowning aristocrats and, like Ugo, are usually members of the Chiaramonte family. Heroes perform superhuman actions to earn their status, but at the same time such extraordinary abilities are passed down through noble families. These stories, therefore, project the fears of Italian communes to remain independent from the French kings and German emperors, yet also represent the desire of the new communal aristocracy to enjoy the privileges of nobility. City-states such as Padua and Florence in which the Carolingian material, including the *Ugo* narrative, circulated, represented themselves as communes whose republican ideals separated them from the true tyrants, such as the Visconti family.

Both Padua and Florence also identified themselves with the Guelf cause and ostensibly pledged their allegiance to the pope in return for his support against tyrants — from both inside and outside Italy — who sought to oppress them. Although, by the fifteenth century, the Guelf party had lost its original purpose of advancing the papal-Angevin cause by defeating the Ghibellines, the institution continued, in the words of historian Alison Brown, as "the guardian of chivalry and conservative ceremonial in Florence" (46). The extreme piety and patriotism of the Ugo character represents a civic attitude that leaders of the Guelf cause tried to develop in Florence.

The urban aristocracy's need for a mythology to legitimize its power helps to explain why the authority of the singer and the discourse of chivalry continued to play such an important role in Florentine society throughout the fourteenth and fifteenth centuries. Andrea's prose epics served as a bridge connecting social groups who could not read to those who read only in vernacular and to the elite who also read texts in Latin. At the same time, the epics revealed the distance that still remained among these groups.

6

Chivalry and Classicism

As much as Andrea da Barberino's epics distance themselves from orality, they also display, like many European texts of the fourteenth and fifteenth centuries, a "resistance to writing." Jesse Gellrich has traced the roots of this late medieval resistance to classical and patristic texts in which writing is conceived as an extension or an imitation of oral utterances. Going back to the *Verbum* would mean a return to authentic language without differentiation. Gellrich's analysis of fourteenth-century English chronicles connects this linguistic nostalgia with a similar desire for political certainty: "this resistance to writing in the chronicle history of England . . . constitutes in its own right historical evidence of a society rooted in a nostalgia for the faded political ideal of feudalism and holding on to its anachronistic myth of the power of ruler in his presence and word" (470–71).

The *Ugo d'Alvernia* narrative expresses the same nostalgia for a landed aristocracy through its long-suffering and noble title character. At the same time, the story ends with the hero's death and frequently deplores the violence of vendettas among aristocratic families and the lack of a seemingly objective, legal bureaucracy to negotiate the conflicts of the knightly class. Like the writers of the English chronicles, Andrea weaves together oral and literary techniques exploiting both the presence of the Word associated with the aristocracy and the power of systematic documentation associated with the communal bureaucracy.

The Carolingian material, including the *Ugo* narrative, acquired popularity in two regions and in two historical periods that shared certain ideologies: the communes of the Trevisan March, particularly Padua, in the early fourteenth century and Tuscany at the turn of the same century.¹ Both communes identified themselves with the Guelf cause and ostensibly pledged their allegiance to the pope in return for his support against tyrants—from both inside and outside Italy—who sought to oppress them. The confused political situation in central and northern Italy, however, produced continual changes among the many varied alliances throughout the Trecento, and the commune of Florence even fought the papacy in the war of the Eight Saints from 1375 to 1378. Despite this political maneuvering, the myth of Guelfism died slowly, especially in Florence where it was used as a unifying battle cry against Ghibelline powers such as Siena and helped certain old, aristocratic families support their claim of being the only true patriotic (and chivalric) Florentines (Brucker 41).

Both Padua and Florence gradually restricted entrance into the ruling oligarchy in an attempt to remain independent by unifying and strengthening the city-state. In Padua, the da Carrara family became signori or lords in 1328, while in Florence by the beginning of the fifteenth century, "a stable, cohesive elite" controlled the commune (Brucker 302). Even though the Florentine commune promoted republican values, its members understood that ties to traditional sources of power such as the Church and emperors were very important to defining and maintaining their power.

The ideological glue of the Florentine commune came from a strong sense of patriotism that included an important religious element (Pini 558). Florentines, like citizens of many other communes, prided themselves on their Duomo and other religious monuments. In particular, the guilds, the confraternities, and the Guelf party used the feast day in celebration of Florence's patron saint, John the Baptist, as a vehicle to express their patriotism (Brucker 15–16). Loyalty to the commune was represented as a religious virtue, just as the "tyrants" of other city-states were described as evil incarnate.

The very structure of the *Ugo d'Alvernia* epic attests to the tensions between chivalric and republican ideals in Guelf communes. Even though Andrea da Barberino and the earlier anonymous poets appropriated the chanson de geste because of the prestige associated with the *Reali di Francia*, they added narrative elements that question the authority of both the French monarchy and the genre, which had once celebrated the royalty's divine calling. As mentioned in chapter five, the narrative has three distinct parts that the singers could have easily separated. The first part of *Ugo d'Alvernia* deals with the unsuccessful seduction of Ugo by Sofia, and clearly came from an earlier chanson de geste (Giacon 55); Andreas

Capellanus refers to the scene of Ugo refusing to love Sofia in his work *De Amore,* written over a century before the Franco-Italian versions of the chanson de geste.[2] This opening section of the Italian *Ugo* story is the only one in which the emperor is depicted favorably. Because of the obvious influence of the *Inferno* on the last two parts of the epic poem, it seems likely that Italian writers added them to the French chanson de geste after 1313. In these latter segments the emperor changes drastically from his favorable characterization at the beginning of the story. The harsh but seemingly principled leader transforms into a cruel and hypocritical tyrant who commits the same sexual crime for which he had condemned his daughter.

Despite the depraved nature of Carlo Martello and his family, the closed, hierarchal social structure associated with the Old French epic never comes under attack but rather is in many respects reinforced. The conflict caused by Carlo Martello and his daughter arises because of their negative character not as a result of any institutional or structural problems. Borrowing heavily from the stories of saints' lives, the singers describe the hero, Ugo, as a virtuous vassal because of his unquestioning loyalty to his signore, Carlo Martello (Meregazzi, "L'Ugo d'Alvernia" 26–29). Ugo's pious behavior reinforces traditional social hierarchy at the same time that it critiques the evil nature of the French monarch and his family.

Hagiographical legends, such as *La Navigazione di San Brandano,* probably influenced the *Ugo d'Alvernia* narrative by establishing a model of the heroic pilgrim who undertakes a spiritual voyage prohibited to most men. Different manuscripts containing the story of Saint Brendan in Latin spread throughout Europe in the Middle Ages, and we know of at least two complete versions produced in Italian. Like the epics, the legend of Saint Brendan was first translated into Franco-Italian and then into Tuscan prose. *La Navigazione di San Brandano* shares several narrative elements with the adventures of *Ugo d'Alvernia.* Both stories recount long trips to visit the otherworld during which the principle characters are attacked by wild beasts and pray constantly to God for protection and guidance.

The saintly qualities of the epic hero include dedication to his patria. While Saint Brendan remains faithful to the Signore in his quest for Terrestrial Paradise, Ugo searches for the otherworld in order to fulfill a promise to his secular signore, the king of France. Ugo's determination to remain a loyal vassal and his patriotism are validated by his saintly status and Christlike suffering in all the versions of the narrative. In his *Ugo d'Alvernia,* for example, Andrea describes the epic hero on his quest for Hell as if he were Christ:

> Et passò per la Puglia, et venne in Calavria, sempre dicendo salmi et orazioni, facendo gran penitenzia . . . ; et molti trovava, che 'l tenevano pazzo; alcuni di lui aveano compassione, alcuni ancora se ne tenevano sollazo, molti il dileggiavano, et chiamavanlo briccone; alcuni ricoglievano del fango della via, et gittavanglielo adosso; ed egli in pace umilmente sopportava, et sempre a Dio si raccomandava. (1:137–38)

> [And he passed through Puglia and came to Calabria continuously reciting prayers and orations, subjecting himself to great penance . . . ; and he came across many who thought he was crazy; some had compassion for him, some were amused by him; many mocked him, and called him a rogue; some gathered dirt from the road and threw it at him; and he tolerated it humbly at peace and always offered himself to God.]

The discourse of chivalry, which at times supported yet also contradicted religious and republican values, played a large role in the development of Florentine and, in particular, Guelf mythology. In the Florentine oligarchy, the reputation of a family determined its power within the city-state, and such status was gained not merely with wealth but also with titles and honors associated with holding public offices. In order to hold certain important positions in the communal hierarchy, one had to claim the title of *cavaliere* (Cardini 28). Even the *ciompi,* the wool workers who led a rebellion against the ruling oligarchy in 1378 and held onto power for six weeks, imitated their supposed enemies by creating knights (28). The distinction of *cavaliere* or *miles* was one of the few ways that new members of the urban aristocracy could cement their authority and gain the prestige of the *nobili* (Cristiani 367). Florentine workers as well as the urban aristocracy adopted the hierarchal values of chivalry much as the latter group espoused republicanism and religious piety to justify social and political authority.

Although the leaders of Florence's guilds enjoyed a certain status in the city-state, their power did not compare to that of the men who held the title of judge or knight. Most guild representatives were excluded from the inner circle of Florentine politics, but at least one member of that group still expressed a good deal of awe and respect for the communal elite, especially the knights. Bartolommeo del Corazza, a wine merchant who was a contemporary of Andrea's, wrote a diary in which he focused on the feasts, dances, jousts, dubbings, and pageants of Florence's elite. He often linked the Guelf party with the knights and the judges who led such events. For example, del Corazza describes a funeral for the Cardinal of Florence on December 30, 1415, at which the captains of the aristocratic Guelf Party appear at Santa Maria del Fiore surrounded by judges and knights; Bartolommeo clearly separated the representatives of the corporate structures, or guilds, from the men distinguished by titles:

> Vennonvi i Capitani della Parte guelfa e donarongli un pallio di drappo nero con drapelloni dell'arme sua e della Parte, con grande cittadinanza, guidici e cavalieri, e donorongli 80 doppieri. Vennevi i Sei della Mercatanzia con tutte le Capitudini, e donògli ogni Arte delle maggiori quattro doppieri, e delle minute ogni Arte due: furono 56. (Corazzini 266)

> [The Captains of the Guelf Party came there and gave him a funeral pall of fine black cloth with embroidered pieces of his and the Party's coats of arms, with great citizens, judges and knights, and they gave him 80 candles. There came the Six of the Merchant's Guild with all the Heads, and each of the great Guilds gave him four candles and the minor Guilds each two: there were 56.]

Bartolommeo also mentions that three ambassadors were dubbed knights that year by the king of Naples, and upon their return to Florence they were presented with gifts from both the commune and the Guelf party. The guildsman then describes the procession which followed:

> Quando entrorono drento, gli andarono incontro una grande e orrevole cittadinanza, e una brigata di giovani.... Fu giuliva cosa a vedere; e drieto a loro e cavalieri e giudici e grande cittadinanza. Auti i sopradetti doni e dal Comune e dalla Parte, andorono per Firenze. (Corazzini 255)

> [When they entered inside the city, great and honorable townspeople and a brigade of young men went to meet them.... It was joyous to see; and behind them knights and judges, and great townspeople. Having received the gifts mentioned above from both the Commune and from the Party, they went through Florence.]

Just as the funeral ceremony that del Corazza describes includes both Florence's titled elite and the representatives of the comune's "republican" guilds, a legend which circulated in fourteenth-century Florence combined a Carolingian tale with the mythology of Republican Rome. This legend claimed that Florence had been founded by ancient Romans and then revived by Charlemagne (Weinstein 22). Giovanni Villani even claims that Charlemagne gave Florence its independence, and the citizens then immediately adopted the republican political structure of ancient Rome, electing two consuls and one hundred senators (129). Along with this tale of rebirth spread a prophecy, stating that another Charles, a French king and Roman emperor, would come and unite the world under his leadership with Florence's help (Weinstein 31). These myths resolved the apparent opposition between republican and neofeudal ideologies, and aggrandized the Guelf party's original allies: the papacy in Rome and the Angevin dynasty. Some in the second half of the fourteenth century also criticized the Guelf party, however, for its role in the conflict between guild corporatism and elitism. One chronicler, Marchionne Stefani, condemned the *arciguelfi* saying that no one was safe from their ruthlessness "even if he were more Guelf than Charlemagne" (Brucker 41). Stefani defines "guelf" in terms of the ideal representative of the chivalric discourse, and at the same time explains how that party abused its authority to persecute men without justifiable cause.

The importance of the vendetta in Florentine society created yet another close link between the mythology of chivalry, fourteenth-century Florentine politics, and the Carolingian epics. Franco Cardini identifies three important signs of communal nobility: fortified homes inside the city, the distinction of *cavaliere,* and the practice of the vendetta (20). In the 1280s the Florentine government enacted statutes to end factional violence by restricting and penalizing the nobles or magnates whose vendettas encouraged bloodshed. Knighthood was the principal way in which the commune defined such magnate status. Like the *Ugo* narrative, then, these statutes express an ambivalence about knighthood. The title of knight clearly connotes nobility, but the title is no longer used to praise men who bravely defend their community—the traditional justification for nobles' privileges—but instead to condemn men who destroy it (C. Lansing 145–63).

Throughout the different stories of Ugo's adventures, the protagonist crusades against the notion of vendetta, which eventually leads to the horrific conflict between the Germans and the French. Many of the souls whom Ugo meets in Hell are taken from classical and medieval epics and condemned for their violence and pride; these warriors and knights did not accept their position in the social order and thus betrayed their patria. Gherardo da Fratta, a character from another chanson de geste rewritten by Andrea, *L'Aspramonte,* presents a negative example of a knight who valued his personal vendetta against Charlemagne more than his loyalty to the Christian cause:

> Quello è Gherardo da Fratta, il quale, per disfare Carlo magno, rinnegò Iddio; e fu tanto disperato, ch'egli portava dipinta Nostra Donna col capo di sotto; e per quello è dannato in questo luogo. (2:134-35)

> [That is Gherardo da Fratta, who in order to undo Charlemagne, renounced God; and was so desperate, that he carried a painting of Our Lady upside down; and for that he is condemned in this place.]

Despite such condemnation of vendetta, even Ugo himself eventually seeks vengeance on the king of France. Ugo allows Carlo Martello to accept the Dark Prince's tribute even though he knows that it will result in the king's eternal damnation. Yet, Andrea distinguishes this vendetta from others perpetrated by earlier heroes because it is an act of God; Ugo simply serves as the vehicle of divine retribution for the king's sins.

The institution of the vendetta, just like the French monarchy, elicits both anxiety and respect from Andrea. The French control over the papacy and the Great Schism left Florence in an unstable political position. The Guelf commune feared that the Church wanted to extend its power into Tuscany. The representation in Andrea's *Ugo d'Alvernia* of a weak papacy that depends on the French to save it from both the evil Saracens and the Germans resembled Florence's similar fears in the last half of the Trecento. Like Ugo's divine vendetta, God punishes the French for their initial refusal to protect St. Peter's city by giving the right to choose the emperor to the Germans. Once again, Ugo is the vehicle for God's actions. In a scene that imitates the passion of Christ, Ugo is forewarned by a miraculous voice that he must die for the sins of his fellow Frenchmen:

> Et venne una boce, e disse che andasse a' suoi, e facesse che tanti Franciosi con tanti Alamanni combattessono; e che a Dio piaceva, che, per li peccati loro, e Franciosi perdessono la corona dello 'mperio, ma non altro onore; e che lui vi doveva morire in questa battaglia. Ugo ne ringraziò Iddio, e tornò in sulla sala. (2:258-59)

> [And a voice came, and said that he should go to his soldiers, and arrange that many Frenchmen battle with many Germans, and that it was pleasing to God, that, for their sins, the French would lose the imperial crown, but not other honors; and that he must die in this battle. Ugo thanked God, and returned to the room.]

In the end, the French are destroyed by their own misdeeds. It is Ugo, leader of a strong city like Florence, who sacrifices his life for his Church and State. He is the only character to receive divine messages; Carlo Martello, unlike Charlemagne in the *Chanson de Roland,* lied when he told Ugo that a divine voice told him to send his vassal to Hell.

Andrea emphasizes that Ugo, not Carlo Martello, received the support of God and of the citizens. When Ugo leaves on his quest for Hell, both the *baroni* and the popolo lament (1:105). After he departs, Carlo Martello sends the giullare or minstrel, Sandino, to try to convince Honida, Ugo's wife, to marry him. Baldovino, Honida's brother, mutilates Sandino and sends him back to Carlo Martello. The text states that the citizens would have killed the minstrel if Baldovino had not insisted that he be sent back to the king of France so that Carlo Martello could see the results of the vendetta (1:117).

The other barons also back Ugo when they elect a new French king after the disappearance of Carlo Martello. At the election, the Pope establishes two criteria: the Monarch should come from an established family and he should be virtuous. These were two qualities that at least some members of the Florentine oligarchy also supported for officeholders in their commune (Brucker 272):

> Il Papa fe qui un lungo sermone, e mostrò a tutti i lignaggi, e uomini valenti, et conchiuse che Guglielmo Zappetta, uomo piccolo di statura, (ma) d'assai, ed era quello a cui si dovea dare la figliuola di Carlo per donna. (2:217)

> [The Pope gave a long sermon here, he showed everyone the important families and virtuous men, and concluded that Guglielmo Zappetta, a man of small stature, but great character, that he was the one to whom Carlo's daughter should be given as wife.]

Ugo refuses the position and eventually the nobles follow the Pope's advice and elect Guglielmo Zappetta (an Italianized version of Capet) who proves to be a completely ineffectual leader. Although Andrea does not mention it, a tale based on a chanson de geste about the life of the first Capetian king was well known in Italy in the Trecento. According to the legend, Hugh Capet was the son of a wealthy butcher who married into an aristocratic family. Dante refers to the epic when he disparagingly describes the "Ciappetta" kings in the twentieth canto of *Purgatorio* as social climbers. Such previous characterizations of the Capetian dynasty could have contributed to Guglielmo Zappetta's portrait as a weak leader who was neither of noble birth nor powerful enough to convince the French barons to fight for Rome's freedom.

Dante reveals a clear anxiety in the *Commedia* about the development of a more flexible social structure that would allow a butcher's son to become king. The representation of Hell in the *Ugo* narrative based on Dante's *Inferno* manifests the same type of concern. Andrea, like Dante, ties the portrayal of the condemned usurers to a broader critique of a society that seemed more fragmented because of *la gente nuova* or newcomers and *i sùbiti guadagni* or quick earnings (*Inferno* 16:l.73). A similar fear of social change and reverence for old aristocratic families occurs in passages from Ugo's trip to the otherworld:

> Enea gli disse, che questi sono una generazione di gente, che non vogliono fare l'arte a modo ch'eglino sanno, e potrebbono viver bene; e per far male lasciano l'arti, e vanno al soldo. (2:164)

> [Enea told him that these are a generation of people, who do not want to work at a trade that they know and with which they could live well; and to do evil they leave their trades and head towards money.]

While the main focus of Dante's anger is the developing monetary system and the continual fluctuation of both economic and social values it implies, the authors of the *Ugo* narrative expand the focus of the attack to another element of late medieval society that promoted social mobility: the university. Dante places the *spiriti magni,* great figures from the pre-Christian world who were increasingly the focus of university studies, in a *nobile castello* surrounded by seven walls (*Inferno* 4:ll.106, 119). Although these characters are in the first circle of Hell, Limbo, their punishment results only from a spiritual sin, their constant but unsatiable desire to see God. Dante obviously revered and pitied these figures, and he even refers to Aristotle as the *maestro* or master of the *filosofica famiglia* or philosophical family (*Inferno* 4:ll.131–32).

The castle with seven walls that appears in all four versions of the *Ugo* narrative is a clear imitation of Dante's *nobile castello*. According to the anonymous poets and Andrea, however, the castle is not so noble. The focus of the description of the castle and its inhabitants in the *Ugo d'Alvernia* narratives changes into a critique of the seven liberal arts and the university as the medieval institution that propagated them. Whereas Dante portrays the poets and philosophers of the classical age in Hell, the anonymous poets in their description of the underworld list the liberal arts and famous scholars from several fields. Although the scholars are of classical origin, they are represented as contemporary scholars at the University of Paris or as those "che vien a inparar a Paria sovra Sayne" [who come to learn in Paris on the Seine].³ The singers of tales condemn the secular values of the masters and ridicule their haughtiness. The scholars' squabbling, for example, creates an unbearably loud din as if they were engaged in real battle:

> Dell muro segondo fin al primier
> Non avé destro de l'un a ll'altro parler
> Per lo gran remor di cridi e del tençer
> Che lli s[c]olier fano in lo sso desputer.

(Stengel, "Huon's aus Auvergne" 51)

[From the second wall until the first, you do not have the opportunity to talk to one another because of the great noise from the shouting and from the quarrelling that the scholars engaged in during their disputes.]

The singers also poke fun at the masters by describing the dialecticians' punishment as an eternal lecture:

> Lo conte d'Alvernia fè un domandament:
> "Ti chen demostri quel maistro che aprent
> Dialeticha a costor che l'intent
> A baxo vixo, no a li altro troment?"
> "No e no avrà fin all çuçement."

(52–53)

[The count from Alvernia posed a question: "Are you revealing that the Master who teaches Dialectics to those with lowered faces does not have another punishment?" "No, and he will not have one until the last judgement."]

Andrea da Barberino's description of the castle is closer to Dante's than those of the anonymous singers; he does not go so far as to place a representative of each liberal art in Hell. Yet, he too attacks the contemporary universities and makes explicit an anti-Aristotelian tendency evident in the earlier versions of *Ugo d'Alvernia*. The anonymous versions list a famous practitioner of each of the liberal arts they condemn. Most of the famous teachers seem like the most obvious choices: for example, Ptolomeus represents the astronomers and Euclid the geometers. One exception is Al-Farabi, who represents the logicians. Al-Farabi was an Arab commentator of Aristotle who had an important influence on late Medieval thought. Like the well-known commentator Averroës, Al-Farabi was famous for the notion of the "double truth," the belief that both revelation and philosophy served as vehicles of enlightenment. In the thirteenth century, several professors at the University of Paris were suspected of teaching heretical principles based on the work of Averroës. In response to this intellectual threat, the Church issued condemnations in the 1270s banning certain principles, including the concept of the double truth.[4] What seems to have disturbed certain clerics about the "radical Aristotelians" is the anxiety-provoking prospect that a discipline known as philosophy could be separated from theology, and that the study of the natural world might one day be distinct from learning the faith (Gilson 559).

Andrea da Barberino makes this anti-Aristotelian attack more explicit in his description of the seven-sided castle when he places Aristotle in Limbo, but allows Plato to escape the punishment. Andrea also states (through the voice of Enea) that scholars who study Nature without referring to God as the creator cannot be saved: "pensa, Ugone, che pochi che studiano in filosofia si possono salvare, imperò ch'eglino non credono se non nella natura" [consider, Ugone, that very few who study philosophy can be saved because they do believe only in nature] (2:107). This remark refers to the debate about whether Christians should accept the Aristotelian notion of causation—the idea that there are secondary agents that control the processes of generation and decay in the natural world.

Motivated by a concern with social mobility, descriptions of the seven-sided castle in all the *Ugo* narratives display a conservative attitude towards universities and the absorption of classical philosophy into Christian theology. Universities contributed to the social mobility of Italian communes by training the notaries and lawyers who, although fewer in number than old aristocratic families and bankers, obtained a great deal of influence in the fourteenth-century Florentine oligarchy (Brucker 269). Andrea includes a direct attack against these professionals:

> E Ugo domandò, che anime erano quelle. Rispuose [Enea]: sono notai, procuratori, ed ogni maniera di gente, che sono ne' palagi dove si piatisce; ancora civili, che inchinono le persone per danari; ed évi molti, chè per ben vestire hanno date sentenzie false, e fatti mille torti, e molte carte false. (2:169)

> [And Ugo asked what souls were those. Enea responded: "They are notaries, lawyers, and every sort of person who is in the palaces where people litigate; although citizens, they exploit people for money; and there are many, who in order to dress well gave false sentences, and made a thousand wrongs, and many false papers."]

Andrea also takes swipes at other figures from classical culture including one of Ugo's companions, Aeneas, whom the singers, following the medieval epic tradition of Dares Phrygius, had portrayed as a traitor. While Dante, the pilgrim, humbly accepts Virgil as his guide, Ugo rejects Aeneas and tells him that he will wait until God sends a more worthy guide. Guillaume d'Orange, the warrior-turned-monk, meets Ugo's standards.[5] Guillaume d'Orange, like Ugo, had remained loyal to his king, Louis, even though the monarch mistreated him. Aeneas walks with Guillaume and Ugo through Hell, but only Guillaume assumes the role of guide. The paralleling of Aeneas and Guillaume not only functions as a critique of the *Commedia* by "popular" writers, but also clearly illustrates the tensions between early humanist and chivalric discourses.

This discursive tension again surfaces when Andrea discusses the mythological founders of his own patria. At one point, Ugo, Aeneas, and Guillaume see a large group of noble Trojans condemned for their pride. Because of his treachery, Aeneas must steal away and hide his identity from his compatriots. Paradoxically, at the same time that Andrea depicts the fallen warriors, he proudly boasts of Fiesole's Trojan ancestry (2:142). Even the Romans, the supposed founders of Florence itself, receive harsh treatment by Andrea; they are described as bloodthirsty warriors who love combat (2:110). Andrea's desire to both establish a connection between his homeland and the ancient world while also distancing himself from classical figures, is yet another illustration of the author's ambivalent attitude towards humanist discourses and the groups that used training in classical texts to promote their own upward movement in the communal hierarchy.

The singers who circulated the *Ugo* narrative shared a disdain for the institutions and philosophical ideas that attacked the status quo and promoted social change. Throughout the late Middle Ages in Italy, Aristotle's translated works, especially the *Politics* and the *Nicomachean Ethics,* had a tremendous influence on writers such as Thomas Aquinas and Marsiglio di Padova, who dealt with social as well as theological issues. Such arguments led to radical notions of a separate, secular government and a limited monarchy (Hyde, *Society and Politics* 190).

These centrifugal concepts conflicted with forces pushing towards a strongly centralized, elitist government in fourteenth-century Florence (Brucker 11). The arciguelfi were often attacked by members of the corporate guilds for their rigidity and nostalgic loyalty to a papacy that could no longer protect the commune. In general, these aristocrats stressed the concept of loyalty to the party and to the commune while criticizing other political groups who were felt to threaten Guelph values and fragment the power of the state.

Chivalric epics, such as Andrea's *Ugo d'Alvernia*, gained considerable popularity in areas controlled by Guelf communes in the late Middle Ages. These texts often promoted the idea that leadership should be earned rather than inherited but that those who qualify to obtain such status must come from an elite class of aristocrats. The principal value emphasized in such epics is loyalty: to a signore, to the patria, and to the Church on which both depend for their ideological power. Urban aristocrats in fourteenth-century Florence depended on the support of coalitions composed of family members, friends, and neighbors in order to receive political favors and gain office (Brucker 21, 28). The apocalyptic scene at the end of Andrea's *Ugo d'Alvernia* represents the fear of chaos created by a breakdown of such social ties:

> Avendo gran pezzo combattuto, s'avevono tagliate l'arme, e le carni; e le budella di tutti si vedevano uscite già fuori del corpo; e per le molte piaghe avevono perduto tanto sangue, che non si sostenevano piue; per questo si scostarono l'uno dall'altro, e in piana terra si gittorono a giacere, picchiandosi il petto, e pregando Iddio che aiutasse l'anima . . . ; *chi piangeva l'amico, e chi il parente, chi il suo signore!* (2:267; emphasis added)

> [Having fought for quite a while, they had torn their weapons and flesh; and one saw that everyone's guts had already come out of their bodies; and because of the many wounds, they had lost so much blood that they could no longer stand up; because of this they moved away from each other, and threw themselves down on flat ground, hitting their chests, and praying to God so that he might help their souls . . . ; *some cried for a friend, some for a relative, and some for their lord.*]

Epics from various historical periods and cultures have often sought to celebrate "transitions from ties of blood, family, and vendetta to the rules of law, communal good, and government" (De Marco Torgovnick 133); the hero manages to vanquish his enemies and establish a new hegemonic order. The *Ugo* narrative reverses this pattern: the protagonist dies as a martyr, but his sacrifice seems meaningless as factional violence has destroyed the social structure at all levels without generating a new one. In *Ugo d'Alvernia*, as in many late Carolingian narratives, authors can never clearly distinguish between clan and government rule. State identities, such as that of the French and the Germans, are determined by the greed and ruthlessness of noble families to protect their own interests; they represent governments that have absorbed factional violence rather than overcome it. Violence creates destruction and chaos, not a new beginning. The late chanson de geste does not offer a new model for social order but simply illustrates the suffering created when people rigidly cling to old ones.

In an ideological and semiotic analysis of the *Chanson de Roland*, Peter Haidu describes how that text represents the growing conflicts between the monarchy and the feudal system during the eleventh and twelfth centuries in France. He interprets the trial, torture, and execution of Ganelon as the symbolic subjection of the upper nobility's codes of honor and vendetta to the king/emperor (145). The *Ugo d'Alvernia* epic also presents contradictory ideological codes that focus on the control of violence. Like the *Chanson de Roland*, the *Ugo* narrative illustrates how the vendettas of noble clans promote a destructive fragmentation of society; at the same time, however, the text questions the idea of centralized power through the representation of the king. The Italian text juxtaposes the city-state's republican values, which promoted shared governance among citizens and the fragmentation of power, with the constant hope that by centralizing political authority in the hands of one noble family, the community might bring a lasting peace to factional violence. Although the death of Ugo reveals the utopian nature of this nostalgic solution, the text still portrays him as a transcendental figure who seems to offer the only possible route to social salvation. The sole hope for peace that *Ugo* suggests is a complete denial of diversity, including the various stylistic and ideological codes that contributed to it.

Andrea da Barberino played dual roles as both author and singer in a society that was rapidly becoming more dependent on written texts. With his epic, *Ugo d'Alvernia*, he appropriated the authority of the aristocratic tradition offered by chivalric texts. At the same time, Andrea also looked towards the future by including in his texts elements of a humanistic discourse which offered a new type of authority that he both desired and feared. Classical literature, Aristotelian thought, the universities, the merchants, and the notaries represented a world of exchange and of flux that Andrea attempted to control by anchoring it in the rigid scheme of his nostalgic fiction.

Epilogue

The Pleasure of Reading and the Power of the Text

The same tendency to combine oral and literary techniques that we have seen in the prose epic encouraged the creation of a new verse form, the cantare, which served as a flexible link between oral traditions and literary texts as well as different social groups. Like many epic narratives, *Ugo* was also translated into ottava rima (the cantare form) in 1488 by Michelagnolo da Volterra, who identified himself as a *trombetto* or trumpeter/soldier in the employ of a captain at Pisa.[1] A great debate still rages among Italianists about the origin of the cantare. Some scholars claim that Boccaccio invented the form while others trace its birth to more anonymous sources such as the *laude* of confraternities.[2] Whatever its origin(s), the cantare developed because of its versatility in addressing various social classes and the corresponding continuum of orality and literacy that existed in Italy during the late Middle Ages.

Texts written in ottava rima are made up of a chain of microtexts. Each cantare begins with a religious invocation and ends with a similar supplication, which also anticipates what will be narrated in its successor. The stanzas of the cantare are made up of eight hendecasyllabic lines—three couplets with an alternating rhyme scheme followed by *endecasillabi baciati* or a rhyming couplet. These stanzas differ from the lasse in several ways. First, they are a closed form of fixed length more like the sonnet than the lassa of indeterminate length. Second, the fixed ottava rima replaces the decasyllabic lines of the lassa that end with the same assonance or rhyme. Although this makes the cantare seem simpler because of its fixed form, it requires more complex—one might say literary—techniques at the level of the macrotext. For example, in the following passage the first stanza is connected to the next ottava by an enjambment that one would not likely find in a text written in lasse (Limentani, "Il racconto" 69):

> Vergine altiera io vi vo narrare,
> benché ingnorança m'abbi a sua bandiera.
> Con umiltà, io vi vo pregare
> che ci iscampi, e sia cosa vera
> quando nostre anime anno apasare
> di questa vita fa chelle non pera,
> sì che abiano parte in ella eterna gloria.
> Or vo seguire la legiadra istoria
>
> Dun ducha che ansuigi fu apellato.
>
> (fol. 1r)

[Noble Virgin I want to tell you a story even though ignorance makes me its banner. With humility, I want to plead with you to save us, and may it be true that when our souls must pass from this life, let them not perish but instead take part in eternal glory. Now I want to return to my beautiful story of a Duke who was called Ansuigi.]

In addition to such formal intricacy, the literary complexity of the *Ugo* cantare is enhanced by the connection of the religious exordium to the narrative events. The sequence of octaves in which Michelagnolo calls on the Virgin to protect our souls presents a great Saracen military threat to the family of the future savior, Ugo, and in particular to his mother, Agnese.[3]

Yet the cantare is similar to the lassa in the flexibility they both allow for the addition or deletion of narrative events; although the microtexts are closed systems, the macrotexts they make up remain open. It is quite possible, however, that the exordial and closing invocations developed as a failed literary technique to secure the order of an epic tradition that the singers of tales continued to rearrange (Cabani 33). Also, unlike the prose translation, the rhyme scheme of the cantare, like the assonance of the lasse, accentuates the text's oral nature. The cantare's elasticity along the oral-literary continuum is the reason for which it arises as a triumphant alternative in the battle of discursive epic forms. These diverse functions also have important ideological significance, which the cantare of *Ugo d'Alvernia* clearly demonstrates.

In his cantare version of *Ugo d'Alvernia*, Michelagnolo da Volterra exhibits how the late epics expand into cycles by going both back into the past to the hero's childhood and forward into the future to narrate the actions of his descendants. His text has several new episodes: we now learn about the lives of Ugo's parents, the hero's enfances, the exploits of his brother Ugolino, and even the destiny of his two children and nephew Busolino. The nephew takes a leading role in this narrative as Michelagnolo even narrates Busolino's childhood. Following the general tendency of the late epic to create hybrid figures, Michelagnolo also adds a new hero of humble origins, the stepfather of Ugo's nephew, Gualtieri, who serves as a trombetto for an aristocratic family.[4] Throughout the text Michelagnolo writes the word *trombetto* in enlarged letters therefore emphasizing the noble acts of a character who did not come from the aristocratic stock of most epic heroes. At the end of the narrative the author also defines himself as a trombetto and thus reveals why he has highlighted Gualtieri's profession in the text. Yet another character who crosses social categories in Michelagnolo's epic is Nida, Ugo's wife. Even though she is a loyal wife in the earlier versions of the *Ugo* narrative, she never takes an active role in defending her husband. Michelagnolo portrays Nida as an Amazonian figure who dons armor and fights with other women in her husband's army.

Following yet another general tendency of the late Carolingian epic that we saw even in the early-fourteenth-century texts of the *Marciano XIII*, the later narrative focuses more on familial politics than on the relationship between the king and his vassal. In a clear demonstration of how the epic's cyclical expansion often had an ideological purpose, Michelagnolo's cantare alters the earlier *Ugo* tales so that the struggle between Carlo Martello and the hero represents a larger battle between two families, the Chiaramonte and Maganza clans.[5] The king now sends Ugo to Hell not because of a suggestion made by a court minstrel but because of two evil knights from the Maganzas, the descendants of Ganelon. Michelagnolo also greatly reduces Ugo's adventures in the East and in Hell, and instead creates new battles between the evil Maganzas and the other members of Ugo's family, especially his brother Ugolino and his nephew Busolino. The cantare returns here to what had been one of the chanson de geste's original functions: providing mythical origins for aristocratic families.

Michelagnolo also makes it explicit that he worked as a trumpeter for an aristocratic Florentine family, the Lenzis, who held important communal offices throughout the Quattrocento (D. Kent 635). The author, in fact, states that Piero di Lorenzo Lenzi served as the *Capitano di Pisa*. In order to hold such a post at that time, the Lenzis must have been supporters of the Medici family—the "veiled tyrants" of Florence. This disparaging epithet referred to the Medicis' accumulation of power in Florence while appropriating the republican institutions of the city. Politically astute, Lorenzo de' Medici used both the chivalric and republican discourses for his own purposes; while he made sure that several important men who supported his family became knights, he always avoided that honor for himself (A. Brown 48).

In a similar fashion, Michelagnolo does make a vague connection between the Chiaramonte family and Tuscany when he refers to Ugo as its ruler after Carlo Martello's demise, but the author never makes a direct link between the French royal family and the Medicis or the family for which he wrote the epic, the Lenzis. Just as the Medici family avoided the public scrutiny of chivalric titles, Michelagnolo links the seigneurial families of Genova and Ferrara, the Malaspinas and the Estes (the real tyrants according to the Florentine aristocracy's point of view), with direct descendants of Ganelon's clan. At the end of the cantare, Ugo and his men arrive in Rome not only to defend the Church from the Saracens, but also from the Maganza clan, who have become allies with the easterners. With the exception of the patriarch Ugo, the whole Chiaramonte clan dies in the fight to free Rome. Whereas Ugo is the only survivor of his faction and returns to Paris an old and lonely man, two pregnant women from the Maganza family survive the war in Rome and then travel to Genova and Ferrara:

> A Genova arivò in suo camini.
> Parturì due figli a un portare,
> mascio et femina in quelli destini.
> Fratello et sorella ebbe a fare;
> di costor due naque e Maleispini.
> E l'altra donna ebbe a navichare
> per lo mare Adriano così amara:
> venne a Vinegia e poi andò a Ferrara
>
> Essendo a Ferrara parturì due figli,
> pur mascio et femina come fé la prima.
> . . . .
> Ingenerorno con gra[n] disoneste;
> chiamòssi poi li Marchesi da Este.

(fols. 162v–163r)

[She arrived in Genova on her journey. She gave birth to two children at one time. A boy and a girl it was fated. The brother and sister had something to do with one another. From those two the Malaspinas were born. And the other lady had to sail on the Adriatic sea so bitter. She came to Venice and then went to Ferrara. In Ferrara she gave birth to two children, also a boy and a girl like the first lady made. They procreated with great dishonesty. They were then called the Marchesi da Este.]

Michelagnolo not only traces the genealogy of the Malaspina and Este families to the evil Maganzas, but also suggests that incestuous relationships produced those noble lineages. While the Maganzas transform into two Italian dynasties in the *Ugo* cantare, the Chiaramonte clan dies out. After returning to Paris, Ugo is attacked by the Germans who want to take control of the empire. As in the earlier versions of the epic, Ugo and the German king die, but since the French king dies first, his people lose the empire. With the death of Ugo, the French royal family becomes extinct: "Della casa di Chiaramonte non rimase / nisuno e fu ispento le gran chase" [No one remained from the Chiaramonte lineage and the great lineage was extinguished] (fol. 165r).

Such selective genealogy brings us back to the contradictory nature of late Carolingian epics, especially those produced in communes that disseminated republican notions of government. Like other late Carolingian epics we have analyzed, the *Ugo* cantare condemns kings and seigneurs at the same time that it justifies the aristocratic privileges of certain families and those who support them. Michelagnolo's text goes one step further by creating a strictly negative genealogy. As we saw in chapter five, a general tendency of the late epic was to combine local traditions with the Carolingian epic. Michelagnolo follows that movement, but with a twist. Instead of using the prestige of the chanson de geste to celebrate an Italian figure, he uses the genre's aura to condemn Italian lords. While his epic still supports the traditional theory that one's social identity is determined largely by blood heritage, he cannot illustrate it in an affirmative way. Once again we see in an even more dramatic fashion the portrayal of chivalry and clan as institutions that should protect their communities, but instead destroy them.

The contradictory nature of Carolingian epics led to their own critical demise. In particular, the oral elements of these texts had already categorized them as inferior to truly literary works; the epics were either satirized by writers such as Ariosto or trivialized by humanists who did not consider them literary. For example, Anton Francesco Grazzini wrote a satirical poem describing the well-known manuscript collection of Stradino, yet another follower of the Medici family who collected Carolingian epics (Maracchi Biagiarelli 54). The following quotation is Grazzini's description of Stradino's library:

Oh come fieno il caso i Rinaldini,
i Nerbonesi e i Cavalieri erranti,
per rinvolger salsiccia e marzolini!

(Verzone 468)

[Oh the stories of Rinaldo, of the Nerbonesi, and of the errant knights should be used to wrap sausage and cheese!]

At the end of his epic, Michelagnolo expresses quite a different opinion as he defends his interest in epics by explaining that he learned about ancient deeds from such texts, but above all else, that he had a good time with them. As another singer, Antonio Pucci, explains, the process of transforming a narrative into rhythm provides him with great pleasure: "il diletto, oltre a quel del sapere, può stare nella melodia delle soave e sonanti rime" [the delight, beyond that of learning, can occur in the melody of soft and sonorous rhymes] (Bettarini-Bruni 148). These singers felt a physical connection to storytelling that was difficult for those who lived in a cultural environment more dependent on books to understand.

Even after the invention of the press, Carolingian epics of writers such as Andrea da Barberino or Michelagnolo da Volterra remained extremely popular. For example, between 1501 and 1516 there were various printings of titles such as *Historia di Carlo Martello, Aiolfo del Barbicone, Aspramonte, Buovo d'Antona, Innamoramento di Carlo Magno, Guerin Meschino, Malagigi, Reali di Francia, Rinaldo e la Spagna* (Beer 335–38). The judgement of the prehumanists and humanists such as Lovati or Grazzini, however, began a critical tradition that exiled these texts and their celebration of pleasure from the canon of medieval literature.

Although humanists did not place the Carolingian epic in the canon of late medieval Italian Literature, Michelagnolo did. At the end of his tale of *Ugo d'Alvernia,* our trombetto listed the stories that he had read. He divided them into three categories: *libri di batagle* [books about battles], *libri picholi e grandi d'inamoramenti* [small and great books about falling in love], and *libri dall'anima da legiere di quaresima* [books for the soul to be read during Lent] (fols. 166r–168r). He subdivided the first category into two groups: narratives about the age of Charlemagne and those that occur before or after that era. Michelagnolo's favorite genre was the Carolingian epic; this becomes clear not only because of its spot on the top of the list but also because of his description. He claims that any man who does not enjoy such narratives is without reason and bestial. He uses the adjective *bellisimi* (very beautiful) for the *libri di battaglie, et buoni bellissimi* (very beautiful and good) for the *libri d'inamoramenti,* and simply *buoni* (good) for the *libri dall'anima*. Such distinctions indicate that Michelagnolo appreciated what the books of love and religious texts had to teach him, but he certainly did not enjoy them to the same extent as his adventure stories. According to Michelagnolo's pleasure principle, Carolingian epics outrank such canonical works as the poems of Petrarca and even Dante's *Commedia*.

What can Michelagnolo's canon of vernacular literature teach us? It illustrates that literacy and orality are not polar opposites but rather form a continuum. Much like rap music today, medieval Carolingian epics in Italy suffered critical devaluation in part because they included an oral component in a culture with strong literary prejudices. Michelagnolo, as a literate man who probably did not read Latin, found himself somewhere in the middle of the literary-oral continuum of his age. As a result, his text embodies both the tensions and the pleasures of such an ambiguous cultural and social status.

Michelagnolo was both a soldier and an avid fan of Carolingian narratives. In his assessment of contemporary vernacular literature he describes the chivalric epics as his favorite genre because they are about battles. He clearly identified with the character Gualtieri whose profession—trombetto—he wrote in large letters throughout the manuscript. Like Gualtieri, Michelagnolo served a "house," a patrician family, whose success or failure would determine the soldier's future. The pleasure that Michelagnolo and so many of his contemporaries drew from reading or hearing Carolingian tales must have been determined not only by their stylistic hybridity as products of both oral and textual traditions, but also by their ambivalent attitude to lineage and faction. Through these texts Italians could consider their own anxieties about the institutions that should have safeguarded them, but often endangered them. Yet they were able to deal with these issues at a safe distance because the epics portray French dynasties rather than the families of their own community. Not all the late epics have such cheerless conclusions as the *Ugo* cantare; for example, the enfances epics like *Bovo* and *Guerrino il Meschino* illustrate how a child hero reclaims a lost lineage. Even these texts, however, describe the violence necessary to maintain such a genealogy as well as the constant threat of losing the familial security that determines social standing. Late medieval Italians had a passion for chivalric epics, and the continued popularity of this genre, even its most pessimistic texts, suggests that Italians must have appreciated the opportunity to consider the threatening aspects of the patrilineal hierarchies that still structured their everyday lives.

Appendix
Chivalric Epics Cited

Title	Language	Form	Approximate Date by Century
Aliscans	F	L	late 12th
Aquilon de Bavière	T/FI	P	early 15th
Chanson d'Aspremont	F	L	late 12th
Aspramonte	T	P	early 15th
Aspramonte	T	C	early 15th
Berte aus grans piés	F	L	late 13th
Berta da li pe grandi	FI	L	early 14th
Berta e Milon	FI	L	early 14th
Bueve de Hantone	F	L	late 13th
Bovo d'Antona	FI	L	early 14th
Chanson de Roland (O)	F	L	late 12th
Chanson de Roland (V4)	FI	L	early 14th
Chanson de Roland (V7)	FI	L	late 13th
Chanson de Roland (C)	FI	L	early 14th
Chevalerie Ogier	F	L	early 13th
Chevalerie Ogier	FI	L	early 14th
Enfances Ogier	F	L	early 13th
Enfances Ogier	FI	L	early 14th
Gaydon	F	L	late 13th
Guerrino il Meschino	T	P	early 15th
L'Entrée d'Espagne	FI	L	early 14th

Title	Language	Form	Approximate Date by Century
Li Fatti de Spagna	FI	P	mid 14th
La Spagna	T	C	15th
Hervis de Mes	F	L	late 12th
Huon de Bordeaux	F	L	late 13th
Karleto	FI	L	early 14th
Macaire	FI	L	early 14th
Le Pèlerinage de Charlemagne	F	L	late 12th
La Prise de Pampelune	FI	L	late 14th
I Reali di Francia	T	P	early 15th
Renaut de Montauban	F	L	early 13th
Renaut de Montauban	FI	L	late 14th
Rinaldino da Montalbano	T	P	15th
Rinaldo da Montalbano	T	P	early 14th
Rinaldo da Monte Albano	T	C	15th
Rolandin	FI	L	early 14th
Storia di Aquilante e Formosa	T	P	late 15th
Le Storie Nerbonesi	T	P	early 15th
Tristan de Nanteuil	F	L	14th
Ugo d'Alvernia	FI	L	late 13th
Ugo d'Alvernia	T	P	early 15th
Ugo d'Alvernia	T	C	late 15th

Languages: F = French; FI = Franco-Italian; T = Tuscan
Form: L = laisses; P = prose; C = cantare

Notes

Citations in this work observe the following style: numbers alone represent page numbers; *l.* and *ll.* refer to lines of verse; colons separating two numbers indicate the first is to volume number or cantare and the second to page number or stanza.

INTRODUCTION

1. Throughout this book I use the names Charlemagne and Roland instead of the various Italianized forms to avoid confusion arising from the many variant spellings in the Franco-Italian and Italian epics. However, I use the Italianized spellings for the names of other characters.

2. In this study, myth or mythology refer to Roland Barthes's use of these terms to mean the representation of historical events as natural and timeless. See his *Mythologies*, 11.

3. Documents, such as a letter by the prehumanist Lovato Lovati, attest to the performance of texts like the *Marciano XIII* (analyzed in chapters one and two) for large groups in the Trevisan March of the late thirteenth and early fourteenth centuries, and contemporary scholars have also hypothesized that the manuscript's hybrid language or code-switching supports this notion. We also know, however, that at least by 1407 the *Marciano XIII*, along with many other Carolingian epics, had a seigneurial audience as it was part of the Gonzaga library in Mantova. For evidence of oral transmission, see Stocchi, "Le fortune della letteratura cavalleresca," 201–17. For information about the epics located in seigneurial libraries, see the following: Bertoni, *La Biblioteca estense*; Bertoni, "Notizie sugli amanuensi degli Estensi," 29–57; Cappelli, "La Biblioteca estense," 1–30; Braghirolli, "Inventaire des manuscrits en langue française," 497–514.

CHAPTER 1. A HYBRID GENRE: THE ITALIAN CHANSON DE GESTE

1. For a discussion of this historical paradigm and how it was superseded by the cycle of "illustrious men" later in the century, see Starn, "Reinventing Heroes in Renaissance Italy," 74–75.

2. For evidence that the transmission of the Carolingian material was wide-

spread in Italy, see Levi, "I cantari leggendari del popolo italiano," 1–171 and Grendler, "Chivalric Romances in the Italian Renaissance," 59–102. For information about the popularity of the Carolingian material in the Trevisan March, see Marchesan, *L'Università di Treviso nei secoli XIII e XIV,* 149–57. For an analysis of the Carolingian material in Tuscany, particularly Florence, at the beginning of the fifteenth century, see chapters five and six.

3. For evidence that Orlando was a popular name in thirteenth-century Florence, see Brattö, "Studi di antroponimia fiorentina," 168–69. For evidence that northern Italians continued to produce epics, even in prose, in the fifteenth century, see Rajna, "Due frammenti di romanzi cavallereschi," 163–78.

4. For the figures at Verona's Duomo, see Lejeune and Stiennon, *La Légende de Roland dans l'art du moyen-âge,* 1:61–71. For the archival evidence, see Rajna, "L'onomastica italiana e l'epopea carolingia," 1–69.

5. Scholars are still debating whether the best term for these hybrid texts is *franco-italiano, franco-veneto,* or *franco-lombardo.* I am using Franco-Italian since it is the most inclusive, but I recognize that this expression has its limitations because it suggests that these texts are written in a standardized language rather than in unique combinations of different dialects with Old French. For an analysis of the issues involved in this linguistic debate, see Wunderli and Holtus, "La 'renaissance' des études franco-italiennes," 4–12.

6. Referring to the *Marciano XIII* narratives, Gaston Paris wrote that "la langue dans laquelle ils sont écrits . . . est complétement *assauvagie,* comme on disait autrefois; elle échappe presque à toutes règles et trahit chez l'auteur une profonde ignorance de l'idiome qu'il prétend écrire." See his *Histoire poétique de Charlemagne,* 164.

7. The editor of the *Entrée d'Espagne,* Antoine Thomas, hypothesized that the author was a cleric because of his knowledge of Latin texts; see the introduction to his edition. Scholars have also proposed that the author had ties to the Visconti court in Milan because he claims to have found Turpin's chronicle in that city; see Dionisotti, "*Entrée d'Espagne, Spagna, Rotta di Roncisvalle,*" 213. Most recently André de Mandach has claimed that the epic was written by Giovanni da Nono, a Paduan writer of noble origin, whose Latin works about the history of his city contain numerous citations of chansons de geste. See De Mandach, "Sur les traces," 48–64.

8. For a history of the debate over the dating of this manuscript, see the introduction to the following edition: Rosellini, *La "Geste Francor" di Venezia,* 18–23. All quotations will be taken from this edition.

9. A *laisse* is the stanza used in the Old French epic, which has an indefinite number of verses that end with the same rhyme.

10. Gautier, *Les Épopées françaises,* 588. Unless otherwise indicated, all translations are my own.

11. Viscardi, *Letteratura franco-italiana,* 25; Limentani and Infurna, *L'Epica,* 42; and Krauss, *L'Epica feudale,* 9.

12. Goldmann states that worldviews are "slices of imaginary or conceptual

reality, structured in such a way that, . . . one can develop them into over-all worlds." See his "The Genetic-Structuralist Method," 160.

13. Segre states that "il testo letterario è nella cultura, non è la cultura: è, semmai, un apporto allo sviluppo della cultura"(22). He describes this aspect of a literary text as its "output" in the making of culture as opposed to "input," a term he uses to describe the analysis of texts as contributing to reality rather than helping to model it. Segre, *Semiotica,* 19–22.

14. There are three extant Franco-Italian versions of this narrative: Marciano IV (V4), Marciano VII (V7), and the Châteauroux manuscript (C). For a description of these manuscripts and modern editions, see the introduction to Cesare Segre's edition of the *Chanson de Roland,* 39–40. For a survey of the Italian epics, which expand the narrative of the *Chanson de Roland* beginning with the Franco-Italian *Entrée d'Espagne,* see Dionisotti, "*L'Entrée d'Espagne, Spagna, Rotta di Roncisvalle,*" 207–41; and Andrea Fassò, "La materia," 65–81.

15. The term *popolo* refers to a political group of non-nobles bound by an oath.

16. While Lansing's book analyzes the role of lineage in thirteenth-century Florence, several prominent historians have focused on the importance of kinship in early-fifteenth-century Florence: F. W. Kent, *Household and Lineage in Renaissance Florence;* Klapisch-Zuber, "'Kin, Friends, and Neighbors,'" 68–93; and Kuehn, *Law, Family, and Women.*

17. Aldo Rosellini, in the introduction to his 1986 edition of the *Marciano XIII,* follows the lead of earlier critics when he describes the narratives of Bovo and the Dane as dissimilar in content from the other tales in the manuscript. He quotes Viscardi to describe the issues presented in the other *Marciano XIII* texts as predominately private, familial, and *essenzialmente borghesi* or essentially bourgeois (62–63).

18. For a discussion of the manuscripts, see the introductions to the three versions of *Bueve d'Hantone* edited by Albert Stimming: *Der festländische Bueve d'Hantone,* vols. 25, 30, 34, 41, and 42. The first version appears in vol. 25, the second in vol. 30, and the third in vol. 34. Volumes 41 and 42 contain notes to the editions. Most Italian critics date the Franco-Italian version of this narrative at approximately the same time as the Old French epics, the late thirteenth or early fourteenth century. For a survey of the dates ascribed to the *Marciano XIII* manuscript by various scholars, see the introduction to Aldo Rosellini's 1986 edition of the manuscript.

19. I describe only the first part of the French narrative, which deals with the conflict between two vassals, Doon and Bueve. The second part of the text represents Bueve's pilgrimage to the East and his conquest of Jerusalem.

20. For a description of the manuscripts and their dates, see Togeby, *Ogier le Danois dans les littératures européennes.*

21. In the Old French version, the role of the coward had been played by a Lombard. The northern Italian author of the *Marciano XIII* manuscript, however, replaced him with a southerner from Puglia.

22. This episode does not occur in the Old French version. Henning Krauss has identified Maximo Çudé as a representation of the contemporary tyrant, Ezzelino da Romano: "Ezzelino da Romano—Maximo Çudé—Historische Realität," 233.

23. Bender, "Les métamorphoses de la royauté," 174. Although Bender was the first to outline this transformation, several scholars have reiterated his description.

24. This is Anne Elizabeth Cobby's interpretation of the text. See her introduction to the following edition: Burgess and Cobby, *The Pilgrimage of Charlemagne*, 2–12.

25. Both the citation in French and the translation are from the Burgess and Cobby edition cited above.

26. Bakhtin, *Rabelais and His World*. Bakhtin states that carnival celebrates a "temporary liberation from the prevailing truth and from the established order; it marked the suspension of all hierarchical rank, privileges, norms, and prohibitions" (10). In describing grotesque realism, Bakhtin says the following: "The essential principle . . . is degradation, that is, the lowering of all that is high, spiritual, ideal, abstract" (19). The editor and translator of Bakhtin's *Dialogic Imagination*, Michael Holquist, in his glossary to the edition defines Bakhtin's use of the term *dialogue*: "A word, discourse, language or culture undergoes 'dialogization' when it becomes relativized, de-privileged, aware of competing definitions for the same things. Undialogized language is authoritative or absolute" (427).

27. Pasero uses this as one of his examples. He refers to vol. 1159 of the following edition: Langlois, *Le couronnement de Louis*.

28. Two other hybrid chansons de geste will be analyzed in this chapter: *Huon de Bordeaux* and *Gaydon*. For a discussion of these texts' hybridity, see C. M. Jones, *The Noble Merchant*, 16–20.

29. See chapter ten of Rossi, *Huon de Bordeaux*, 587–607. For a description of the patrician families of Arras, see Lestocquoy, *Les dynasties bourgeoises*.

Chapter 2. The Conflicting "Family Values" of the *Marciano XIII* Manuscript

1. Leslie Morgan notes that "throughout Ms. 13, families are important at all levels, not only the royal: Aquilon, the hero and advisor seen throughout Ms. 13, is the father of Naimes, the advisor par excellence, so there is a 'house' of advisors." Morgan, "Unity of Composition," 23.

2. In a very thorough and recent study of chivalry in late medieval Italy, Stefano Gasparri questions the characterization of Italian *cavalleria* as bourgeois, which began with Salvemini's study early in this century. See Gasparri's *I milites cittadini*, 10–11. For another critique of Salvemini's emphasis on class conflict in late medieval Florence, see Ottokar, *Il Comune di Firenze*, 32.

3. The following is a description of a celebration that occurred in Padua in 1300: "Hoc anno milites et nobiles et alii iudices Paduae et frataleae Paduae fuerunt in astiludis et aliis solaciis cum pulchris vestibus, quas omnes donaverunt

hominibus curialibus, publicam laetitiam propter Paduae maximam libertatem."
Annales Patavini, Rerum Italicarum Scriptores, 8, 1: 208.

4. Some scholars use an alternate spelling of the writer's name: Giovanni di Nono.

5. For an example of this type of conflict, see Kuehn, *Law, Family, and Women*, 129–42.

6. These responsibilities continued throughout the marriage. Women engaged in numerous activities such as gift-giving and mourning rituals to maintain ties between different generations and families within a clan. Sharon Strocchia has adopted the term *lavoro di parentela* or the work of kinship to describe how the unity of clans often depended on the ability of women to create strong bonds with the kinship network. See her "La famiglia patrizia fiorentina," 130.

7. For a detailed comparison of the two texts see the introduction to Carla Cremonesi's edition of the romance epic and Adler, "Structural Meaning," 101–8.

8. Da Barberino, *I Reali*, 466–67. All citations and quotations refer to Vandelli and Gambarin's edition.

9. I borrowed the term "epic of revolt" from William Calin's book on the rebellious vassal epics: *The Old French Epic of Revolt*.

10. Franco-Italian narrative appears in the manuscript *Marciano fr. XVI*. For the history of the Rinaldo narrative in Italy, see Rajna, "Rinaldo" 58–127, 213–41; and Melli, "I 'Cantari di Rinaldo,'" 102–56.

11. The most accessible version is edited by Elio Melli.

12. This, however, is not the first time that the emperor's family had been associated with sins of a sexual nature. In both Latin and vernacular texts, Roland is described as the product of an incestuous affair between Charlemagne and his half sister (either Berta or Gilles). For information about this legend, see De Gaiffer, "La Légende de Charlemagne," 490–503; Roncaglia, "Rolando e il peccato di Carlomagno," 315–47; Keller, "Le péché de Charlemagne," 39–54. Leslie Morgan relates this legend to the importance placed on Berta Big-Foot's physical deformity in the *Marciano XIII* codex. Such deformities were often attributed to sexual sins, which could be inherited. See Morgan, "Berta," 40–43.

CHAPTER 3. HYBRID IDENTITIES: MONSTERS, WILD MEN, AND WARRIOR WOMEN

1. Bernheimer, *Wild Men*, 144–45. Bernheimer views the identification with the wild man as an example of the aristocracy's "radical archaism" in the fourteenth and fifteenth centuries.

2. I am adopting Inge Boer's definition of *cultural cross-dressing* as "a sense of blurring the boundaries not only in gender roles but also in cultural roles." Boer points out that this term stresses "the fact that it is directed toward the assumption of a culturally constructed model, i.e. the Orient." See her "This is not the orient," 212–13.

3. Carolyn Dinshaw coined the expression "queer touches" in "Chaucer's

Queer Touches," 75–92. In both this chapter and the next, I use the word "queer," as Dinshaw and other contemporary scholars do, to describe narrative elements that subvert the category of the normal in sexual, gender, class, or race power relations.

4. *Bovo* is the spelling used in the *Marciano XIII* manuscript, whereas *Buovo* is a variant adopted by Andrea da Barberino in his work *I Reali di Francia*.

5. The term *velu* is used in line 14800, and Varocher is described as a wild man at 14882.

6. Roger Bartra makes a similar point about nature when he claims: "Nature was paradoxically a symbolic and artificial space that sanctioned the elaboration of models of behavior proceeding from the anomalies of a natural order." See his *Wild Men in the Looking Glass*, 96.

7. For example, Krauss quotes the following verses from the chanson de geste, *Les Narbonnais*, in which it is explained that Lombards cannot be good knights because they are merchants (211): "Par Dieu, Lonbart, trop estes bobancier. / Ne devez pas a franc home tencier. / Chevalerie n'est pas vostre mestier, / Mes trosiax vandre et monoie changier" (ll. 1608–11).

8. Krauss argues that the character Varocher represents a new, democratic *Volksheer* in Italy. See his *Ritter und Bürger*, 221.

9. Krauss, *L'Epica feudale*, 202. Krauss qualifies this interpretation when he states that the generic mediation of the chanson de geste, with its feudal values, prohibits Varocher from completely embodying a bourgeois self-consciousness.

10. Sinclair, *Tristan de Nanteuil, chanson de geste inédite*, 161. For an analysis of the character's disguise, see Sinclair, *Tristan de Nanteuil. Thematic Infrastructure*, 34–42.

11. For an analysis of other literary traditions that might have influenced the figure of the warrior woman in late medieval epic (especially reworkings of Ovid's *Metamorphosis* IX), see Bendinelli Predelli, "La donna guerriera," 13–31.

12. Wettan Kleinbaum, *The War Against the Amazons*, 51–58. Kleinbaum comments on Benoît's Amazons "as a hybrid of both male and female virtues" (51). She attributes this "faintly positive image" to the influence of courtly love (58).

13. For a more complete analysis of how Boccaccio measures women according to their ability to act like men, see Jordan, "Boccaccio's In-Famous Women," 25–47 and Joseph Benson, "Boccaccio's *De mulieribus claris*," 9–31.

14. Tomalin, *Fortunes of the Warrior Heroine*, 25. Tomalin refers to this contradictory argument as "double-think." Jordan discusses parallels between Boccaccio's view of women in *De mulieribus claris* and his description of the popolo in *De casibus virorum illustrium;* the ideological similarities echo those shared by the figures of the warrior woman and the wild man in the early Italian epic. See her "Boccaccio's In-Famous Women," 43–44.

15. Bendinelli Predelli notes that the children of Amazons were usually considered bastards in western literature. See her *La donna guerriera*, 15.

16. Allaire, "Warrior Woman," 35–36. Allaire points out that women watching male military games from a balcony is a common image in classical and medi-

eval literature that defines the "feminine" as "passive observation and confined space."

17. Zemon Davis discusses how in the late Middle Ages the "relation of the wife—of the potentially disorderly woman—to her husband was especially useful for expressing the relation of all subordinates to their superiors." See her "Women on Top," 127.

18. Although documents refer to Andrea as a *canterino* or public singer, and he might have recited this very narrative in a Florentine piazza, in many ways he distances himself from the oral tradition even as he depends on it.

19. The narrative ends with Antonio di Giovanni da Bacherato, a Florentine citizen, claiming to have finished writing the story in 1487.

20. She pledges a vow of chastity first to the goddess Diana and then to the Virgin Mary. On fol. 20v there is a drawing of Formosa participating in a joust. The only thing that distinguishes her from the other knights is a figure of Diana on her helmet. Once again, her sexual difference is marked at the same time that it is effaced by the symbol of chastity.

21. There is one exception—a fifteenth-century cantare describes Braidamonte as a legitimate member of the family. See Tomalin, *Fortunes of the Warrior Heroine*, 56.

22. Manuscript 1904 of the Biblioteca Riccardiana, fol. 66r. All quotations are taken from this manuscript. I have added accents and punctuation to manuscript transcriptions.

23. "Where the role of [the warrior woman] is treated seriously woman is correspondingly respected and active." See Tomalin, *Fortunes of the Warrior Heroine*, 10.

24. For instance, Judith Brown concludes that the number of working women in Tuscany dropped in the last half of the fourteenth century and that very few women entered the work force for the next two centuries. See her "A Woman's Place," 208–9.

25. Helen Solterer notes that the inclusion of women in tournament literature "emerges as one factor distinguishing the earlier, brutal combats from the later, more 'entertaining' spectacles." See her "Figures of Female Militancy, 528."

26. Minutoli, *Storia di Rinaldino da Montalbano*, 260. I am indebted to Gloria Allaire for this reference.

27. Schiesari, "In Praise of Virtuous Women?" 70–71. Schiesari notes that although chastity "would bring with it a certain freedom, nevertheless that choice is limited since the very concept . . . is inscribed within the male-centered discourse of *virtù* as an ideal of masculinity that women could only achieve by denying their difference as women."

Chapter 4. Masculinity, Sexuality, and Orientalism in the Medieval Italian Epic

1. All citations and quotations refer to Peter Wunderli's edition: Da Verona, *Aquilon de Bavière, roman franco-italien en prose*.

2. By using the term Orientalism, I am referring not only to Edward Said's thesis that the West has attempted to use its knowledge of eastern cultures to contain and dominate them (40), but I am also alluding to Homi Bhabha's notion that the stereotyping involved in colonial discourse is a kind of fetishism (26).

3. François Suard says that "une incertitude relative pèse désormais sur le héros, dont le sexe lui-même n'est plus à jamais déterminé." Suard, "L'épopée française tardive," 455.

4. Andrea da Barberino lived from approximately 1371–1431. See Catalano, "La data di morte," 84–87.

5. Ms. 2226 of the Biblioteca Riccardiana, fol. 41r. All subsequent quotations of *Guerrino il Meschino* will be taken from the same manuscript. I am indebted to Gloria Allaire for allowing me to read her transcription of this lengthy manuscript. All translations from the manuscript in this chapter, however, are my own.

6. For example, Andrea describes their war cries as "bestialj più che ordinate" (fol. 3v). The earlier Franco-Italian epics, *Berta da li pe grandi* from the *Marciano XIII* (Rosellini 248) and the *Entrée d'Espagne* (Thomas 2:218), also portray Christian knights bringing good table manners to the easterners.

7. Although many medieval definitions of sodomy included all nonprocreative sexual practices, by the High Middle Ages the term meant homosexual activity in everyday language. See Boswell, "Dante and the Sodomites," 66.

8. For another example, see my analysis of the Roland/Dama Roenza encounter in chapter three.

9. Since the medieval exegetical tradition often conflated sodomy with other types of "unnatural" behavior, including the misuse of rhetoric, several critics have suggested that the sinners of Inferno 15 and 16 are guilty of nonsexual sins: see, for example, Kay, *Dante's Swift and Strong* and Vance, "Differing Seed."

10. While the Florentine government tried to repress male homosexuality, it chose a different approach regarding prostitution. Since the government believed it was better for young men to have sex with *meretrici* rather than with other men, the government encouraged a controlled, and well-organized development of prostitution as an alternative to homosexuality. See Mazzi, *Prostitute e lenoni,* 181.

11. Jeffrey Richards says that sodomy was seen "almost exclusively as a sin of the city, the court, and the upper and professional classes." See his *Sex, Dissidence and Damnation,* 138.

12. For details about the long history of this legend among Christian theologians, crusaders, and poets, see Eckhardt, "Le cercueil flottant de Mahomet," 77–88.

13. Antonio Franceschetti traces the development of this famous debate from its appearance in the *Entrée* through later versions in *Li Fatti de Spagna* and *La Spagna.* See his "Saracens in Early Italian Chivalric Literature," 205–6. For an analysis of the Roland/Ferragu debate see Bradley-Cromey, *Authority and Autonomy,* 149–54. On page 150, Bradley-Cromey states that "it is his role as dialectician for his faith which most aptly depicts a Roland elevated to the function of *orator.*"

14. In her analysis of Castilian epic and ballad, Louise Mirrer describes these strategies as "linguistic markers generally seen to constitute powerless language—the language that women, even today, are supposed to speak. He [the Muslim protagonist] uses polite expressions, flattery, and meek, self-effacing, and naive utterances." See her "Representing 'Other' Men," 175.

15. This same debate appears in *L'Entrée d'Espagne*. See Bradley-Cromey, *Authority and Autonomy*, 150–52 and Adler, "Didactic Concerns," 107–9.

16. In a sermon to the Florentines, San Bernardino says that men who do not marry become Sodomites: "Guai a chi non toglie moglie avendo el tempo e cagione legittima! chè non pigliandola doventano soddomiti." See Cannarozzi, *Le prediche volgari*, 1:416. He repeats the same notion in a sermon to the Sienese, saying that the husbands should not spend time away from their wives because they might become Sodomites: "Non si díe partire il marito dalla donna, come molti fanno, che stanno tre o quattro o sei anni di fuore . . . e tu stai con disonestá e in peccato, e talvolta in vizio di sodomia." See Bargellini, *Le prediche volgari*, 402. Jeffrey Richards notes "that the medieval popular perception of homosexuality was that it was something that occurred in the absence of women or marriage." See his *Sex, Dissidence and Damnation*, 138.

17. All quotations are taken from the manuscript Palatino 101, vol. 2, of the Biblioteca Medicea Laurenziana.

18. Steven Kruger discusses how "medieval anti-Semitic and homophobic discourses . . . operated through an association between the (religiously or sexually) queer and the feminine, misogynistically conceived." See his "Racial/Religious and Sexual Queerness," 33.

19. Cannarozzi, *Le prediche volgari*, 419. "Se tu, marito, guadagni, e non ài chi conservi, la casa va male. Non avendo donna, la roba tua va male."

20. Although I am aware of the dangers involved in accepting evidence of queer sexuality from strictly homophobic sources, I believe Rocke's research does prove that many Florentines constructed sodomy as a set of social and sexual practices that were more common among young men. I cannot agree, however, with Rocke's assumption that the court records can be used as a guide for describing homosexual relationships in Renaissance Florence.

21. While explaining why he will not rest until he finds his true lineage, Guerrino insists that all parents should be respected for having followed God's divine commandments (fol. 81r).

22. For the Florentine government's persecution of sodomites in the first half of the fifteenth century, see Trexler, *Public Life in Renaissance Florence*, 379–80.

Chapter 5. Orality, Literacy, and the Prose Epic

1. I have used very general dates for two reasons. First, scholars have had great difficulty dating with precision the manuscripts of early Carolingian epics written by anonymous authors. Second, the shift from Franco-Italian to Tuscan occurred gradually as the different versions of the *Ugo* text studied in this article illustrate.

2. See Kittay and Godzich's analysis of the relationship between prose and the development of state bureaucracy in France. Kittay and Godzich, *The Emergence of Prose,* 102.

3. Some versions of this narrative use *Ugone* instead of *Ugo* or alternate between the names.

4. Bäuml describes narrative techniques associated with primary orality as a fictional "character" of medieval written texts. See "Medieval Texts," 43.

5. Dante followed a thirteenth-century tradition that associated prose with truthfulness. Baranski, "La lezione esegetica di *Inferno* I," 86. Zumthor, *Langue, texte, énigme,* 246.

6. For a description of how medieval and Renaissance Italians learned to read, see Grendler, *Schooling,* 142–61. For a discussion of reading *sotto voce* in the medieval period, see Ong, *Orality and Literacy,* 119.

7. See Gloria Allaire's book for more information about these narratives and their attribution to Andrea da Barberino.

8. The Hamilton manuscript 337 of the Kupferstich-Kabinett of Berlin; the N III 19 manuscript of the Biblioteca Nazionale di Torino; and the manuscript 32 of the Biblioteca Del Seminario Vescovile di Padova. A large portion of the Berlin manuscript was published by A. Tobler and E. Stengel in various articles; see the bibliography in Meregazzi, "L'Episodio del Prete Gianni, 9–10. The manuscript in Turin was badly damaged by a fire; however, a short extract of the manuscript had already been published in Renier, *La discesa di Ugo d'Alvernia allo Inferno.* For published extracts of the Paduan manuscript, see Meregazzi, "L'Episodio del Prete Gianni," 9–10. There is also a fragment of a fourth *Ugo* narrative in lasse: De Bartholomaeis, "La discesa di Ugo d'Alvernia all'Inferno," 3–54. The unedited cantare written by Michelagnolo da Volterra is contained in the manuscript Palatino 82 of the Biblioteca Medicea Laurenziana in Florence. An article describes yet another manuscript found in southern France that contains a second version of the Italian cantare, but I have not been able to locate the codex: Anglade, "Notice sur un manuscrit de *Ugo d'Alvernia,*" 108–16.

9. All citations and quotations from Andrea da Barberino's text refer to the following edition: Zambrini and Bacchi Della Lega, *Storia di Ugone d'Alvernia volgarizzata nel secolo XIV da Andrea da Barberino, non mai fin qui stampata.*

10. For an analysis of this episode in *L'Entrée d'Espagne,* see Bradley-Cromley, *Authority and Autonomy,* 27–54. For the development of the "Ogier en Orient" narratives in fourteenth-century manuscripts, see Togeby's book on Ogier le Danois.

11. All three episodes appear in the three manuscripts that were used as the basis for Zambrini and Bacchi Della Lega's edition of Andrea da Barberino's *Ugo d'Alvernia.* Gloria Allaire, however, recently discovered two manuscripts of Andrea da Barberino's prose *Ugo* that greatly reduce the protagonist's journey to Hell. Allaire has conjectured that the two manuscript traditions represent a reworking of the material by the author rather than the intervention of a scribe. See Allaire, "Due testimoni sconosciuti di Andrea da Barberino," 121–30 and "Un manoscritto rediano," 43–48.

12. For a detailed study of the close similarities between manuscript P and the first part of Andrea da Barberino's *Ugo d'Alvernia,* see Vitale-Brovarone, "De la Chanson de Huon d'Auvergne," 395–96.

13. Manuscript P, fol. 18v. The author of the manuscript P might have made a consistent error when he used this formulaic description. If one replaces "a" with "e" ("to" with "and") in the second verse, the passage makes more sense.

14. Many of Andrea's modifications of the *Ugo* material derive from the commentary tradition. For a discussion of the development of titles in Latin commentaries in the twelfth and thirteenth centuries and the corresponding changes in the practice of producing and reading such texts, see Parkes, "The Influence of the Concepts of *Ordinatio* and *Compilatio* on the Development of the Book," 115–41.

15. Andrea confuses the Carolingian kings Charlemagne (768–814) and Charles le Chauve (843–77) with the Merovingian King Charles Martel (719–41). Charles Martel was probably used in this narrative because of his legendary licentiousness.

16. For a comprehensive discussion of the commentaries of the *Commedia* and their medieval predecessors, see Parker, "The Medieval Roots of Commentary," 25–49.

17. Although Andrea often writes sentences with several clauses, the syntax of his sentences is not as complex as the prose of other vernacular writers of the Trecento, particularly Boccaccio. Andrea's prose is a compromise between the simple style of the earlier epics and the heavily Latinized texts of Boccaccio.

18. M. B. Parkes points out that the realization of these principles of *ordinatio* and *compilatio* in late medieval commentaries led to "fat volumes, embracing as many as possible of the writings of a single *auctor,* and constructed from independent 'booklets' or units." In a similar fashion, Andrea compiled adventures of the Carolingian heroes from various sources and then reorganized them into "fat" epics. See Parkes, "The Influence of the Concepts of *Ordinatio* and *Compilatio* on the Development of the Book," 123.

19. Giovanni Villani describes the need to write such organized, chronological history in the first chapter of his chronicle. See Villani, *Cronica di Giovanni Villani,* 15.

20. See chapter one for an analysis of this ideological tendency.

Chapter 6. Chivalry and Classicism

1. For information about the Carolingian material in the Trevisan March, see Marchesan, *L'Università di Treviso nei secoli XIII e XIV,* 149–57.

2. "Huic autem opinioni argumentum praestat validum Caroli Magni regis filia, quae ab Ugone Alverniae expressissime postulavit amari; ipse tamen, quia alterius eiusdem regis filiae ligabatur amore, ipsam quidem recusavit amare nolens incestus scienter incurrere crimen." Capellanus, *De amore,* 200. Although Capellanus refers to the attempted seduction of Ugo by Sofia, several details differ

in his version. The emperor is Charlemagne instead of Charles Martel, and Ugo is in love with a second daughter of the king rather than with the daughter of another nobleman.

3. This citation is taken from the P manuscript. For a comparison between this description and a similar one in the Berlin manuscript, see the following article: Stengel, "Huon's aus Auvergne," 54. I have checked all of Stengel's transcriptions with a microfilm of the P manuscript.

4. Ironically, the most famous of the so-called Averroists, Siger de Brabant, never mentions the notion of a second truth reached through reason. He clearly states that natural reason has its limits, and if philosophical inquiry contradicts the faith, one must accept the one and only truth: divine revelation. Gilson, *La Philosophie au moyen âge,* 562.

5. Andrea produced another romance epic, *Le Storie Nerbonesi,* based on the French chanson de gestes, *Les Narbonnais,* with numerous additional episodes collected from other epics in the Guillaume cycle.

Epilogue. The Pleasure of Reading and the Power of the Text

1. The cantare is contained in the manuscript Palatino 82 of the Biblioteca Medicea Laurenziana in Florence.

2. For a summary of the debate, see Balduino, "Le misteriose origini dell'ottava rima," 25–47.

3. For a detailed discussion of the various and complex uses of the invocation in the cantare tradition, see Cabani, *Le forme del cantare epico-cavalleresco,* 23–46.

4. The first example occurs on fol. 74r.

5. As previously noted, Gloria Allaire has recently discovered an alternative manuscript tradition of Andrea da Barberino's prose *Ugo* in which the protagonist's journey to Hell is greatly reduced.

Bibliography

Adler, Alfred. "Didactic Concerns in the *Entrée d'Espagne.*" *L'Esprit Createur* 2, 3 (1962): 107–9.
———."The Structural Meaning of *Berta da li pe grandi.*" *Italica* 27 (1950): 101–8.
Allaire, Gloria. *Andrea da Barberino and the Language of Chivalry.* Gainesville: University of Florida Press, 1997.
———. "The Chivalric 'Histories' of Andrea da Barberino." Ph.D. diss., University of Wisconsin, 1993.
———. "Due inediti di Andrea da Barberino nella Biblioteca Palatina di Parma." *Pluteus* 8–9 (1990–98): 19–25.
———. "Due testimoni sconosciuti di Andrea da Barberino nel Codice Barberiniano Latino 4101 della Biblioteca Vaticana." *Pluteus* 6–7 (1988–89): 121–30.
———. "Un frammento di un romanzo sconosciuto di Andrea da Barberino(?)," *Cultura Neolatina* 58, 1–2 (1998): 101–20.
———. "Un manoscritto rediano delle *Storie Nerbonesi* e dell'*Ugone d'Alvernia.*" *Studi e problemi di critica testuale* 47 (1993): 43–48.
———. "Portrayal of Muslims in Andrea da Barberino's *Guerrino il Meschino.*" In *Medieval Christian Perceptions of Islam*, edited by John Tolan, 243–69. New York: Garland Press, 1996.
———. "The Warrior Woman in Late Medieval Prose Epics." *Italian Culture* 12 (1994): 33–43.
Anglade, J. "Notice sur un manuscrit de *Ugo d'Alvernia.*" *Romania* 45 (1918–19): 108–16.
Annales Patavini. Rerum Italicarum Scriptores, vol. 8, 1. Città di Castello: Si Lapi, 1906.
Bakhtin, M. M. *The Dialogic Imagination.* Edited by Michael Holquist. Translated by Caryl Emerson and Michael Holquist. Austin: University of Texas Press, 1981.
———. *Rabelais and His World.* Translated by Hélène Iswolsky. Bloomington: Indiana University Press, 1984.
Balduino, Armando. "Le misteriose origini dell'ottava rima." In *I cantari: struttura*

e tradizione (Atti del convegno internazionale di Montreal: 19–20 marzo 1981), edited by M. Picone and M. Bendinelli Predelli, 25–47. Florence: Olschki, 1984.

Bancourt, Paul. *Les musulmans dans les chansons de geste du cycle du roi.* 2 volumes. Aix en Provence: L'Université de Provence, 1982.

Baranski, Zygmunt G. "La lezione esegetica di Inferno I: allegoria, storia e letteratura nella Commedia." In *Dante e le forme dell'allegoresi,* edited by Michelangelo Picone, 79–97. Ravenna: Longo, 1987.

Bargellini, Piero, ed. *Le prediche volgari.* Milan: Rizzoli, 1936.

Barthes, Roland. *Mythologies.* Translated by Annette Lavers. New York: Hill & Wang, 1972.

Bartra, Roger. *Wild Men in the Looking Glass: The Mythic Origins of European Otherness.* Translated by Carl T. Berrisford. Ann Arbor: University of Michigan Press, 1994.

Bäuml, Franz H. "Medieval Texts and the Two Theories of Oral-Formulaic Composition: A Proposal for a Third Theory." *New Literary History* 16 (1984–85): 31–49.

———. "Varieties and Consequences of Medieval Literacy and Illiteracy." *Speculum* 55 (1980): 237–65.

Beer, Marina. *Romanzi di cavalleria: Il "Furioso" e il romanzo italiano del primo Cinquecento.* Rome: Bulzoni, 1987.

Bellomo, Manlio. *Ricerche sui rapporti patrimoniali tra coniugi: Contributo all storia della famiglia medievale.* Milan: Giuffrè, 1961.

Bender, Karl, "Les métamorphoses de la royauté de Charlemagne dans les premières épopées franco-italiennes." *Cultura Neolatina* 21 (1961): 164–74.

Bendinelli Predelli, Maria. "La donna guerriera nell'immaginario italiano del tardo medioevo." *Italian Culture* 12 (1994): 3–31.

Bernheimer, Richard. *Wild Men in the Middle Ages.* Cambridge: Harvard University Press, 1952.

Bertoni, Giulio. *La Biblioteca estense e la coltura ferrarese ai tempi del duca Ercole I (1471–1505).* Turin: Loescher, 1903.

———."Notizie sugli amanuensi degli Estensi nel Quattrocento." *Archivum romanicum* 2 (1918): 29–57.

Bettarini-Bruni, Anna. "Intorno ai cantari di Antonio Pucci." In *I cantari: struttura e tradizione (Atti del convegno internazionale di Montreal: 19–20 marzo 1981)*, edited by M. Picone and M. Bendinelli Predelli, 143–60. Florence: Olschki, 1984.

Bhabha, Homi K. "The Other Question . . ." *Screen* 24, 6 (November–December 1983): 18–36.

Bloch, R. Howard. *Etymologies and Genealogies: A Literary Anthropology of the French Middle Ages.* Chicago: University of Chicago Press, 1983.

Boccaccio, Giovanni. *De mulieribus claris.* In *Opere in versi,* edited by Pier Giorgio Ricci, 705–83. La letteratura italiana: storia e testi, vol. 9. Milan: Ricciardi, 1965.

———. *Decameron.* Edited by Vittore Branca. Turin: Einaudi, 1980.

Boer, Inge. "This is not the orient: theory and postcolonial practice." In *the point of theory*, edited by Mieke Bal and Inge Boer, 211–19. New York: Continuum, 1994.

Boni, M., "I manoscritti marciani della *Chanson d'Aspremont* e *l'Aspramonte* di Andrea da Barberino." *Convivium* 17.2 (1949): 253–72.

Boswell, John E. "Dante and the Sodomites." *Dante Studies* 112 (1994): 63–76.

Bradley-Cromey, Nancy. *Authority and Autonomy in "L'Entrée d'Espagne."* New York: Garland, 1993.

Braghirolli, Willelmo. "Inventaire des manuscrits en langue française possédés par Francesco Gonzaga I, Capitaine de Mantoue, mort en 1407." *Romania* 9 (1880): 497–514.

Branca, Vittore, ed. *Mercanti scrittori: Ricordi nella Firenze tra medioevo e rinascimento*. Milan: Rusconi, 1986.

———. "Notizie di manoscritti: Un poemetto inedito di Andrea da Barberino?" *Lettere italiane* (January–March 1990): 89–90.

Brattö, Olof. *Studi di antroponimia fiorentina. Il libro di Montaperti (An. MCCLX)*. Göteborg: Elanders Boktryckeri Aktiebolag, 1953.

Brown, Alison. "The Guelf Party in 15th-Century Florence: The Transition from Communal to Medicean State." *Rinascimento* ser. 2, vol. 20 (1980): 41–86.

Brown, Judith. "A Woman's Place Was in the Home: Women's Work in Renaissance Tuscany." In *Rewriting the Renaissance: The Discourses of Sexual Difference in Early Modern Europe*, edited by Margaret W. Ferguson, Maureen Quilligan, and Nancy J. Vickers, 206–24. Chicago: University of Chicago Press, 1986.

Brucker, Gene. *The Civic World of Early Renaissance Florence*. Princeton: Princeton University Press, 1977.

Bruns, Gerald. "What Is tradition?" *New Literary History* 22, 1 (Winter 1991): 1–21.

Burgess, Glyn S., and Anne Elizabeth Cobby, ed. and trans. *The Pilgrimage of Charlemagne and Aucassin and Nicolette*. New York: Garland, 1988.

Butler, Judith. "Performative Acts and Gender Constitution." In *Performing Feminisms: Feminist Critical Theory and Theatre*, edited by Sue-Ellen Case, 270–82. Baltimore: Johns Hopkins University Press, 1990.

Cabani, Maria Cristina. *Le forme del cantare epico-cavalleresco*. Lucca: Fazzi, 1988.

Calin, William. *The Old French Epic of Revolt: Raoul de Cambrai, Renaud de Montauban, Gormond et Isembard*. Geneva: Droz, 1962.

Cannarozzi, C., ed. *Le prediche volgari*. 7 vols. Pistoia: Tip. Cav. Alberto Pacinotti, 1934.

Capitani, Ovidio, "Dal comune alla signoria." In *Storia d'Italia. Comuni e Signorie: Istituzioni, società e lotte per l'egemonia*, vol. 4, edited by G. Galasso, 137–78. Turin: UTET, 1981.

Capellanus, Andreas. *De amore*. Edited by E. Trojel. Munich: Max Niemeyer Verlag, 1964.

Cappelli, A. "La Biblioteca Estense nella prima metà del sec. XV," *Giornale storico della letteratura italiana* 14 (1889): 1–30.
Cardini, Franco. "'Nobiltà' e cavalleria nei centri urbani: problemi e interpretazioni." In *Nobiltà e ceti dirigenti in Toscana nei secoli XI–XII: Strutture e concetti,* 13–28. Florence: Papafava, 1982.
Catalano, Michele. "La data di morte di Andrea da Barberino." *Archivum romanicum* 23 (1939): 84–87.
Chojnacki, Stanley. "Subaltern Patriarchs: Patrician Bachelors in Renaissance Venice." In *Medieval Masculinities: Regarding Men in the Middle Ages,* edited by Clare A. Lees, 73–90. Minneapolis: University of Minnesota Press, 1994.
Compagni, Dino. *Cronica.* Edited by Gino Luzzatto. Turin: Einaudi, 1968.
Cook, Robert. "'Méchants romans' et épopée française: pour une philologie profonde." *L'Esprit Createur* (Spring 1983): 64–74.
Corazzini, G. "Diario Fiorentino di Bartolommeo di Michele del Corazza (Anni 1405–1438)." *Archivio storico italiano* 14 (1894): 233–98.
Corti, Maria. *Il viaggio testuale. Le ideologie e le strutture semiotiche.* Turin: Einaudi, 1978.
———. "Modelli e antimodelli nella cultura medievale." *Strumenti Critici* 12 (1978): 3–30.
Cremonesi, Carla, ed., *Berta da li piè grandi: Codice Marciano XIII.* Milan: Varese, 1966.
———. *Berta e Milon—Rolandin.* Milan: Goliardica, 1973.
———. *Le Danois Oger. Enfances-Chevalerie.* Milan: Goliardica, 1977.
Cristiani, Emilio. "Sul valore politico del cavalierato nella Firenze dei secoli XIII e XIV." *Studi Medievali* 3 (1962): 365–71.
Da Barberino, Andrea. *L'Aspramonte.* Edited by Luigi Cavalli. Naples: Fulvio Rossi, 1972.
———. *I Reali di Francia.* Edited by Giuseppe Vandelli and Giovanni Gamberin. Bari: Laterza, 1947.
———. *Storia di Ugone d'Avernia volgarizzata nel secolo XIV da Andrea da Barberino, non mai fin qui stampata.* Edited by F. Zambrini and A. Bacchi Della Lega. 2 vols. Bologna: Romagnoli, 1882.
———. *Le Storie Nerbonesi: romanzo cavalleresco del secolo XIV.* Edited by I. G. Isola. Bologna: Romagnoli, 1887.
Da Pisa, Guido. *I fatti di Enea.* Edited by Francesco Foffano. Florence: Sansoni, 1900.
Da Verona, Raffaele. *Aquilon de Bavière: Roman franco-italien en prose (1379–1407).* Edited by Peter Wunderli. 2 volumes. Tübingen: Max Niemeyer Verlag, 1982.
Daniel, Norman. *Islam and the West: The Making of an Image.* Edinburgh: Edinburgh University Press, 1960.
Dante Alighieri. *La Divina Commedia.* Edited by C. H. Grandgent, revised by Charles S. Singleton. Cambridge: Harvard University Press, 1972.
———. *Il Convivio.* Edited by Maria Simonelli. Bologna: Pàtron, 1966.
De Bartholomaeis, Vincenzo. "La discesa di Ugo d'Alvernia all'Inferno secondo

il frammento di Giovanni Maria Barbieri." *Memorie della R. Accademia delle Scienze dell'Istituto di Bologna, Classe di scienze morali* 2, 10 (1925–26): 3–54.
De Gaiffer, Baudoin. "La Légende de Charlemagne. Le péché de l'empereur et son pardon." In *Recueil de travaux offert à M. Clovis Brunel. Mémoires et documents publiés par la société de l'école de Chartes* 12, vol. 1, 490–503. Paris: Société de l'école de Chartes, 1955.
De Mandach, André. "Sur les traces de la cheville ouvrière de l'*Entrée d'Espagne*: Giovanni di Nono." In *Testi, cotesti e contesti del franco-italiano,* edited by Günter Holtus, Henning Krauss, and Peter Wunderli, 48–64. Tübingen, Max Niemeyer Verlag, 1989.
De Marco Torgovnick, Marianna. "The Godfather." In *Crossing Ocean Parkway,* 109–36. Chicago: University of Chicago Press, 1994.
Delbouille, Maurice. "Les chansons de geste et le livre." In *La technique littéraire des chansons de geste,* 295–407. Paris: Les Belles Lettres, 1959.
Delcorno Branca, Daniela. "Fortuna e trasformazioni del *Buovo d'Antona.*" In *Testi, cotesti e contesti del franco-italiano,* edited by Günter Holtus, Henning Krauss, and Peter Wunderli, 285–306. Tübingen: Max Niemeyer Verlag, 1989.
———. *Romanzo cavalleresco medievale.* Florence: Sansoni, 1974.
Dinshaw, Carolyn. "Chaucer's Queer Touches/A Queer Touches Chaucer." *Exemplaria* 7, 1 (1995): 75–92.
Dionisotti, C. "*Entrée d'Espagne, Spagna, Rotta di Roncisvalle.*" In *Studi in onore di Angelo Monteverdi,* edited by G. G. Marcuzzo. Vol. 1, 207–41. Modena: Società Tipografica Editrice Modenese, 1959.
Douglas, Mary. *Purity and Danger: An Analysis of Concepts of Pollution and Taboo.* London: Routledge, 1966.
Duby, Georges. *La société chevaleresque.* Paris: Flammarion, 1988.
Eckhardt, Alexandre. "Le cercueil flottant de Mahomet." In *Mélanges de philologie romane et de littérature médiévale offerts à Ernest Hoepffner par ses élèves et ses amis.* Reprint, Geneva: Slatkine, 1974.
Eusebi, Mario, ed. *La chevalerie d'Ogier de Danemarche.* Milan: Varese, 1963.
Fassò, Andrea, ed. *Cantari d'Aspramonte (inediti) (Magl. VII 682).* Bologna: Commissione per i testi di lingua, 1981.
———. "La materia di Francia nei poemi e nei romanzi italiani." In *Sulle orme di Orlando: leggende e luoghi carolingi in Italia,* edited by Anna Imelde Galletti and Roberto Rodi, 65–81. Padua: Interbooks, 1987.
Folena, G., "La cultura volgare dell'umanesimo cavalleresco nel Veneto." In *Umanesimo europeo e umanesimo veneziano,* edited by Vittore Branca, 141–58. Florence: Sansoni, 1963.
Foligno, C. "Epistole inedite di Lovato de' Lovati e d'altri a lui." *Studi Medievali* 2 (1906): 37–58.
Folz, Robert. "Charlemagne en Allemagne." In *Charlemagne et l'épopée romane,* Actes du VIIe Congrès International de la Société Rencesvals, vol. 1, 77–101. Paris: Les Belles Lettres, 1978.
Franceschetti, Antonio. "Saracens in Early Italian Chivalric Literature." In *Ro-

mance Epic: Essays on a Medieval Literary Genre, edited by Hans-Erich Keller, 203–11. Kalamazoo: Medieval Institute Publications, 1987.
Friedman, John Block. *The Monstrous Races in Medieval Art and Thought.* Cambridge: Harvard University Press, 1981.
Friscia, Alberto. "Le Personnage de Rainourt au Tinel dans la *Chansons d'Aliscans.*" *Annales de l'Université de Grenoble* 21 (1909): 43–98.
Gadamer, Hans-Georg. *Truth and Method.* Translated by Joel Weinsheimer and Donald G. Marshall. New York: Crossroad, 1989.
Garber, Marjorie. *Vested Interests: Cross-Dressing & Cultural Anxiety.* New York: Routledge, 1992.
Gasparri, Stefano. *I milites cittadini. Studi sulla cavalleria in Italia.* Rome: Istituto Storico Italiano Per Il Medio Evo, 1992.
Gautier, Léon. *Les Épopées françaises. Étude sur les origines et l'histoire de la littérature nationale.* 1892. Reprint, Osnabrück: Otto Zeller, 1966.
Gellrich, Jesse. "Orality, Literacy, and Crisis in the Later Middle Ages." *Philological Quarterly* 67 (Fall 1988): 461–73.
Giacon, Carla. "La redazione padovana dell'*Huon d'Auvergne:* studio, edizione, glossario." Tesi di laurea, Università degli Studi di Padova, 1960–61.
Gilson, Etienne. *La Philosophie au moyen-âge.* Paris: Payot, 1962.
Goldmann, Lucien. "The Genetic-Structuralist Method in the History of Literature." In *Towards a Sociology of the Novel,* translated by Alan Sheridan, 156–71. London: Tavistock, 1975.
Gorra, Egidio. *Testi inediti di Storia Trojana preceduti da uno studio sulla leggenda trojana in Italia.* Turin: Loescher, 1887.
Green, D. H. "Orality and Reading: The State of Research in Medieval Studies." *Speculum* 65 (April 1990): 267–80.
Greenblatt, Stephen. "Towards a Poetics of Culture." In *The New Historicism,* edited by Aram Veeser, 1–14. New York: Routledge, 1989.
Grendler, Paul F. "Chivalric Romances in the Italian Renaissance." In *Studies in Medieval and Renaissance History,* edited by J.A.S. Evans and R. W. Unger, 59–102. New York: AMS, 1988.
———. *Schooling in Renaissance Italy:* Literacy and Learning, 1300–1600. Baltimore: Johns Hopkins University Press, 1989.
Grignani, Maria A., ed. *Navigatio Sancti Brendani/La navigazione di San Brandano.* Milan: Bompiani, 1975.
Guessard, F., and S. Luce. *Gaydon, chanson de geste publiée pour la première fois d'après les trois manuscrits de Paris.* Anciens Poètes de la France, vol. 7. 1862. Reprint, Nendeln: Krauss, 1966.
Haidu, Peter. *The Subject of Violence: The "Song of Roland" and the Birth of the State.* Bloomington: Indiana University Press, 1993.
Hayes, Colleen. "French Medieval Literature in the Nineteenth Century: A Nationalist Perspective." Paper presented at the conference "Reinventing the Middle Ages and the Renaissance: Constructions of the Medieval and Early Modern Periods," Arizona State University, February 1995.

Hays, Dennis, and John Law. *Italy in the Age of the Renaissance 1380–1530.* London: Longman, 1989.

Heers, Jacques. *Le clan familial au moyen-âge.* Paris: Presses Universitaires de France, 1974.

Herbin, Jean-Charles, ed. *Hervis de Mes.* Geneva: Droz, 1992.

Herlihy, David, and Christiane Klapisch-Zuber. *Tuscans and Their Families: A Study of the Florentine Catasto of 1427.* New Haven: Yale University Press, 1978.

Hiestand, Ruldolf. "Aspetti politici e sociali dell'Italia settentrionale dalla morte di Federico II alla metà del '300. In *Testi, cotesti e contesti del franco-veneto,* edited by Günter Holtus, Henning Krauss, and Peter Wunderli, 27–47. Tübingen: Max Niemeyer Verlag, 1979.

Holtus, Günter. "Lessico franco-italiano = lessico francese e/o lessico italiano." *Medioevo romanzo* 10 (1985): 249–56.

———. *La versione franco-italiana della "Bataille d'Aliscans": Codex Marcianus fr. VIII [=252].* Tübingen: Max Niemeyer Verlag, 1985.

Horrent, Jacques. "L'histoire légendaire de Charlemagne en Espagne." In *Charlemagne et l'épopée romane,* Actes du VIIe Congrès International de la Société Rencesvals, vol. 1, 125–56. Paris: Les Belles Lettres, 1978.

Husband, Timothy. *The Wild Man: Medieval Myth and Symbolism.* New York: The Metropolitan Museum of Art, 1980.

Hyde, J. K. "Contemporary Views on Faction and Civil Strife in Thirteenth- and Fourteenth-Century Italy." In *Violence and Civil Disorder in Italian Cities 1200–1500,* edited by Lauro Martines, 273–307. Berkeley: University of California Press, 1972.

———. *Padua in the Age of Dante.* New York: Barnes & Noble, 1966.

———. *Society and Politics in Medieval Italy: The Evolution of the Civil Life, 1000–1350.* London: Macmillan, 1973.

Jameson, Fredric. *The Political Unconscious: Narrative as a Socially Symbolic Act.* Ithaca: Cornell University Press, 1981.

Jauss, Hans Robert. *Toward an Aesthetic of Reception.* Translated by Timothy Bahti. Minneapolis: University of Minnesota Press, 1982.

Jones, Catherine M. *The Noble Merchant: Problems of Genre and Lineage in "Hervis de Mes."* Chapel Hill: University of North Carolina Press, 1993.

Jones, Philip. *Economia e società nell'Italia medievale.* Turin: Einaudi, 1980.

Jordan, Constance. "Boccaccio's In-Famous Women." In *Ambiguous Realities: Women in the Middle Ages and Renaissance,* edited by Carole Levin and Jeanie Watson, 25–47. Detroit: Wayne State University Press, 1987.

Joseph Benson, Pamela. "Boccaccio's *De mulieribus claris*: An Ambiguous Beginning." In *The Invention of the Renaissance Woman: The Challenge of Female Independence in the Literature and Thought of Italy and England,* 9–31. University Park: Pennsylvania State University Press, 1992.

Kay, Richard. *Dante's Swift and Strong: Essays on Inferno XV.* Lawrence: Regents Press of Kansas, 1978.

Keen, Maurice. *Chivalry.* New Haven: Yale University Press, 1984.

Keller, Hans-Erich. "The *Mises en prose* and the Court of Burgundy." *Fifteenth-Century Studies* 10 (1984): 91–103.

———. "Le péché de Charlemagne." In *L'imaginaire courtois et son double,* Actes du VIe Congrès de la Société Internationale de Littérature Courtoise, 39–54. Naples: Edizioni Scientifiche Italiane, 1991.

Kelly (-Gadol), Joan. "Did Women Have a Renaissance?" In *Women, History, and Theory: The Essays of Joan Kelly,* edited by Catherine R. Stimpson, 19–50. Chicago: University of Chicago Press, 1984.

Kent, Dale. "The Florentine *Reggimento* in the Fifteenth Century." *Renaissance Quarterly* 23 (Winter 1975): 575–638.

Kent, Francis William. "La famiglia patrizia fiorentina nel Quattrocento. Nuovi orientamenti nella storiografia recente." In *Palazzo Strozzi metà millenio 1489–1989. Atti del Convegno di Studi (Firenze 3–6 luglio 1989),* edited by Paola Gori, 70–91. Rome: Istituto della Enciclopedia Italiana, 1991.

———. *Household and Lineage in Renaissance Florence: The Family Life of the Capponi, Ginori, and Rucellai.* Princeton: Princeton University Press, 1977.

Kinoshita, Sharon. "The Politics of Courtly Love: *La Prise d'Orange* and the Conversion of the Saracen Queen." *The Romance Review* 86, 2 (1995): 265–87.

Kittay, Jeffrey, and Wald Godzich. *The Emergence of Prose: An Essay in Prosaics.* Minneapolis: University of Minnesota Press, 1987.

Klapisch-Zuber, Christiane. "'Kin, Friends, and Neighbors': The Urban Territory of a Merchant Family in 1400." In *Women, Family and Ritual in Renaissance Italy,* translated by Lydia G. Cochrane, 68–93. Chicago: University of Chicago Press, 1985.

Krauss, Henning. *L'Epica feudale e pubblico borghese.* Translated by Andrea Fassò. Padua: Liviana, 1980.

———. "Ezzelino da Romano—Maximo Çudé—Historische Realität und epischer Strukturzwang in der frankoitalienischen *Chevalerie Ogier.*" *Cultura Neolatina* 30 (1970): 233–49.

———. "Ritter und Bürger—Feudalheer und Volksheer: Zum Problem der feigen Lombarden in der altfranzösischen und frankoitalienischen Epik," *Zeitschrift für romanische Philologie* 87 (1971): 209–22.

———. "Von Varocher zu Ispinardo." In *Das Epos in der Romania. Festschrift für Dieter Kremers zum 65. Geburtstag,* edited by Susanne Knaller and Edith Mara, 193–205. Tübingen: Gunter Narr, 1986.

Kristeva, Julia. *Strangers to Ourselves.* Translated by Leon S. Roudiez. New York: Columbia University Press, 1991.

Kruger, Steven. "Racial/Religious and Sexual Queerness in the Middle Ages." *Medieval Feminist Newsletter* 16 (Fall 1993): 32–36.

Krygier, Martin. "Tipologia della tradizione." *Intersezioni* 5, 2 (1985): 221–49.

Kuehn, Thomas. "Il diritto di famiglia e l'uso del diritto nelle famiglie fiorentine nel Rinascimento." In *Palazzo Strozzi metà millenio 1489–1989: Atti del Convegno di Studi (Firenze, 3–6 luglio 1989),* edited by Paola Gori, 108–25. Rome: Istituto della Enciclopedia Italiana, 1991.

———. *Law, Family, and Women: Toward a Legal Anthropology of Renaissance Italy.* Chicago: University of Chicago Press, 1991.
Labalme, Patricia, ed. *Beyond Their Sex: Learned Women of the European Past.* New York: New York University Press, 1980.
Langlois, Ernest, ed. *Le couronnement de Louis.* Paris: Champion, 1984.
Langmuir, Gavin I. *Toward a Definition of Antisemitism.* Berkeley: University of California Press, 1990.
Lansing, Carol. *The Florentine Magnates: Lineage and Faction in a Medieval Commune.* Princeton: Princeton University Press, 1991.
Lansing, Richard H., trans. *Dante's "Il Convivio" ("The Banquet").* New York: Garland, 1990.
Larner, John. "Chivalric Culture in the Age of Dante." *Renaissance Studies* 2 (October 1988): 117–30.
———. *Italy in the Age of Dante and Petrarch (1216–1380).* London: Longman, 1980.
Latini, Brunetto. *Li livres dou Tresor.* Edited by F. J. Carmody. 1948. Reprint, Geneva: Slatkine Reprints, 1975.
———. "Il Tesoretto." In *Poeti del Duecento,* vol. 2, edited by Gianfranco Contini, 175–277. Milan: Ricciardi, 1960.
Latour, Bruno. "Visualization and Cognition: Thinking with Eyes and Hands." *Knowledge and Society: Studies in the Sociology of Culture Past and Present* 6 (1986): 1–40.
Le Goff, Jacques. *Histoire de la France urbaine.* Vol. 2. Paris: Seuil, 1980.
Lejeune, Rita, and Jacques Stiennon. *La Légende de Roland dans l'art du moyen-âge.* 2 vols. Bruxelles: Arcade, 1967.
Lestocquoy, J. *Patriciens du moyen-âge: Les dynasties bourgeoises d'Arras du XIe au XVe siècle.* Arras: Nouvelle Société du Pas-de-Calais, 1945.
Levi, Ezio. "I cantari leggendari del popolo italiano nei secoli XIV e XV." *Giornale storico della letteratura italiana* 16 (1914): 1–171.
Limentani, Alberto. "Il comico nell'*Entrée d'Espagne* e il suo divenire una preghiera en 'la lois aufricaine.'" In *Interpretation. Das Paradigma der europäischen Renaissance-Literatur. Festschrift für Alfred Noyer-Weidner zum 60. Geburtstag,* edited by Klaus W. Hempfer and Gerhard Regn, 61–82. Wiesbaden: Max Niemeyer Verlag, 1983.
———. "L'Epica in 'lengue de France': l'*Entrée d'Espagne* e Niccolò da Verona." In *Storia della cultura veneta dalle origini al Trecento,* vol. 2, edited by Gianfranco Folena, 338–68. Vicenza: Pozza, 1976.
———. "Il racconto epico: funzioni della lassa e dell'ottava." In *I cantari: struttura e tradizione (Atti del convegno internazionale di Montreal: 19–20 marzo 1981),* edited by M. Picone and M. Bendinelli Predelli, 49–74. Florence: Olschki, 1984.
Limentani, Alberto, and Marco Infurna, eds. *L'Epica.* Bologna: Il Mulino, 1986.
Luzzatto, Gino. "Tramonto e sopravvivenza del feudalismo nei comuni italiani del medio evo," *Studi Medievali* 3 (1962): 410–19.
Manuscript 32 of the Biblioteca Del Seminario Vescovile di Padova.
Manuscript Palatino 82 of the Biblioteca Medicea Laurenziana.

Manuscript Palatino 101, vol. 2, of the Biblioteca Medicea Laurenziana.
Manuscript 1904 of the Biblioteca Riccardiana.
Manuscript 2226 of the Biblioteca Riccardiana.
Maracchi Biagiarelli, Berta. "L'Armadiaccio di Padre Stradino." *La Bibliofilia* 84 (1982): 51–57.
Marchesan, Angelo. *L'Università di Treviso nei secoli XIII e XIV e cenni di storia civile e letteraria della città in quei tempi.* Treviso: Turazza, 1902.
Martines, Lauro. *Power and Imagination. City-states in Renaissance Italy.* New York: Knopf, 1979.
Masaro, Carla. "Un episodio della cultura libraria volgare nella Firenze medicea: la biblioteca dello Stradino (1480 cs.-1549)." *Alfabetismo e cultura scritta* (forthcoming): n.p.
Mazzi, Maria Serena. *Prostitute e lenoni nella Firenze del Quattrocento.* Milan: Mondadori, 1991.
Meek, Mary Elizabeth, trans. *Historia Destructionis Troiae by Guido delle Colonne.* Bloomington: Indiana University Press, 1974.
Melli, Elio, ed. *I Cantari di Rinaldo da Monte Albano.* Bologna: Commissione per i testi di lingua, 1973.
———. "I 'Cantari di Rinaldo' e l'epica francese." *Atti della Accademia delle Scienze dell'Istituto di Bologna, Classe di scienze morali, Rendiconti* 57 (1968–69): 102–56.
Meregazzi, Luisa A. "L'Episodio del Prete Gianni nell'Ugo d'Alvernia." *Studi Romanzi* 26 (1935): 1–69.
———. "L'Ugo d'Alvernia: poema franco-italiano." *Studi Romanzi* 27 (1937): 1–87.
Meyer, P. "De l'expansion de la langue française en Italie pendant le moyen-âge." In *Atti del Congresso Internazionale di Scienze Storiche*, vol. 4, 61–104. Rome: Tipografia della R. Accademia dei Lincei, 1903.
Minnis, A. J. "Literary Theory and Literary Practice." In *Medieval Theory of Authorship*, 160–210. Philadelphia: University of Pennsylvania Press, 1988.
Minutoli, Carlo, ed. *Storia di Rinaldino da Montalbano: Romanzo cavalleresco in prosa.* Bologna: Romagnoli, 1865.
Mirrer, Louise. "Representing 'Other' Men: Muslims, Jews, and Masculine Ideals in Medieval Castilian Epic and Ballad." In *Medieval Masculinities: Regarding Men in the Middle Ages,* edited by Clare A. Lees. Minneapolis: University of Minnesota Press, 1994.
Moore, R. I. *The Formation of a Persecuting Society: Power and Deviance in Western Europe, 950–1250.* Oxford: Basil Blackwell, 1987.
Morgan, Leslie. "Berta ai piedi grandi." *Olifant* 19, 1–2 (Fall 1994-Winter 1995): 37–56.
———. "*Bovo d'Antona* in the *Geste Francor* (V13): Unity of Composition and Clan Destiny." *Italian Culture* 16, 2 (1998): 15–38.
Murray, Alexander. *Reason and Society in the Middle Ages.* Oxford: Oxford University Press, 1978.

Mussafia, Adolf, ed., *Altfranzösiche Gedichte aus venezianischen Handschriften. Prise de Pampelune.* Vol. 1. Vienna: Druck und Verlag von Gerold's John, 1864.
Newth, Michael A., trans. *The Song of Alivcans.* New York: Garland, 1992.
Nichols, Stephen. "Augustine and the Troubadour Lyric." In *Vox intexta: Orality and Textuality in the Middle Ages,* edited by A. N. Doane and Carol Braun Pasternack, 137–61. Madison: University of Wisconsin Press, 1991.
Ong, Walter J. *Interfaces of the Word.* Ithaca: Cornell University Press, 1977.
———. *Orality and Literacy: The Technologizing of the Word.* London: Methuen, 1982.
Osella, Gicaomo. "Su Andrea da Barberino." *Convivium* 2 (1942): 363–80.
Ottokar, Nicola. *Il Comune di Firenze alla fine del Dugento.* 1926. Reprint, Turin: Einaudi, 1962.
Paris, Gaston. *Histoire poétique de Charlemagne.* 1905. Reprint, Geneva: Slatkine Reprints, 1974.
Parker, Deborah. "The Medieval Roots of Commentary in the Renaissance." In *Commentary and Ideology: Dante in the Renaissance,* 25–49. Durham: Duke University Press, 1993.
Parkes, Malcolm B. "The Influence of the Concepts of *Ordinatio* and *Compilatio* on the Development of the Book." In *Medieval Learning and Literature: Essays Presented to Richard William Hunt,* edited by J.J.G. Alexander and M. T. Gibson, 115–41. Oxford: Clarendon Press, 1976.
Pasero, Nicolò. "Niveaux de culture dans les chansons de geste." In *Essor et fortune de la chanson de geste dans l'Europe et l'Orient latin,* Actes du IXe Congrès International de la Société Rencesvals pour l'Étude des Épopées Romanes, vol. 1, 3–25. Modena: Mucchi, 1984.
Petrucci, Armando. *Writers and Readers in Medieval Italy: Studies in the History of Written Culture.* Edited and translated by Charles M. Radding. New Haven: Yale University Press, 1995.
Picone, Michelangelo. "Strutture poetiche e strutture prosastiche nella *Vita Nuova.*" *Modern Language Notes* 92 (1977): 117–29.
Picone, Michelangelo, and M. Benedinelli Predelli, eds., *I cantari: Struttura e tradizione. Atti del convegno internazionale di Montreal: 19–20 1981* (Florence: Olschki, 1984).
Pini, Antonio I. "Dal comune città-stato al comune ente amministrativo." In *Storia d'Italia—Comuni e signorie: istituzioni, società e lotte per l'egemonia,* vol. 4, edited by G. Galasso, 451–587. Turin: UTET, 1981.
Piron, Maurice. "Le cycle carolingien dans les traditions du pays de Liège." In *Charlemagne et l'épopée romane,* Actes du VIIe Congrès International de la Société Rencesvals, vol. 1, 177–88. Paris: Les Belles Lettres, 1978.
Rajna, Pio. "Due frammenti di romanzi cavallereschi," *Rivista di filologia romanza* 1 (1872): 163–78.
———. *Le fonti dell'Orlando Furioso.* 1900. Reprint, Florence: Sansoni, 1975.
———. "L'onomastica italiana e l'epopea carolingia," *Romania* 18 (1889): 1–69.

———. "Le origini delle famiglie padovane e gli eroi dei romanzi cavallereschi." *Romania* 4 (1875): 161–83.

———. *Ricerche intorno ai Reali di Francia per P.R., seguite dal Libro delle storie di Fioravante e dal Cantare di Bovo d'Antona*. Bologna: Collezione di opere inedite o rare dei primi tre secoli della lingua, 1872.

———. "Rinaldo da Montalbano." *Il Propugnatore* 3,2 (1870): 58–127, 213–41.

———."La rotta di Roncisvalle nella letteratura cavalleresca italiana," *Il Propugnatore* 3, 2 (1870): 384–409; 4, 1 (1871): 52–78, 333–90; 4, 2 (1871): 52–133.

Renier, R. *La discesa di Ugo d'Alvernia allo Inferno, secondo il codice franco-italiano della Nazionale di Torino*. Scelta di curiosità letterarie inedite o rare, vol. 194. Bologna: Romagnoli, 1883.

Renzi, Lorenzo. "Il francese come lingua letteraria e il franco-lombardo. L'Epica carolingia nel Veneto." In *La Storia della cultura veneta dalle origini al Trecento*, vol. 1, edited by Gianfranco Folena, 563–89. Vincenza: Pozza, 1976.

Richards, Jeffrey. *Sex, Dissidence and Damnation: Minority Groups in the Middle Ages*. New York: Routledge, 1990.

Rocke, Michael. *Forbidden Friendships: Homosexuality and Male Culture in Renaissance Florence*. New York: Oxford University Press, 1996.

Roncaglia, Aurelio. "Rolando e il peccato di Carlomagno." In *Symposium in onorem Prof. M. de Riquer*, 315–47. Barcelona: Quaderns Crema, 1986.

Rosellini, Aldo, ed. *La "Geste Francor" di Venezia. Edizione integrale del Codice XIII del Fondo francese della Marciana*. Brescia: La Scuola, 1986.

Rosmarin, Adena. *The Power of Genre*. Minneapolis: University of Minnesota Press, 1985.

Rossi, Marguerite. *Huon de Bordeaux et l'évolution du genre épique au XIIIe siècle*. Paris: Champion, 1975.

Rubin, Miri. "The Eucharist and the Construction of Medieval Identities." In *Culture and History 1350–1600*, edited by David Aers, 43–63. New York: Harvester Wheatsheaf, 1992.

Ruggieri, Ruggero, ed. *Li Fatti de Spagna: Testo settentrionale trecentesco già detto "Viaggio di Carlo Magno in Ispagna."* Modena: Società Tipografica Modenese, 1951.

———. "Les Lombards dans les chansons de geste." In *Actes et Memoires du Société Rencesvals IVe Congrès International*, 37–45. Heidelberg: Carl Winter, 1969.

———. *L'Umanesimo cavalleresco italiano da Dante all'Ariosto*. Naples: Fratelli Conte, 1977.

Rychner, J. *La chanson de geste. Essai sur l'art épique des jongleurs*. Genève-Lille: Droz, 1955.

Sacchetti, Franco. *Il Trecentonovelle*. Edited by Emilio Faccioli. Turin: Einaudí, 1970.

Said, Edward. *Orientalism*. New York: Vintage Books, 1979.

Sainte-Maure, Benoît de. *Le Roman de Troie*. Edited by Léopold Constans, vol. 4. 1908. Reprint, New York: Johnson Reprint Corp., 1968.

Salvemini, Gaetano. *La dignità cavalleresca nel Comune di Firenze e altri scritti*. Edited by Ernesto Sestan. 1896. Reprint, Milan: Feltrinelli, 1972.

Schiesari, Juliana. "For a Genealogy of Gender Morals in Renaissance Women," *Annali d'Italianistica* 7 (1989): 66–87.

Segre, Cesare. *La Chanson de Roland*. Milan: Ricciardi, 1971.

———. *Semiotica, storia, e cultura*. Padua: Liviana, 1977.

———. *La Tradizione della "Chanson de Roland."* Milan: Ricciardi, 1974.

Simpson Shen, Lucia. "The Old-French 'Enfances' and Their Audience." Ph.D. diss., University of Pennsylvania, 1982.

Sinclair, Keith V., ed. *Tristan de Nanteuil, chanson de geste inédite*. Assen: Van Gorcum, 1971.

———. *Tristan de Nanteuil: Thematic Infrastructure and Literary Creation*. Tübingen: Max Niemeyer Verlag, 1983.

Solterer, Helen. "Figures of Female Militancy in Medieval France." *Signs* 16, 3 (1991): 522–49.

Stallybrass, Peter, and Allon White. *The Politics and Poetics of Transgression*. London: Methuen, 1986.

Starn, Randolph. "Reinventing Heroes in Renaissance Italy." *Journal of Interdisciplinary History* 17, 1 (Summer 1986): 67–84.

Stengel, Edmund. "Huon's aus Auvergne Höllenfahrt nach der Berliner und Paduaner Hs." *Festschrift der Universität Greifswald* (May 1908): 1–85.

———. "Huons Suche nach dem Hölleneingang." *Festschrift der Universität Greifswald* (1912): 1–51.

———. "Huons von Auvergne Keuschheitsprobe." In *Mélanges de philologie romane e d'histoire littéraire offerts à M. Maurice Wilmotte*, 685–713. Paris: Honoré, 1910.

———. "Karl Martels Entführung in die Hölle und Wilhem Capets Wahl zu seinem Nachfolger: Stelle aus der Chanson von Huon d'Auvergne nach der Berliner Hs." In *Studi letterari e linguistici dedicati a Pio Rajna*, 873–91. Florence: Ariani, 1911.

———. "Roms Befreiung durch Huon d'Auvergne und dessen Tod." In *Miscellanea di studi critici in onore di Vincenzo Crescini*, 267–90. Turin: Bottega d'Erasmo, 1927.

Stimming, Albert, ed. *Der festländische Bueve de Hantone: Gesellschaft für romanische Literatur*. Vols. 25, 30, 34, 41, and 42. Dresden: Dresden Publikationen, 1911–1920.

Stocchi, Manlio Pastore. "Le fortune della letteratura cavalleresca e cortese nella Treviso medievale e una testimonianza di Lovato Lovati." In *Tomaso da Modena e il suo tempo: Atti del Convegno Internazionale di Studi per il VI centenario della morte*, 201–17. Treviso: Comitato Manifestazioni Tomaso da Modena, 1980.

Stock, Brian. *Listening for the Text: On the Uses of the Past*. Baltimore: Johns Hopkins University Press, 1990.

Strocchia, Sharon. "La famiglia patrizia fiorentina nel secolo XV: La problematica della nonna." In *Palazzo Strozzi metà millenio 1489–1989: Atti del Convegno di Studi (Firenze, 3–6 luglio 1989)*, edited by Paola Gori, 126–37. Rome: Istituto della Enciclopedia Italiana, 1991.

Suard, François. "L'épopée française tardive (XIVe–XVe s.)." In *Études de philologie romane et d'histoire littéraire offertes à Jules Horrent à l'occasion de son soixantième anniversaire*, edited by Jean Marie D'Heur and Nicoletta Cherubini, 449–60. Liège: Gedit, 1980.

———. "La tradition épique au XIVe et XVe siècles." *Revue des Sciences Humaines* 55, 183 (July–September 1981): 95–107.

Subrenat, Jean. *Étude sur Gaydon, chanson de geste du XIIIe iècle*. Provence: Editions de l'Université de Provence, 1974.

Thomas, Antoine, ed. *L'Entrée d'Espagne, chanson de geste franco-italienne*. 2 vols. 1913. Reprint, New York: Johnson Reprint, 1968.

Tobler, A., "Die Berliner Handschrift des Huon d'Auvergne." *Sitzungsberichte der Könglich Preusischen Akademie der Wissenschaften zu Berlin* 1 (1884): 506–20.

Togeby, Knud. *Ogier le Danois dans les littératures européennes*. Munksgaard: DSL, 1969.

Tomalin, Margaret. *The Fortunes of the Warrior Heroine in Italian Literature: An Index of Emancipation*. Ravenna: Longo, 1982.

Trexler, Richard C. *Public Life in Renaissance Florence*. New York: Academic Press, 1980.

Vance, Eugene. "The Differing Seed: Dante's Brunetto Latini." In *Mervelous Signals: Poetics and Sign Theory in the Middle Ages*, 230–55. Lincoln: University of Nebraska Press, 1986.

———. *From Topic to Tale: Logic and Narrativity in the Middle Ages*. Minneapolis: University of Minnesota Press, 1987.

Verzone, C. ed. *Le rime burlesche ed inedite di A. F. Grazzini*. Florence: Sansoni, 1882.

Villani, Giovanni. *Cronica di Giovanni Villani*. Edited by I. Moutier. 4 vols. 1944. Reprint, Frankfurt: Minerva GMBH, 1969.

Viscardi, Antonio. *Letteratura franco-italiana*. Modena: Società Tipografica Modenese, 1941.

Vitale-Brovarone, Alessandro. "De la *Chanson de Huon d'Auvergne*, à la *Storia di Ugone d'Avernia* d'Andrea da Barberino: techniques et méthodes de la traduction et de l'élaboration." In *Charlemagne et l'epopée romane*, Actes du VIIe Congrès International de la Société Rencesvals, vol. 2, 393–403. Paris: Les Belles Lettres, 1978.

Vitullo, Juliann. "Orality, Literacy, and the Prose Epic: The Case of Andrea da Barberino's *Ugo d'Alvernia*." *The italianist* 13 (1993): 29–45.

Warner, Marina. *Alone of All Her Sex: The Myth and the Cult of the Virgin Mary*. New York: Knopf, 1976.

Weinstein, Donald. "The Myth of Florence." In *Florentine Studies: Politics and Society in Renaissance Florence*, edited by Nicolai Rubinstein. London: Faber & Faber, 1968.

Wettan Kleinbaum, Abby. *The War Against the Amazons*. New York: McGraw Hill, 1983.

White, David Gordon. *Myths of the Dog-Man*. Chicago: University of Chicago Press, 1991.
White, Hayden. *Tropics of Discourse*. Baltimore: Johns Hopkins University Press, 1978.
Wittkower, Rudolf. "Marvels of the East: A Study in the History of Monsters." *Journal of the Warburg and Courtauld Institutes* 5 (1942): 159–97.
Wolfzettel, Freidrich. "Zur Stellung und Bedeutung der 'Enfances' in der altfranzösischen Epik." *Zeitschrift für französische Sprache und Literatur* 83 (1973): 317–48; 84 (1974): 1–32.
Wunderli, Peter. "Roland théologien dans *l'Aquilon de Bavière*." In *Essor et fortune de la chanson de geste dans l'Europe et l'Orient latin*, Actes du IXe Congrès International de la Société Rencesvals pour l'étude des épopées romanes, vol. 2, 759–81. Modena: Mucchi, 1982.
Wunderli, Peter, and Günther Holtus. "La 'renaissance' des études franco-italiennes." In *Testi, cotesti, e contesti, del franco-italiano*, edited by Günter Holtus, Henning Krauss, and Peter Wunderli, 3–23. Tübingen: Max Niemeyer Verlag, 1989.
Zambon, Francesco. "La 'Materia di Francia' nella letteratura franco-veneta." In *Sulle orme di Orlando: Leggende e luoghi carolingi in Italia*, edited by Anna Imelde Galletti and Roberto Rodi, 53–64. Padua: Interbooks, 1987.
Zemon Davis, Natalie. "Women on Top." In *Society and Culture in Early Modern France*, 124–51. Stanford: Stanford University Press, 1975.
Zumthor, Paul. *Langue, texte, énigme*. Paris: Seuil, 1975.

Index

Adenet le Roi, 37
Aliscans, 60, 62–63
Allaire, Gloria, 68, 75
Aquilon de Bavière, 74, 81–85, 88–89
Aristotle, 123–25, 127
Astolfo, 81–83
Aubert, David, 94
Augustine, St., 51, 65

Bäuml, Franz M., 93, 96, 112
Bellomo, Manlio, 70
Bakhtin, M.M., xiv, 26, 140n.26
Bender, Karl, 11, 24
Bernardino, St., 80, 86–87, 89, 145n.16
Berta (Charlemagne's half-sister), 40–41, 141n.12
Berta (Pepin's wife), 36–40
Boccaccio, 65, 89, 98
bourgeois, 5, 14, 19–20, 60–61, 82, 98
Bovo d'Antona, 16–21, 27–28, 46, 53–55
Braidamonte, 68–70, 73
Brown, Judith, 70
Bruns, Gerald, xii
Bueve de Hantone, 16–21, 53–55, 139nn.18–19
Buovo d'Antona. *See* Bovo d'Antona
Butler, Judith, 71

Cantare d'Aspramonte, 66
Capellanus, Andreas, 115–16
Cardini, Franco, 119
Cereta, Laura, 72
Chanson d'Aspremont, 65

Chanson de Roland, 6, 10, 16, 28, 31, 121, 127, 139n.14
Charlemagne, xi, 11, 21–29, 34–37, 40–44, 46–47, 56–59, 67, 81, 119, 121, 141n.12
Chevalerie Doon de Mayence, 60
Chevalerie Ogier, 59
chivalry (knighthood), 15, 31–33, 71–72, 85, 98, 117–19
Chrétien de Troyes, 45
Chronique de Turpin, 81
Cicero, 108
communes (It. *comuni*), xi, 4, 16, 95, 117–19, 126
Compagni, Dino, 14, 30, 108
Couronnement de Louis, 26

Da Barberino, Andrea, 54–55, 75, 94–99, 143n.18, 146nn. 17–18. —epics, *I Reali di Francia*, 53–55, 108, 115, 133; *Le Storie Nerbonesi*, 55–59; *L'Aspramonte*, 66–67, 119–20, 133; *Guerrino il Meschino* 75–81, 85, 89–90, 133–34; *Ugo d'Alvernia* 99–13, 114–27, 146nn. 8,11
Da Nono, Giovanni, 33
Da Pisa, Guido, 111
Da Verona, Raffaele, 81–85
Da Volterra, Michelagnolo, 128
Dama Roenza, 68–70
Dante, 11, 79, 96–97, 100, 103, 116, 121–22, 125, 133
Dares, 125

Del Corazza, Bartolommeo, 117–18
Delcorno Branca, Daniela, 53–54
Delle Colonne, Guido, 65
Di Padova, Marsiglio, 125
Dinshaw, Carolyn, 53
Douglas, Mary, 84–85

enfances epics, 87–89
Entrée d'Espagne, 5, 10, 81, 100, 138n.7
Estoria de Bernaldo, 108

Fatti de Spagna, 24
Fonte, Moderata, 72
Formosa, 68, 70, 85–86
Franco-Italian, 5, 81, 93, 101, 112, 138 n.5
Friedman, John, 52

Galaziella, 63, 65–68, 73
Garber, Marjorie, 53
Gaufrey, 60
Gautier, Léon, 6–8
Gaydon, 27–29, 60
Gellrich, Jesse, 114
Ghibellines, 14, 16, 30, 113, 115
Giamboni, Bono, 12
Girolami, Remigio, 14
Godzich, Wlad, 97, 106
Goldmann, Lucien, 9
Grazzini, Anton Francesco, 132–33
Green, D. H., 93
Guelphs, 14, 16, 24, 30, 95, 113, 115, 117–19, 126
Guerrino, 75–81, 85, 89–90
Guillaume d'Orange (It. Guglielmo d'Oringa), 60–63, 100, 103–4

Haidu, Peter, 127
Heers, Jacques, 33–34
Herlihy, David, 87
Hervis de Mes, 26–27, 37
Huon de Bordeaux, 27–29, 75
Hyde, J. K., 13

Infurna, Marco, 9, 11

Jameson, Fredric, 9–10
Jauss, Hans R., xiv
Jerome, St., 52
Jones, Catherine M., 26–27, 37
Jones, Philip, 13

Kittay, Jeffrey, 97, 106
Klapisch-Zuber, Christiane, 70, 87
Krauss, Henning, 9, 11–14, 54, 61
Kristeva, Julia, 30
Krygier, Martin, xii–xiii

Langmuir, Gavin, 83
Lansing, Carol, 13
Larner, John, 12, 14
Latini, Brunetto, 3, 12, 79
Latour, Bruno, 106
Limentani, Alberto, 9, 11
Luzzatto, Gino, 13

Marciano XIII, xiv, 5–7, 16, 30–31, 45–47, 61, 88, 137n. 3, 140n. 1. —narratives: *Bovo d'Antona* 16–21, 88, 133–34; *Enfances Ogier* 21–22, 88; *Chevalerie Ogier*, 22–24; *Karleto* 34–36, 88; *Berta da li pe grandi*, 36–40; *Berta e Milon* 36–43; *Rolandino*, 36–43, 88; *Macaire*, 43–45, 55–59
Mary, St., 75, 81, 83–85, 129, 143n. 20
Mazzi, Maria Serena, 87
Mazzuoli, Giovanni (lo Stradino), 72, 132–33
Medici, Lorenzo de', 131
monstrous races, xv, 51–55
Moore, R. I., 90
Morgan, Leslie Z., 36
Muhammad, 74, 78, 80, 82

Navigazione di San Brandano, 116

Ogier, 16, 21–24, 43, 45–46
orality, xv, 93–103, 114, 128–34
orientalism, xv, 53, 62, 74–90, 141n. 2, 144n. 2

Paris, Gaston, 138n.6
Pasero, Nicolò, 26
Pèlerinage de Charlemagne, 24–26
Penthesilea (Fr. Panthesilée), 64–65, 72–73
Pepin, 36–40
Perry, Milman, 93
Petrarca, Francesco, 134
Plato, 124
popolo, 14, 15, 16, 20, 60, 139n. 15
Primera Crónica General, 108
Prise d'Orange, 61
Prise de Pampelune, 59
Pucci, Antonio, 133

Rainourt, 60–62
Rajna, Pio, 7–9, 11
Renaud/t (It. Rinaldo), xi, 24, 45–46, 69–70, 79, 94
Renaut de Montauban, 24, 45–46, 53
Rinaldo da Montalbano, 68–70, 79, 133
Rocke, Michael, 80, 87
Roland, xi, 4, 10, 28, 40–43, 46–47, 68, 70, 74, 79, 81, 83–85
Roman de Troie, 63–65
Rossi, Marguerite, 75
Rubin, Miri, 84
Ruggieri, Ruggero, 3

Sacchetti, Franco, 32, 72
Sainte-Maure, Benoît de, 63–65

Salvemini, Gaetano, 31–33
Saracens, 52, 62, 65–73, 74–90, 120
Scrovegni, Enrico, 32
Simpson Shen, Lucia, 88
sodomy, 79–80, 85–87, 89–90, 144nn. 9–11, 145n. 20
Stallybrass, Peter 62–63
Stock, Brian, xi–xiii
Storia di Rinaldino da Montalbano, 72
Suard, François, 94

Tristan de Nanteuil, 63

Ugo d'Alvernia, xi, 99–113, 114–27, 128–32

Vance, Eugene, 45
Varocher (Ispinardo), 43–46, 55–60
Villani, Giovanni, 108–9, 119
Virgil, 100, 110–11
Viscardi, Antonio, 9, 11, 30
Vitry, Jacques de, 78, 90
warrior women (Amazons), xv, 52, 61–73, 130, 142n. 11

White, Allon, 62–63
White, Hayden, 55–56
wild men, xv, 55–61
Wunderli, Peter, 82

Yvain, 45

Juliann Vitullo is associate professor of Italian at Arizona State University. She specializes in both medieval and Italian-American culture, with interests in gender and ethnic studies.